D1458185

Chanctonbury Ring

An Autobiography

By the same author

THERE IS A TIDE
WHOM THEY PIERCED
CHRISTIANITY AND MARXISM
I WENT TO MOSCOW
THE FAITH TO-DAY
CAMBRIDGE SERMONS
BISHOP'S JOURNAL
THE CROSS AND THE SICKLE

Chanctonbury Ring

An Autobiography

Mervyn Stockwood

HODDER AND STOUGHTON   SHELDON PRESS
LONDON SYDNEY AUCKLAND TORONTO   LONDON

The author wishes to thank the following for the use of their illustrations:

The Times for the picture of the author with the Archbishop of Canterbury and the Bishop of Barking after his consecration as Bishop of Southwark.

The *Daily Express* for the picture of the author in his consistory court.

Bill Bates for the picture of the author at a Foyle's luncheon with Barbara Cartland and Sir Arthur Bryant.

Jane Bown, the *Observer*, for the picture of the author in the out-of-door pulpit of Christchurch, North Brixton, with Sir John Betjeman.

Wessex Newspapers for 'Swan song in Bath'.

Jeffrey Millan for the picture of the author with Malcolm Muggeridge at Chanctonbury Ring.

British Library Cataloguing in Publication Data
Stockwood, Mervyn
    Chanctonbury ring.
    1. Stockwood, Mervyn   2. Church of England
    —Bishop—Biography
    I. Title
    283'.092'4   BX5199.S/

ISBN 0 340 27568 5

Hodder and Stoughton Editorial Office: 47 Bedford Square, London WC1B 3DP.

Contents

1

Early Years

It was my first month with a reversed collar, a Sunday night in the winter of 1936. I was asked to visit a woman who was seriously ill with tuberculosis. Immediately after the service I hurried round to the dingy house in which she and her three-year-old son Jimmy had one room. The gas had failed and, as there were no pennies for the meter, the only light was a candle stuck into a bottle. She was already dead, or, as the neighbour put it, she had gone to join her daughter who had been struck down by the same disease in the previous year. My chief concern was for Jimmy. He was lying in the same bed, breathing with extreme difficulty. The women standing by said it was tears, but I suspected pneumonia. I telephoned the doctor, who quickly examined him and, wrapping him in a blanket, took him to hospital. With difficulty his life was saved. Now an orphan, he was sent to a children's home.

Such was my introduction to the ministry, but it was only the first of many shocks for which my upbringing at school, university and theological college had done little to prepare me. It was a traumatic first month. It affected the course of my ministry.

My earliest memory is riding upon my father's back in search of cockles at Bridgend market in South Wales. I suppose I must have been nearly two, and the Great War had been declared a few months previously. My father, like my grandfather, was a solicitor. He maintained my mother and their three children in modest comfort.

The house seemed large and there were rooms upstairs which I was afraid to visit after dark. The garden was a source of delight, and, as the war continued, was the scene of many imaginary battles between the British and the Germans. I, being the youngest, was expected to represent the Germans and to suffer defeat—a point which will doubtless give the psychologists several clues to my subsequent complexes and inhibitions.

Much time was spent with my brother Alick. My father had joined the army, my mother was engaged in war work, and my sister disappeared to boarding school. He was two years older and,

7

although we had the usual squabbles and I was the more aggressive, we got on happily. In the afternoon Bessie, the servant, took us for walks and her favourite haunt was the asylum, which I dreaded, especially when the inmates passed us in their crocodile. I must have told my mother of my fears because the route was changed. Instead, Bessie took us through the woods and by the river, never failing to tell me that a big fish would eat me if I misbehaved. Now that the Bessies of the world scarcely exist, I sometimes wonder what threats modern parents use to inculcate good conduct.

For a while the war made little impression. Friends came to the house in uniform and I can still see my mother looking through the casualty lists with an anxious face. Sometimes a band played in the street and that, for some reason, terrified me. Occasionally we were taken to charity concerts in aid of the Red Cross, but I am sure I did not understand what was involved. But in 1916, when I was three, came the battle of the Somme, and my father was killed. He was little more than a stranger to me, but I vividly remember the day the telegram arrived and my mother opening it. I also recall looking out of the bedroom window that evening in my pyjamas with my chin cupped in my hand, feeling I had lived for years and years and was steeped in the agonies and sufferings of the world and always would be. A curiously vivid impression that has never left me, a blend of sorrow and loneliness. Perhaps the hallmark of my life. I don't know.

A few months later the home was sold, and my mother, who was awarded by the Government a pension of less than £3 per week, which, while allowing for inflation, was hardly a princely sum, embarked upon a new life. I often wonder how she made ends meet. It is true that some years later the pension was raised to £3. 6s. 0d. and a law society provided a grant for educational purposes, but for a long time poverty was close to the door.

In 1917 we moved to Bristol, and a kindly headmistress took us in. It was a satisfactory arrangement because it meant that while my mother went to work, my brother and I attended school and shared the life of the boarders.

As I was very young I was excused lessons in the afternoons and was taken walks by a Mrs Skinner, a war widow. She is not without importance in my life because the walks usually ended inside All Saints' Church, Clifton, which in later years was to have a considerable, if not a determining, influence upon me.

All Saints', unfortunately destroyed by bombs in 1940, was a large and magnificent building, quite different from the smaller church that took its place thirty years later; it was sometimes called the Anglo-Catholic cathedral of the West Country. It attracted vast congregations, and was constantly used by many people, often hundreds, throughout the week. The lofty roof, the imposing high altar, the great sanctuary lamps, the multiplicity of stained glass, the graceful side-chapels, the priests moving up the aisles in cloaks and birettas, combined to produce an atmosphere of mystery and awe. I cannot imagine anybody talking above a whisper, or entering without kneeling to say a prayer. My earliest religious impressions date from these afternoon visits. I enjoyed them; I felt at home in the church; I began to develop a sense of mystery and worship.

Not everything was serious, even in those days. On Sundays the school attended All Saints' for High Mass. I suppose the building held about a thousand people, and it was usually full. Men sat on one side of the church and women on the other. As I was a child I was allowed to sit next to the school mistress. The service was long, but there was continual movement at the altar and I enjoyed the colours and incense; the singing, All Saints' having its own choir school, was of a high standard. On this particular occasion the mistress, a Miss Mahaffey, experienced an embarrassing moment. At a particular point in the service when it was customary for the congregation to kneel, she slipped on her hassock, and, as she lurched forward, her wig fell to the ground. As she groped for her lost property the girls tried to smother their laughs, but I was too young to understand. I assumed that things like that happened to people when they went to church.

On another occasion as we were queuing in the aisle to get into our places, I had forgotten to remove my cap, on which were inscribed my initials. A ferocious-looking man, called a sacristan, and wearing a cassock, seized my cap and said, "Men and boys are not allowed to wear hats in church." Fifty years later when I was preaching at the consecration of the rebuilt church, I told the congregation the story before adding, "That little boy is now standing in this pulpit. Today he is allowed to wear a hat in church."

In the summer of 1919, after a long illness which kept me on the sick list for the greater part of a year, I went as a boarder to the Downs School, which sixty years later is still a thriving institution. I was five years old and I could not understand why my mother should send me away. I remember, as though it were yesterday, the sense of gnawing despair which gripped me as she walked out of the front door. I cried myself to sleep, thinking I was the most pitiable creature in a cruel world. I was too young to understand that the move was one of the consequences of my father's death. Having no home, my mother had no alternative. But I adapted myself quickly. The headmaster, Wilfred Harrison, and his wife were the essence of kindness. I think I helped to fill a heart-searing gap in their lives. Their son David, the same age as myself, had died a few months earlier in the terrible influenza epidemic that had swept Europe, causing the death of millions. They gave me David's toys. I took his teddy bear to bed. The older boys in the dormitory never laughed at me. I think they instinctively knew it was grief shared.

Today private education is a bone of political contention. If I had been married and had had a son I often wonder what I would have done. Like many of the Left I believe private education to be a cause of class division. At an early age a child is removed from the mass of his fellows and placed in a privileged group, upon which so much can depend. I once heard Nye Bevan reply to the question, "Why do parents pay for their sons to be educated?"—a question which probably expected the answer, "Because it is better."—"In order to acquire an expensive accent." And there is truth in it. To be privately educated may lead to the possession of a key that can open gates which might otherwise remain shut. But so can most forms of private education, for example physical and artistic. Few object to parents spending money on such privileges in out-of-school hours, although the consequence may eventually place the recipients in a different social milieu or financial bracket. My guess is, if independent schools were eliminated, parents keen to 'better' their children would arrange an additional system to operate in the evenings and at weekends. This would certainly be true in the case of church schools, which are arguably divisive. If they were abolished, believing parents might be constrained to provide opportunities for their children to be educated in their beliefs, not only as private individuals but as a group. However these arguments were not to concern me for many years. I was still on the receiving end, and at the bottom rung.

Private schools were often of poor quality or worse, and when they became liable to inspection thousands disappeared. The Downs School was better than most, though its teaching standards would not be acceptable today. I doubt whether many members of the staff were qualified, but it was a happy school. The headmaster had a quiet influence on us. He was a man of integrity and deep religious conviction. He cared. Half a century later, as a very old man, he still wrote to us.

In retrospect, my chief criticisms of the system at that time would be two: first, we rarely met boys, still less girls, who came from a different background. When the local state school challenged us to a football match it was declined. The two schools belonged to different worlds.

Second, the excessive emphasis placed upon sport and athletic prowess. Few things seemed to matter as much as a straight bat in the summer term and a stiff upper lip in the winter. The headmaster, together with his brother, had played for Dorset. Consequently cricket was a priority in the curriculum. We played three times a day. Sixty years later I can even remember the slots: 12.30–1.00, 2.15–3.30, 5.30–6.30. I loathed the game and was bored to desperation. When I nominated David Sheppard, a former captain of England, to be my Suffragan Bishop of Woolwich, I told him it was the most generous act of forgiveness in my life!

In other terms we played football and hockey, but I never shone at any games other than running short distances. I have always been a swift mover; in middle age even, when I was challenged by a dozen soldiers to enter the hundred yards, I hit the tape first—to their dismay.

My criticism of the emphasis placed on sport goes deep because it raises the question of the purpose of education. Even today school magazines are sent to me with pages devoted to the happenings of the football and cricket elevens. Of course opportunities must be provided for those who enjoy these activities, and all boys and girls need physical exercise; but what of other interests and pursuits? I resent, and that is a modest word, the hundreds of hours, more likely thousands, that I was compelled to spend on playing-fields between the ages of five and eighteen. Life is all too short and there are so many exciting things to do and skills to master. The tough masculine programme may have prepared us to lead troops in difficult situations, but it did little to introduce us to the more delicate arts and leisure occupations which can do so much to enhance a man's perception and understanding of life. Apart from a short interlude in the Isle of Wight, it was not until I went to Cambridge that I began to be educated at these levels. When I reached the university it was like passing from Sparta to Athens.

For two terms I attended a boarding school at Bembridge. It was founded shortly after the Great War by a former Liberal Member of Parliament, J. H. Whitehouse. He was the Warden, or headmaster, and he had a distinguished band of governors including Dean Inge, C. F. G. Masterman, C. R. Nevinson and Isaac Foot. Two of the 'Feet' brothers, Dingle and John, were my contemporaries, and some years later Robin Day was at the school. Although we had to play

11

some games, we were given several afternoons each week to read in the library, make excursions to the country, or go to the photography room or pottery shed. More important, we were encouraged to think our own thoughts and to do our own thing. The Warden was essentially a nonconformist who had little use for Establishment attitudes. He expected the boys to value their independence and to speak their minds. But there was too much liberty, and basic educational requirements were ignored. My mother, realising that examinations lay ahead, returned me to the Downs School for another three years and to its more conventional setting. But I am grateful to Bembridge for its emphasis upon singularity and upon the need to be true to oneself rather than to toe the conventional line.

In September 1926 I began life at Kelly College, Tavistock, where I remained for four years. I endured it rather than enjoyed it. I was not unhappy but, like John Betjeman, I hated being 'summoned by bells' from morning to night. I have never fitted easily into institutional life. I am by nature an individualist and I like living among individualists, not zombies. Years later I was to choose as suffragan bishops men with strong convictions but with outlooks and attitudes different from my own. I am not suggesting I was a rebel; I accepted, without question, the usual standards. But I had interests for which the curriculum made small provision and I did not share the enthusiasms which were fostered by public opinion. It never mattered to me who won school matches, or what a visiting officer thought of the military training corps. I grudged the time which was spent on such boring interludes, preferring to hide in the library or walk on Dartmoor. I escaped to the countryside whenever possible because I soon learnt to love the moors. Sometimes I was accompanied by a friend, but often I would walk by myself. I have never been bored with my own company, and Dartmoor has a majestic loneliness which is well suited to dreamy adolescence.

The most valuable contribution that a boarding school makes to the development of character, be it fee-paying or a state orphanage, is to teach the individual the art of living in community. Boys and girls who have to share studies and dormitories with colleagues whose temperaments are different from their own, and sometimes uncongenial, are better prepared for the complex society which awaits them when they leave school. To be a good mixer is a requisite of every parson, and a boarding school is a good training ground. But there are limitations. Most boys come from the same social stratum and it is possible to leave school without any real understanding of the conditions of the majority. I think that while I was at Kelly I imagined I belonged to that section of society which was destined to rule, and it did not occur to me to study the conditions and aspirations of those who did not belong to the ruling class. It is true we had a college mission, or settlement, in a poor part of Devonport, to which we contributed money each term. There were occasional visits and exchanges, but of a condescending nature. I vividly recall a school coach taking us to the club for a table-tennis match, having been warned previously that when the game was over we were not to accept invitations to dance with the local girls as they might be infectious or lousy. Worse still, on our way back to Tavistock from Plymouth—and I can recall the precise point on the road—the master in charge ordered us out of the coach to take deep breaths of Dartmoor air in order to rid ourselves of the germs that we might have picked up in 'the slums'!

A further serious limitation was the extent to which we were confined to our own sex for the greater part of the year. Later, as a parish priest I noticed how easy it was for boys and girls to mix and make friends, whereas we were shy and gauche. Moreover the system failed to take into account the development of the sexual instincts. Human nature being as it is, a boy is likely to form a romantic attachment with a member of his own sex, if he cannot fall in love with a girl. This is not necessarily bad, in fact it may be good, but it should be faced realistically and not brushed under the carpet.

On political matters, I remember no serious discussion. It was assumed that we and our parents were Conservatives or, less probably, Liberals. Just as at my preparatory school, the General Strike was regarded as an act of treachery by a malevolent rabble, so at Kelly there was contempt and ridicule for the Labour Party. Our ignorance of politics and civics in the widest sense was appalling. Schools are more enlightened today; even so I remember visiting Clifton College many years after the end of the Hitler war to find that at a mock election in the school each vote for the Labour candidate was multiplied by three. It was assumed that as no rational person would vote anything but Tory such a device was necessary to make the exercise a worthwhile piece of fun. The only clue that I have of subsequent wider interests is that while I was at Kelly I started to read *The Times* and the *Manchester Guardian*; the more radical papers were not available.

My religious development was more definite and independent. From an early age I followed my own path. The prospectus of the Downs Schools stated that the religious teaching was in accordance with the tenets of the Church of England. This meant on weekdays school prayers at assembly and private prayers with Bible readings in the dormitory, morning and evening. On Sundays we learnt the collect and the catechism before going to Matins at the local church. Judged by modern standards it was excessive, but it seemed natural to us. At times we were bored, especially by the dreary church services.

In the holidays I attended All Saints' Clifton, except when I went with my mother to Oakfield Road church, a free church with a Unitarian bias, to sit under a distinguished scholar, Dr Gustav Beckh. Although his sermons were too difficult for me to understand, I was impressed by his immense learning, and I sensed that his literary masterpieces were of a higher standard than those to which I had been accustomed. I told the clergy at All Saints' of these visits and met with disapproval, but I continued to accompany my mother occasionally. The impressions, most of them unconscious at the time, were not without influence. As the years passed I became increasingly convinced that orthodoxy and intellectual integrity were not necessarily identical, and that creeds too frequently shrouded rather than expressed Truth.

In 1926 Dr Beckh resigned. His large congregation was devastated. During his last months it was said that up to a thousand people attended his services, sitting on the chancel and pulpit steps, on chairs in the aisles and under the tower.

I sometimes wonder how he might have affected my development had he remained at Oakfield Road. As it was he gave me a respect for the honest doubt that is part and parcel of the experience of most of us in our spiritual pilgrimage.

All Saints' Clifton, however, was my natural home and in the holidays I went to High Mass on most Sunday mornings. I look back with gratitude to All Saints' which taught me the dignity, beauty and reality of corporate worship. It was a remarkable church and I always think of it with deep affection. Nevertheless it was here that I first came into collision with ecclesiastical dogmatism. The cause was trivial, but the consequences were considerable. I had been taught by a priest on the staff to go to confession and, as it was the custom of the church, I took it in my stride. On one occasion I was cross-examined by Father Stothert about keeping the fast before receiving the Sacrament. (For those who are ignorant of ecclesiastical minutiae, let me explain that in those days there was a custom, though not a rule, to abstain from food before going to Holy Communion.) At Kelly, where fasting Communion was not taught, we had the service occasionally in the middle of the morning, after breakfast. When I mentioned the matter to Father Stothert he told me not to go again. I argued with him and, greatly daring, said there was no rule about fasting in the Anglican prayer book. We reached a deadlock and he told me that unless I obeyed he could no longer give me absolution. I told a friend who referred the matter to the Bishop of Bristol, Dr Nickson, who had confirmed me. Nickson said that matters of this sort had to be left to the individual's conscience. Father Stothert refused to have further dealings with me. From that day I have been distrustful of ecclesiastical regulations and legalism. In the last resort, which is supreme—the Church or private judgment? I do not regret the contretemps because it helped to convince me that a man must find his own way to Truth, grateful for the help he derives from Church systems, but not subservient to them. The passing years have increased the irritation, and never more so than during the debates in the General Synod on canon law, when as a bishop I was an unwilling and occasional participant. Christianity is a religion of the Spirit, of God's encounter with men, of the search for freedom and truth. Rules and regulations have their place in the list of priorities, but near the bottom. "The letter killeth but the Spirit giveth life," should be inscribed on every Prayer Book.

These difficulties did not prevent me from going to All Saints', even though it began to dawn on me that I did not altogether belong; nor did they hinder the development of a friendship with its vicar, Canon M. P. Gillson, who was an impressive man, remarkably handsome, and, in the strict sense of the word, an aristocrat. I can see him now quietly sweeping into church with a dignity and aloofness which were almost unique. I am told he ruled the congregation with a rod of iron, and I believe it, because I cannot imagine anybody daring to argue with him. I had respect and affection for him. Although he was remote, and few people succeeded in penetrating the barrier of reserve, he was the essence of kindliness towards me. I visited the vicarage frequently in the holidays and was often invited to meals. When I grew older I used to stay with him and once he took some of us to the Continent where, among other things, we went to the Passion Play at Oberammergau. The town was draped with swastikas, as Hitler had been in the theatre on the previous day. While we were in Munich the Nazis burnt down a synagogue.

We rarely discussed religion, but his Christian approach to life taught me lessons I shall never forget. He invariably treated me as a contemporary and, although it made me old for my years, I was so anxious to keep abreast of him that I began to take a keen interest in reading, painting, music and travel, in the hope that I should be able to talk sensibly to him at the dinner table. He had a loathing of emotion and undignified behaviour. He was remote, and he expected me to be remote. He took a keen interest in my education and in term time wrote frequently to me. I still treasure his letters. As the years passed, I realised that I had modelled myself unconsciously on him, and I know that many of my attitudes and reactions are due to his influence. Friendly, yes; but always aloof. Our friendship continued until 1939 when he left Bristol to retire to Blandford. He died in 1950, aged eighty. He left the world with as much dignity as he had shown passing through it, stooping down to pick a flower.

Religion at Kelly was treated seriously, but without emotion. We went to chapel each morning, and on Sundays twice. The headmaster, Norman Miller, was an arresting preacher, but I think more should have been done to provide us with a solid, intellectual basis for our faith. A boy living in a scientific age is bound to question the fundamental assumptions of Christianity. Physics, psychology and anthropology encourage an approach to life that is different from the approach of traditional orthodoxy and it is difficult for a young person to relate what he learns in the classroom to what he hears in chapel. I remember being accused of a dirty mind when in a divinity lesson I said I could not believe in the Virgin Birth!

In 1929 I came under the influence of Bryan Green and there began a friendship which deepened with the passing of the years and which frequently brings us together half a century later. When I first knew him he was regarded as an enthusiastic 'hot gospeller'. He conducted missions for young people in many parts of the country. He came to Clifton and I was taken to hear him. This unconventional evangelism was not in keeping with the restrained dignity of All Saints'. Although I disliked his methods I admired the freshness of his approach and decided to go to the mission each night. I did not have a conversion experience and I refused to fill in one of his cards, but I learnt many things about personal religion which helped to mould my future ministry.

I found it more difficult to work with members of his team. In those days they belonged to the 'Low Church' puritanical section and they struck me as life-deniers rather than life-affirmers. Music, art, drama, colour, wine are the gifts or a beneficent God to make glad the heart of man. Of course they can be abused, but to reject them outright is to misunderstand the Christian doctrine of Creation.

We shall meet Bryan Green later, but I have an early memory of an incident which could have ended in a disaster. As we had not met for some months we stayed talking into the early hours of the morning. We are both owls by nature and only larks of necessity. Round about two o'clock I suggested we should go to bed and I asked for a soft drink. He went to the kitchen and brought back a glass of what was supposed to be lime juice. In fact it was disinfectant, Chloros. I took a gulp and fell to the floor, choking. I felt my throat contracting and I wondered whether my host would have to say a requiem for me. Bryan was as scared as I was. He hurried to the telephone and called a doctor, who quickly restored me.

As my time at Kelly drew to a close, the headmaster asked me about future plans. I told him I had considered ordination and schoolmastering. Perhaps I would combine both by becoming a school chaplain. In any case it meant continuing my education at a university. I put my name down for Cambridge. Meanwhile I had to raise the funds. Luckily I was awarded three non-academic bursaries, but as there was still a gap I decided to teach for two years at a preparatory school in Shrewsbury, a beautiful town that I quickly came to love.

Although Kingsland Grange had no official connection with Shrewsbury School many of the boys went on to it. We lived under its eye and adopted some of its customs. The academic standard of Kingsland Grange was high. The outgoing headmaster, W. B. C. Drew, who believed in the virtues of a classical education, did not hesitate to cane Latin and Greek into the recalcitrant. Many evenings saw a queue outside the gym waiting to be thrashed. The boys appeared to bear him no grudge, especially those who won scholarships.

Drew's successor was a clergyman, P. C. West, whose methods and practices were different. He respected sound learning, but his primary interests were the boys and their happiness. Academic standards and discipline suffered. It was not always easy for the masters who were responsible for scholarship preparation. To a young master who was enthusiastic about his work it was irksome; but, as the months passed, I began to grasp the strength and wisdom of West's approach. The boys became accustomed to his régime and the natural consequences of the reaction disappeared. What is more, they started to respond to his kindliness and courtesy. He was invariably gentle and gracious. I never once saw him irritated,

17

nor did I hear him speak an angry word. As I look back, I realise that West had a great influence upon me. He taught me something of the art of personal relationships. I have worked in a team for most of my life and I have tried to treat the members of it as West treated us.

We certainly had a happy staff-room. My colleagues, who were senior to me, must have found me young and impetuous. However the only complaint they expressed concerned my failure to play Bridge, which they did on most days. Cards had always bored me. It meant I had to find my own amusements. I went to concerts and films, and I learnt to dance. My chief hobby was necessarily less expensive; I joined a library and started to read. Within a few weeks I developed a passion for books. As soon as school was over I went to my room and, apart from the interruptions of meals and dormitory duty, read late into the night. I averaged four to five books a week and covered considerable ground. Fiction, biography, travel, history and philosophy constituted my diet. I acquired knowledge and improved my education. I am sure that books did as much to prepare me for the priesthood as did my studies at theological college. Fiction and biography bring the reader to grips with human nature and widen his sympathies. It is difficult for a keen novel reader to sit in judgment upon his fellows; he tends towards broadmindedness.

English history and biographies of public men quickened my interest in the political life of the country, but I remained a staunch Conservative. Ramsay MacDonald formed his 'National Government' in 1931 and I campaigned for the Tory candidate at the ensuing election. On the night of the poll I went to the market place in Shrewsbury to hear the result. While I waited I became involved in an argument with a socialist. Tempers were frayed. He challenged me to a fight. A colleague, fearful lest an ill report should reach the school, hurried me away and the brawl was abandoned. How much I had to learn, and unlearn.

The two years at Shrewsbury gave me an unexpected introduction to rural life. A friend of my uncle, Charles Stockwood, at that time the Archdeacon of the Isle of Man, was Jim Chitty, rector of Yockleton, on the road towards Welshpool. When he heard I was in the neighbourhood he and his wife invited me to their house and I was immediately treated as one of the family. Not only did I spend several weekends with them during the term but also a part of my vacations, especially when I went to Cambridge, as it was an ideal place to study and to cram for exams. Within a matter of months the rector persuaded the Bishop of Hereford to license me as a lay reader although I was only eighteen. Thus I began my active ministry in the Church of England.

Chitty was one of the old school. He wore a white bow-tie, a symbol of his brand of Victorian evangelicalism. He disliked popery, clerical collars, weekday services, radicalism and new-fangled ideas. He loved his parish and his people, but best of all he loved his garden. As we walked through the rectory grounds on summer evenings I tried to interest him in ecclesiastical chatter, but he soon tired and the talk reverted to gladioli, rhubarb and quinces. Sometimes we were joined by his old friend, Arthur Baring-Gould, before sitting down for a late supper which invariably concluded with stilton cheese and a glass of port. In addition to opening my eyes to village life, Chitty introduced me to the hobby that was to give me so much relaxation in later life, especially during the busy years at Southwark. He was a first-class fisherman and the trout in the Salopian streams had a healthy respect for his cunning. I used to sit on the banks, an enthusiastic disciple, and watch him. Although I was too clumsy and inexperienced to share his success, I spent many happy hours with a rod in my hand. The catch was usually nil, but it taught me something about patience, concentration and inner serenity. How little did I know how much I was to need all three virtues in the years ahead.

I began at Christ's College, Cambridge in the autumn of 1932, having jumped the financial hurdles partly by my own efforts but mainly through the generosity of friends. I decided to read history because an agnostic schoolmaster had told me that it was the only subject which could prevent an ordinand from becoming an intolerant bigot. It is not for me to say whether he was right but I have never regretted his advice. Perhaps all politicians should be compelled to follow suit. They would talk less nonsense about the present and the future if they understood the past. Although I enjoyed my studies I was not impressed by the dons who were supposed to teach me. The supervisors and lecturers, with few exceptions, were intolerably dull, and I suspect that many of them had relied upon the same notes for thirty years. When I had finished my historical studies I remained at Cambridge to read theology. Canon Charles Raven, Regius Professor of Divinity, ornithologist and botanist, a future master of Christ's College and Vice-Chancellor of the university, would electrify his audiences, and his liberal and scholarly approach made an immense impact upon me. He was the 'de Chardin' of an earlier generation whose greatness was never recognised by his

Church. But, as for the rest, the position was worse, if anything, than it had been when I was reading history: the other lecturers were indescribable. One, who attained great academic heights, spent the greater part of a lecture arguing that St Paul was let down a wall at the time of his escape in a sack and not a basket. Nearly fifty years have passed but I have kept his notes as a reminder of the dangers of misplaced knowledge. A lecturer should encourage an aptitude for learning among his pupils rather than bore them. Sack or basket!

Although I worked hard and kept a chart of the hours spent each day in academic studies, I had an interesting social life. Recently I discovered in a drawer an engagement diary covering my last year at Cambridge. It reminded me that I had at least one lunch, tea or dinner date on each day. Some people may regard such conviviality as a waste of time, whereas I see it as an essential factor in educational development. Technical knowledge is important, but it is no substitute for education. In the Epistle to the Romans we are told to be "given to hospitality". It should be a hallmark of Christian witness.

My circle of friends included active members of the University Conservative Association. I had joined the party in my early days, partly I regret to admit because I was attracted by its tie, a silver background with cerise stripes. I still have it. This incident had important consequences. I was asked to be the Tory representative in Christ's College. Within a few days I was hard at work and in the first term we had twenty recruits. I attended several meetings and Kenneth Pickthorn, soon to become a Member of Parliament, asked me to dine in his rooms at Corpus Christi to meet leading members of the Government. It was sometimes disillusioning. I remember a Cabinet Minister making a devastating attack upon Winston Churchill, describing him as an irresponsible public nuisance. Ten years later he spoke of Churchill as the greatest Englishman of the century. He was not the only humbug. Others expressed their views on farming, mining and unemployment, and they rarely impressed. The 'National Government' seemed to lack drive and initiative. I began to feel there was a lack of competence with which to deal with the problems of the country. At the same time I was becoming aware of the distressed areas, the dole, hunger marches and the unemployment queues. Although it did not occur to me to transfer my political allegiance, I became restive.

The socialists were active and among them were men who were to become famous as Labour politicians or notorious Communist spies.

The Soviet Union was still a paradise for the Left Wing, and the Marxists attracted some of the most brilliant, idealistic and creative undergraduates. I was bewildered by their opinions but challenged by their sincerity and sense of purpose. At the same time I was offended, because it seemed that they wanted, in the interests of a new type of society, to wreck the culture and conventions which I had been taught to regard as sacrosanct. And, of course, I was shocked by their hostility to Christianity. To them it was the tool of reactionaries to maintain a class-structured society and the rights of private property. Nevertheless, when the hunger marchers passed through the city they were the first to welcome them. They took them to their rooms in college and gave them meals and clothes. I had an uncomfortable feeling that the Christians were letting them do their work for them.

In his autobiography, Stephen Spender, whose friendship I have enjoyed since we first met in the early days of the war at Blundell's School, Tiverton, where he was a temporary master and I the school missioner, criticised the boorishness, snobbery and materialism of Oxford. He could have said the same of Cambridge, though I should want to put forward the plea of ignorance as a partial justification. We were woefully unaware of historical, social and economic trends. We were unprepared. Although I was reading history, the syllabus stopped short at the end of the nineteenth century, while of America and Russia there was scarcely a mention.

Religion at Cambridge in the 1930s was at a disadvantage. Optimistic liberalism was still the vogue. Man was the master of his destiny and, with the help of the League of Nations, the world was progressing towards the scientific Utopia. College chapels were badly attended and only outstanding preachers, like William Temple of York or Barnes of Birmingham, were able to draw congregations to the University Church.

I attended my college chapel on Sundays but King's became my spiritual home, and to it I went most days. It is difficult to explain to those who have not lived in Cambridge the ethos of King's. It is superb; the architecture, the liturgy and the music.

In my third term I was introduced to Edward Wynn, the Dean of Pembroke, who many years later when he was Bishop of Ely was to institute me to the living of Great Saint Mary's, the University Church. He had a genius for getting on with undergraduates, who flocked to his rooms. He was a delightful host with a fund of amusing stories and an infectious laugh. He became my confessor

21

and I invariably turned to him for advice. The chaplain of Christ's, Frank Woolnough, struck me as a creeping opportunist and a schemer. I avoided him. Alas, I was to meet many of his kind in the years ahead.

My friendship with Wynn led to an interesting development which was to influence my future ministry. Universities have a plethora of religious societies, sometimes of an extremist nature, especially the 'hot gospel' Christian unions. I lacked enthusiasm for organisations outside the official Church. I disliked their exclusiveness and I felt they absorbed too much time. But there was to be one exception. As I became better acquainted with Wynn I took an increasing number of my friends to his rooms. In turn they brought their friends. One evening I suggested to Wynn that we should meet in Pembroke chapel on Thursday mornings for a Communion service and have breakfast together afterwards. It was unofficial and we neither claimed to be a society nor gave ourselves a name. Invitations depended upon personal contacts. Numbers were limited to thirty. We belonged to no party within the Church and made no attempt to toe a particular line. We were men and women of diverse views who were brought together on a basis of friendship. Many were to hold responsible positions in Church and State though the number of casualties in the war was to be sadly above average. For me it was a further step in the direction of broadening sympathies, of a distaste for categories.

In the July of 1935 I moved to my theological college, Westcott House, and came under the influence of its Principal, B. K. Cunningham.

Most Anglican theological colleges owe allegiance to a particular party within the Church of England. They tend to produce a definite type, conscious of a group affiliation and critical of other traditions. In fact, in my judgment, theological colleges have, for the most part, done considerable damage to Anglicanism.

Cunningham, better known by us as the 'Professor' or B.K., stood above party and attracted ordinands of all schools of thought. It would be wrong, however, to suggest that his teaching was nondescript. He was an ardent Anglican with a deep devotion to the Establishment and to the liturgy. He believed that Christian character was a more effective weapon for a priest than ecclesiastical shibboleths. It was impossible for him to think of the workings of the Holy Spirit within the restrictions of partisan formulae. He understood human nature better than most and he knew how to deal with his men. He rarely reprimanded; instead he convinced us by

22

the indefinable quality of his life. Of course he had his weaknesses, but they endeared him to us. He was an impenitent snob, and admission was usually confined to the products of the public schools and senior universities. He once said, half in jest, that his job was to provide a gentleman in holy orders for every parish. When I saw him, shortly before his death, a Welsh college had been evacuated to Cambridge. Westcott, which was half empty on account of the war, had to provide accommodation. The 'Professor' looked out of his study window at the lawn where the Welshmen were having tea. He remarked with a sigh, "Mervyn, boy, the war has at last come to Westcott." B.K. was the child of an age that had ceased to exist. He disliked modern England and did not understand it. But he knew intuitively that a fresh approach was necessary, although he failed to understand its implications.

B.K. was a Scot, and though he was generous with his pounds, he held fast to his pence. He would cheerfully make out a three-figured cheque for a deserving cause, but a trifling bill would distress him. One Sunday he asked me to go to his rooms after a late evening service to join him over a bottle of whisky which had been given to him by a friend. He started to extract the cork and then, putting the bottle on the table, remarked, "It's too expensive, boy; we'll have tea instead." On another occasion he asked me to go with him to London to see the pantomime at Drury Lane Theatre. When we reached the box office he said, "I shall sit in the stalls, but you buy your own ticket and sit where you like." But it was impossible to be offended because I knew that, had I been in distress, he would have given me a hundred pounds or more without turning a hair. As indeed he did, when shortly before my ordination I had to go into hospital for an operation.

I was attached to the 'Professor' and I think he was fond of me. Perhaps his greatest contribution to his students was his insistence on charity in personal relationships. He expected us to refrain from all unkind and negative criticism of our fellows. St Paul's panegyric on love in his Epistle to the Corinthians was more than a poem; it was an order for the day that Christians must obey. That was why Westcott was the most loving and caring community in which I have ever lived. I could wish that all clergy had had the experience, for soon after ordination it did not take me long to realise that a weakness, perhaps a curse, of the clerical profession is gossip and scandal-mongering. It was, perhaps, the major cause of unhappiness in my episcopate.

It was during my last term that I became increasingly interested in the political situation. There were two reasons, Abyssinia and the abdication of Edward VIII.

On October 3rd 1935, I was staying with John Collins at a residential library near Chester. Collins, later to achieve fame as a canon of St Paul's Cathedral and leader of the Nuclear Disarmament Campaign, was Vice-Principal of Westcott House. He, like myself, adhered to the Conservative party. On that afternoon we read in the late editions of the local paper that Mussolini's fascist troops had invaded Abyssinia. For me, and I think for him, and for thousands more of our generation, it was a traumatic moment. I had been led to believe that the League of Nations had put an end to war. The slaughter of 1914–18 would never be repeated, as national and international disputes would be settled by discussion and arbitration. How wrong we were! Italy was embarking upon an imperialistic war against a virtually defenceless people using the latest weapons, not excluding gas. We thought that the democracies would rally to the defence of Ethiopia. Not a bit of it. The so-called 'National Government' connived, and within a matter of months put forward the infamous Hoare-Laval pact which set out to carve up the country to Mussolini's advantage. Hoare was forced to resign while Laval, who subsequently was as ready to appease the Germans as he had been the Italians, was shot as a traitor. Meanwhile our Government did nothing. Anthony Eden made half-hearted protests from the Foreign Office and gave way to Lord Halifax. As Halifax was a dedicated Churchman and held almost in religious veneration, I believed he was bound to withstand Mussolini. Far from it. At the conclusion of the Italian invasion, Halifax went to Rome and toasted the King at a public banquet as 'Emperor of Ethiopia'—an action which brought from the lips of another great Churchman, Sir Stafford Cripps, the remark, "The trouble with Edward is that as he enters the doors of the Foreign Office he hangs up his bowler hat on his crucifix."

The attitude of the Vatican was worse. The Cardinal who dealt with foreign affairs, and who was to become Pius XII, described his countrymen's war as a "just and righteous crusade in which the cross and the sword had gone hand in hand." So much for papal infallibility!

When I left Cambridge in December 1936 the issue was still in doubt, but I had become disillusioned. I began to question the motives of the Government. More important, I was anxious to discover the nature of the powerful interests that induced Church and State to condone Mussolini's war of aggression. It still did not

24

occur to me that the Labour Party was a feasible alternative, not least because of its muddled attitude towards the combating aggression with armed forces, and its lack of leadership. I was sufficiently naïve to believe that if good men in all parties would combine to thwart evil, there would be an end to war.

During my last days at Westcott House the country was shaken by the news that the King intended to marry Mrs Simpson, even though it might necessitate his abdication. It was of such over-whelming importance that little else seemed to matter. Hour by hour radio and newspapers issued bulletins. One might have thought that the Second Advent, with the Final Judgment, had arrived.

I have always been a monarchist and it is likely that in the Civil War I should have been on the side of King Charles, though with reluctance. But the twentieth century is not the seventeenth. The monarch is no longer a ruler but a figurehead and, in my judgment, it is better to have a figurehead who is trained to do the job, and who is rooted in national history, than to have a president, who is likely to be unqualified for a representative role on account of his political involvements. But I cannot believe that it matters much which member of the Royal Family sits on the throne, so long as he discharges his duties faithfully. As a Churchman I hoped that Edward VIII would conform, but if he refused, the nation had his brother to take his place. As matters turned out, what a happy exchange it was! George VI and his Queen superbly expressed the unity of the nation during a grave period in its history.

What worried me was the fuss and the near hysteria. I was more concerned with the war in Abyssinia, the rise of Hitler and un-employment at home, because in each case the fate of millions of people was involved, rather than with the matrimonial affairs of two people, even though one was a King who was threatening to hand over his responsibilities to his brother if he did not get his own way. It seemed to me to reflect a curious scale of priorities. And the pompous self-righteous radio sermon of the Archbishop of Canterbury, Cosmo Lang, made matters worse.

It was the challenge to priorities that hastened my political develop-ment. I knew I had to ask questions and search my conscience. What were the things that really mattered? How should a Christian look at life? Was the Church, as exemplified by Archbishop Lang, right in making such a fuss about personal sexual morality, while remaining so silent on great social evils?

Shortly before his death, in the course of my duties, I had a simple meal with the Duke of Windsor and his wife. He was now virtually unknown and forgotten. He was old and ill. I should like to have told them that the event which had brought so much unhappiness to themselves had sped one of his subjects along the path to a greater understanding of life. The Abdication was not the cause of the journey, as the seeds were already germinating, but it was prominent among the occasions.

A few days after the Abdication I put on a clerical collar and was ordained in Bristol Cathedral.

2

Coming to Heel

St Saviour's mission district was in the poorer part of St Matthew Moorfields, a large parish in the East End of Bristol. I was given supervision of the area which meant I was responsible for about two thousand people. Unemployment was rife and many families were on the means test. It is difficult to describe the squalor, misery and hopelessness to a generation that is largely ignorant of real want. Housing and overcrowding were deplorable. Within a few yards of the mission building was a family of nineteen and another of sixteen. I remember one house where there were twelve sons. They slept six in a bed, three at the top and three at the bottom. There were no bathrooms and no inside lavatories. It did not take me long to change my attitude towards birth control and when, some years later, I became chairman of the Health Committee of the Bristol City Council I immediately pressed for the building of a municipal birth-control clinic.

The mission church was an ugly concrete building at the end of a street. On weekdays a wooden screen hid the altar and the main hall was used for secular activities. In the mornings we ran a rehabilitation centre for the unemployed. The men had nowhere to go; in the summer they sat for hours on the kerb stones, and in the winter in clusters at the street corners. Some had been without work for years and their only activity was to report at the labour exchange, where in most instances they were told they were unwanted. I quickly realised I was unprepared and inadequate for the situation. I had imagined that with few exceptions there were jobs for those ready to work hard, and I remember Christopher Chavasse, the Master of an Oxford college and subsequently Bishop of Rochester, saying that he had never known a converted Christian who had been unable to find employment. It did not occur to him, nor to me, that whole areas could be reduced to pitiful and unwelcome idleness by the cruel facts of a harsh economy over which the victims had no control. Moreover, I was appalled by the scales of relief. I had often met people who had to husband their resources and to count their pennies, and I myself had been brought up in a home which by many standards was considered poor, but I had never encountered families who were denied the basic necessities of life, and I was horrified when men came to me for bread and coal tickets and for clothes and shoes for their children. The main difference between being a parson in such an area in the 1930s and one in the 1980s is that a parishioner can now tell him to go to hell! Formerly he would not have dared because he knew he might have to creep to him for charity. Hence commonsense demanded no unnecessary enemies. Today the welfare state guarantees a minimum standard and society's casualties are no longer dependent upon Lady Bountifuls in clerical collars. Thank God for the change. I prefer to meet parishioners as equals, without enforced patronage on my side or false subservience on theirs.

Although the men kept their thoughts to themselves I knew they had little use for either Church or parson. We represented the privileged classes and, although we were ready to dress the sores caused by the economic cancer, we were seen to be too much part of the status quo to want a major operation for removing the cancers. I had not yet read or studied sufficiently to appreciate the position, but as the months went by economic attitudes started to come into perspective. It was considered fitting for me to dispense charity, but it was intolerable that I should seek to alter, still less to overthrow, the economic foundations of society, even though the change might result in the elimination of the need for charity.

The first months were disillusioning. I had hoped to gain the men's friendship, but I discovered that for them I was a creature from an alien world. I dressed differently; I spoke differently; I had a guaranteed livelihood, while labour excahnges and means tests did not overshadow every aspect of my domestic scene. I was most conscious of frustration when I celebrated the Holy Communion in my concrete church. The service ought to have been a symbol of brotherhood and justice, but I was aware that it did not occur to my unemployed parishioners that we intended to take practical steps to act upon our principles. To them religion was escapism or play-acting, while the parson with his foreign culture was divorced from the rough-and-tumble in which they lived. But our relationships were correct, and I was treated with the politeness which was normally extended to a well-intentioned relieving officer, or undertaker.

In the afternoons we had clubs for mothers and in the evenings for boys and girls. They were appreciated but I didn't know how much they achieved. The mothers listened to talks on home training and housekeeping, but they knew they had neither the facilities nor the finance to take action. I shall never forget their courage and good humour, but it was little short of a miracle if they 'managed'. Food and clothes were short, and sometimes furniture, cots and baby clothes were pawned to meet necessary bills and rents. I tried to help the families in the greatest need, but it was unsatisfactory. Jealousy was inevitable and the scroungers probably did better than their more honest neighbours. I remember an old woman who, when she saw me approaching her house, hurriedly grasped a Bible and spread it on her knees in the hope of impressing me: "There's nothing better than reading the Good Book, Mister," she said. "Yes, there is," I replied, "and that's reading it the right way up." She was impenitent and added, with a wicked grin, "Right side up or wrong side down, how about a coal ticket for Christmas?" It was useless to be angry. The old soul was cold and her one chance of a good fire lay in thawing the parson's heart.

I enjoyed the work with the young people. They were a rough and ready lot, but providing one ruled them with an iron hand in a velvet glove, they were co-operative and loyal. As soon as I arrived I decided to redecorate the hall. It was a loathsome chocolate brown, disfigured and crumbling. A group got to work and when we reopened the club a month later it was a cheerful blue and primrose. I told the members of the club that the hall was theirs to ruin or to keep decently. They responded magnificently. I never saw a pencil mark on the walls.

I encouraged them to run their own affairs, and to assume responsibility. It was not easy. If you are born into the world with a conviction that society has a grudge against you, you are inclined to believe that your place is on the front bench of the opposition, attacking the government, suspicious of authority, and refusing to co-operate. I remember a mother passing the door of the hall on the morning of our Christmas party, with a child at her side: noticing the tree laden with presents she pointed to a doll that was rather better than the rest, and said to the child, "Er's a lovely one, ain't she? But I bets 'er ain't for thee but for one of 'is toffs."

I made it clear to the youth clubs that religion was not an extra for the few and that I hoped that members would remain for prayers. To most it was strange as they had had no dealings with the Church. I gave them responsibility for running the short epilogue and they read the prayers and the lessons. Their simple reverence was impressive.

Some came forward for confirmation instruction and we soon had a dozen or more at the weekly Communion service. But it was hard to persuade the majority. They felt the Church belonged to an alien world. Moreover they were honest, and when jobs were scarce and money was short, they knew that unless they looked after themselves and forgot their Christian ideals they would remain in the unemployment queue. It was all right for those who were safely removed from the cut and thrust of economic struggle, but it was another matter for those who were below the bread-line. My ideas started to change and I wondered how the clergy would have reacted if we had had to share the lot of our people; if we had been unemployed and on the means test; if we had been dependent upon soup kitchens and coal tickets. Perhaps our readiness to leave the Kingdom of Heaven to the other side of the grave would have been less obvious and, because we were hungry, we would have joined the hunger marches.

These were difficult months and I began to wonder whether I had chosen the right path. Perhaps it would have been better if I had remained a schoolmaster. The Church to which I was supposed to have given my life seemed so divorced from the lives of the people I was trying to serve. Worse still, the clergy in the area who might have encouraged me seemed to be indifferent to the harsh facts of unemployment and poverty. They were concerned with taking services for the few who attended and visiting them when they were ill. They were kind to me and I was grateful for their patience. I must have been an awkward colleague. Only the Bishop of Bristol, C. S. Woodward, understood the trauma in which I found myself; when I told him that I was so unhappy in the ministry that I wanted to quit he helped me to maintain my balance and carry on.

And help came unexpectedly from another direction. My mission church in Moorfields was sponsored by Blundell's, a public school in Tiverton in Devon. They paid half of my salary and contributed to the expenses. More important, some boys came to Bristol at weekends to live in the area and to share our lives. Whether or not these visits achieved anything or were dismissed by the unemployed as condescension on the part of do-gooders I hesitate to say. There was ribald laughter at the opening of the mission when some of the governors of the school appeared in smart chauffeur-driven cars in morning dress and top hats.

Once a week I made the seventy-mile journey to Blundell's to talk to the boys, take a confirmation class and stay in one of the boarding houses. The headmaster, Neville Gorton, who was ordained, was one of the most exciting men I have had the joy to know. Fantastic, is probably the right adjective. He was a law unto himself and disregarded most public-school conventions. On one occasion, for instance, when the Officers Training Corps was being visited by a formidable General, he thought it would be more profitable to visit the inmates of the local workhouse.

Another time Gorton preached in chapel on the eve of the confirmation service to be taken by the Bishop of Exeter. As usual he was incomprehensible. The notes of his address were jotted down on cigarette packets, most of which he dropped on the steps as he mounted the pulpit. When he had finished his sermon he hurriedly retraced his steps and leaning on the desk said, "I don't suppose you have understood a word of my sermon. What I mean to say is, being a gentleman is not enough; you need a damn good conversion."

The chaplain, R. A. Abigail, was of a different persuasion. He was a major in the Officers' Training Corps and often appeared in khaki. At the beginning of the Michaelmas term he put up a notice with regard to training for the army and the Church: "The following boys will take Cert A (a military exam) and Confirmation." I liked the order. He certainly believed in muscular Christianity. Shortly before I was due to take a confirmation class, there was a knock on the door and a boy was summoned to appear before Abigail to be beaten as he had kicked a football through a school window. The boy, who was about to listen to me speaking on the virtues of love and non-violence, returned flushed and rubbing his behind. Ten minutes later the boy was summoned again by Abigail: "Bend over," he said. "The hole in the window is larger than I supposed. Another two." The boy returned, still stroking his behind, while I continued my address on love and non-violence.

The following year Abigail, as senior chaplain, addressed all the boys on the eve of their confirmation although they had been prepared by four priests, among whom were Neville Gorton and myself. The headmaster and I sat on the back bench in the classroom. He occasionally took snuff. Abigail, whose idea of Churchmanship was to spread the Union Jack on the altar on Remembrance Sunday, was determined to undermine Gorton and myself, who had encouraged weekly attendance at the sacrament of Holy Communion. I do not think I am being unfair to the Reverend Major, in vestments of khaki, if I summarise his sermon thus: "We are on a journey. Up to the present we've survived on short rations, prayer and Bible reading. Now the journey is more difficult. There are many stiff hills to climb. We need petrol in our tanks. And that, boys, is what the Bishop of Exeter will give you tomorrow—free and for nothing. But there is an even more powerful support, Holy Communion.

31

Once a month. I know there are people who say you should go every Sunday, but that is fanaticism. Of course if you should be faced with great temptations, let me be frank with you and say 'dirty thoughts or masturbation', then I suggest twice a month." To which Gorton exclaimed in a loud whisper to me, audible to all and sundry, "Bloody fool, it won't work anyway!"

One of my confirmands found himself in trouble. He was a clever boy due to sit for an Oxford scholarship. When I arrived at the school for my weekly visit his housemaster said to me, "Peter will have to be expelled, he is guilty of a grave offence. He has been found in bed with a junior boy." I asked the housemaster if he would allow me to deal with the matter as I was outside school discipline. He agreed. I sent for Peter. I asked him to have tea with me. I remember we had an almond cake with icing on the top. He told me that his affair with James had been the most wonderful experience in his life and that everybody had behaved so foully that when he left me he was going to commit suicide. I said, "Keep calm. I'm dealing with this and I will see you through. But tell me, and I apologise for the question, did you have it off with James?" "Of course not," he replied. "Silly ass," I said. "If you are going to be hanged why not for a sheep rather than a lamb?" That reduced the temperature. I went to Gorton and told him the story. He dismissed me and sent for Peter. "Peter," he said, "Michael is leaving this term and I want you to succeed him as head prefect." Yes, Gorton was a genius. In his day Blundell's was a school of unusual achievement. It was alive and brimful of ideas. I used to meet some of the most famous artists and poets in Gorton's house. He would ask them to come to the school to enthuse the boys. Eric Gill, the sculptor, was a frequent visitor. He enabled the boys to build a superb central altar in the middle of the chapel. It was written up in *The Times*. Alas, Gorton's successor, a curious man, removed it.

It was during this Blundell's period that I met Stephen Spender who was a temporary schoolmaster. Thus began a friendship which still persists. I married him to his second wife, Natasha, in the chapel of the Blundell's School mission in Bristol. It was the first time I had married a divorced person. Contrary to what most people think, a Church of England priest has the right to marry a divorced person, no matter what his bishop may say.

Gorton left Blundell's to become the Bishop of Coventry. I chaplained him at his enthronement in the bombed cathedral. He failed to turn up for the complicated rehearsal and at the last moment when we were leaving his house I said, "Gorty, you have forgotten to put on your pectoral cross. Let me get it for you." "No," he answered. "You won't know where it is. I'll get it . . . Oh damn! Ethel has gone off with the key of the front door." He then forced a lavatory window, retrieved the cross, but could not find the chain on which to hang it around his neck. As a substitute he used a boot lace.

When he died I was asked to write the Blundell's chapter in his biography. I approached Heathcote Amory, subsequently Chancellor of the Exchequer, for his views, as he was chairman of the governors of the school. He said in his reply that while he was not quite sure what was the orthodox definition of the word saint, in his judgment Gorton was the most saintly man he had met.

Eccentric, erratic, unpredictable and often incomprehensible, but I shall never forget this ill-dressed man in knickerbockers, sometimes with one or no stockings, making his way in the early morning to Blundell's chapel to ponder the last chapters of St John's Gospel. He was a wonderful friend to me and an anchor in the early years of my ministry. I am amused to think that it was Brendan Bracken, Churchill's great friend, who had been a boy at Sedbergh when Gorton was a housemaster, who was responsible for making him a bishop. An indefensible method of appointment possibly but more effective than some of the products of the present system. He was a great man.

The Member of Parliament for the Bristol East constituency was Sir Stafford Cripps. I had been brought up to believe that he was a Red ogre and a traitor to his class. The worst fears of his opponents were confirmed when he made what appeared to be slighting references to the reactionary influences emanating from Buckingham Palace, though he was careful not to make mention of the King. The fury that he unleashed was on the scale that years later was to descend on Aneurin Bevan, and on his successor in his Bristol constituency, Tony Benn.

Although I was still a member of the Conservative party, I was so disillusioned by the Chamberlain Government, both because of its spinelessness in its dealings with Hitler, Mussolini and Franco, and because of its deplorable record in home affairs, a record which included the miseries, indignities and poverty of my parishioners, that I went to a meeting early in 1938 in the hall of All Hallows Easton, within half a mile of my mission, to listen to Sir Stafford Cripps speak on his criticisms of the present and his hopes for the future. Little did I realise that this meeting was to be a determining event in my life.

Sir Stafford proved to be so different from the newspaper assessments. He spoke quietly and with restraint. He was obviously of outstanding intellectual calibre. He never made personal criticisms of his opponents, nor descended to the vulgar depths of his critics. He was a brilliant advocate of his socialist views but he was inspired by his Christian faith. When A. J. P. Taylor writes in his *English History 1914–1945* (page 360) that "Cripps took up Marxism with the rigidity of a convert," he is talking rubbish. Of course the mistake may be due to Taylor's possible inability to distinguish between Marx and Mark. Cripps was a dedicated Christian, his inspiration was the Bible, his strength emanated from his prayers. And, as members of my congregation will testify, whenever he was in Bristol on a Sunday he came to the Communion service to receive the Sacrament.

After the meeting I decided I must get down to serious reading on social and political matters. I avidly ploughed through dozens of books. I joined the Left Book Club. I attended lectures and conferences. Within a few months I joined the Labour party. However, my stay in my new home was of short duration because almost immediately Cripps and most of his East Bristol party were expelled by the Labour caucus for his advocacy of an united popular front against Hitler and fascism. The Labour Party Conference, like its national executive, has a record for crass stupidity and suicidal fantasies, but I doubt whether its most ardent admirer would now seek to approve its blind foolishness on this occasion. Had Cripps succeeded, had those in all parties who appreciated the evils of Nazism and the paralytic ineptitude of Chamberlain, Hoare and Halifax, rallied around him, Churchill and Duff Cooper, the Second World War might have been avoided. But perhaps it was already too late. Who knows?

Like most converts, and because of my conviction that war was imminent, I had the enthusiasm of an evangelist. My sermons placed greater emphasis upon social justice, though my inspiration was derived from the Old Testament prophets and from the teachings of Jesus. I have always challenged those who have accused me of preaching party politics from the pulpit to quote a single sentence that cannot be justified by Scripture. The challenge has never been accepted.

What I did as a private citizen was another matter. Just as many a parson appeared on a Conservative party platform, so now I appeared on Labour platforms; though after my expulsion with Cripps I turned elsewhere for hospitality. The trouble is, if a priest of the

Church of England supports Conservative causes he is not accused of partisanship; it is another matter when his sympathies lie on the other side. Years later a woman said to one of my archdeacons. "Your Bishop is such a good man, but what a pity he spoils his witness by backing the Labour party." To which the archdeacon replied, "But hasn't *your* Bishop (who happened to be a close neighbour) equally strong convictions?" "Oh no," said my critic. "He's simply a member of the Conservative party." Peter Kirk, a Conservative Member of Parliament, was more perceptive. In the book, *One Army Strong*, he writes, "While no one seems to see anything strange in a clergyman being a Conservative councillor, and there are quite a number of them, Canon Stockwood was widely assailed for sitting on his own local council as a Labour party representative."

My main political activity was to address a meeting on Clifton Downs, Bristol's substitute for Hyde Park Corner, on Sunday evenings under the auspices of the Christian Socialist movement of which Cripps and Lansbury were supporters. It was a new experience and a frightening one. I had never spoken in the open air, except at Sunday School rallies. Now I had to stand to my feet, to cope with hecklers and outwit them, and to be sure of my facts, and above all never to lose my temper, but to defeat my opponents with kindly humour and a laugh. These were difficult lessons and it was a long time before I mastered them.

As I look back I am surprised by my energy. When the war came, and I had no car and there was no public transport on Sunday evenings, I walked three miles from my mission church to the Downs and three miles back, arriving home near midnight.

It was not long before these meetings scandalised my fellow clergy. Invitations to preach in other churches declined, and some were cancelled. One senior cleric, who had been a friend, when meeting me on the Downs as I was making my way home said in response to my good-night greeting, "Get away, you Red traitor." I think my beloved bishop, Dr Woodward, must have heard about the encounter because a few weeks later he said to me, "Stockwood, are you speaking on the Downs next Sunday? If so I am passing near your church and will give you a lift in my car." As he deposited me he said, "You're a brave chap. I don't always agree with you, but thank God, you've got courage."

I was to cause Dr Woodward more embarrassment and of a more serious nature. In fact one that was to have widespread repercussions affecting my future ministry.

In the winter of 1939–40 I preached to the Student Christian Movement in Cambridge. In my address I said that a British zinc firm was still supplying the Japanese, Hitler's ally, with products for making armaments. I urged the workers to strike. I do not defend the fiery language of my youthful outburst, but on the main principle—of aiding and abetting our potential enemies with weapons for the benefit of the shareholders and our own destruction—my views have not changed. It was typical of the Chamberlain Government and its short-sighted supporters.

My outburst gave my Conservative critics in Bristol their opportunity. They had already written to Dr Woodward and to the press urging that I, and three priests who thought alike, should be forbidden to preach. Now they took two further steps. First, they wrote to Neville Gorton at Blundell's to the effect that I was unfit to be the priest of the school mission, still less to prepare his boys for confirmation. Gorton was more than their match. While he did not attempt to defend the temper of my sermon in Cambridge he asked my critics whether or not they approved or disapproved the facts and the implications. There was silence. In fact one of the governors of Blundell's, Sir Lionel Goodenough Taylor, called on me at the mission church to rebuke me, but ended up by asking me to join him on a fishing holiday in Wales. We remained close friends until he died in his nineties twenty years later. His cottage on the Mendips became a regular retreat and resting place. On the day of the announcement of my appointment to the Bishopric of Southwark it was to him and his wife that I went to hide from the press.

The second step was more serious. I was reported to the police as a dangerous influence. It was at the time of Hitler's victories, Dunkirk and the threat of invasion. I was warned that I might be arrested. Once again Dr Woodward intervened, but I never knew from day to day what might happen. In fact the Bishop referred the matter to William Temple, the future Primate of All England, but at that time the Archbishop of York.

The progress of events must seem scarcely credible to those who are unaware of the postal delays that occurred during the war. Temple, having become aware of my existence, wrote to me in the summer of the following year asking me to visit him at the farmhouse at which he was staying at Bicknoller in Somerset. The letter did not reach me for several days. Meanwhile he telephoned me. Now a young clergyman, aged twenty-eight, does not expect an Archbishop to phone him. I assumed the call came from Charles Claxton, a neighbouring parson, subsequently the Bishop of Blackburn, who was a good friend and prone to jokes. The conversation went something like this:

"It's the Archbishop speaking."

"Sez you."

"It is the Archbishop."

"I'm sorry, Charles, I am busy. I'll call you tomorrow. Let's have lunch."

"I am sorry, Stockwood, to disappoint you. I am not Charles, but the Archbishop of York. I wrote to you a few days ago inviting you here. If you don't believe me, I am speaking to you from Bicknoller Post Office and the postmistress will identify me."

I was horrified and probably terrified. My arm trembled. I could scarcely hold the mouthpiece. "Yes, Your Grace . . . no, Your Grace . . . Please forgive me, Your Grace . . ."

Even worse was to follow. The Archbishop said that as he was staying in a remote farm he would meet me at the Windmill restaurant at St Audries between Bridgwater and Minehead. I set off in good time but, as the tyres on my car were nearly worn out, and as it was difficult to get replacements in the war, I had three punctures and I was late, at least half an hour. The Archbishop was waiting in the rain in green plus-fours and open-necked white shirt. I was covered in confusion and did not know how to voice my apologies. "Your Grace," I said, "I am ashamed to have kept you waiting like this. I do not ask you to forgive me." "Don't worry, Stockwood," he said, "on the contrary it's such a relief to see you alive and well. I was afraid lest the Bristol Tories had you put into prison." We made for the farmhouse. Our conversation was interrupted only once. Some children knocked on the door to ask for milk. As the farmer's wife was out, Temple went to the dairy to fill their jugs. I doubt whether they had any idea who he was.

A few days later the Archbishop's letter, written in his own hand, arrived. I quote it as it gives an insight into his character and his humility:

Lower Wearcombe
Bicknoller
Somerset

August 25th 1941

My dear Stockwood,

My wife and I are here until the beginning of next week and it has occurred to us how very pleasant it would be if by any piece of amazing luck you had any engagements bringing you to Taunton or its neighbourhood and could come out to see us. Of course we know it is most unlikely, but it seemed worthwhile to ask. We should be free on Thursday, Friday or Saturday—if we knew you were coming and should be delighted to see you for lunch or tea or any other time.

The buses from Taunton would bring you to Wulfston Moor, about half a mile from this house, the next turning after the Bicknoller turning. They run as follows: (here follow the details of the alternatives). Also from Bridgwater to St. Audries which is about a mile away: (here follow the details of the alternatives).

I would meet you at either Wulfston Moor or St. Audries if I knew to which you would come—only I realise that almost certainly you can't come at all. Could we have a telegram? Bicknoller is a telegraph office.

Yours sincerely,

William Ebor

Years later when I was a bishop and feeling prelatical I would look at Temple's letter to a young man of twenty-eight in the feeble hope that it would keep me humble.

And so began a friendship which was to endure until his death. We often exchanged letters. I visited him again at Bicknoller and sometimes in Lambeth. It was typical of his kindness that he and his wife allowed my mother and me to use their cottage for a week to rest after a series of air raids on Bristol. All expenses paid.

William Temple was an outstanding Archbishop, a saintly priest, a great man.

To return to Bristol and to the start of the rumpus in the summer of 1940. I had had enough and was determined to leave. In March 1939 Eric Abbott, the Warden of Lincoln Theological College, and future Dean of Westminster Abbey, had asked me to join him as chaplain where Michael Ramsey, later to become Archbishop, had recently been Sub-Warden. War broke out within a few months and owing to declining numbers Abbott withdrew the invitation. In December B. K. Cunningham asked me to return to Westcott House as Vice-Principal. I packed my bags, but at the last moment the council refused to approve the appointment. I suspect my address to the Student Christian Movement on arms was my undoing. No explanation was given; I unpacked my bags.

Two academic jobs came my way at a school in Vancouver and Exeter University, but the war again upset plans.

In November 1940 it seemed that at last I had the firm offer which would enable me to kick the dust from my feet and to take over a parish in downtown Sheffield. Everything was arranged for me to see the Bishop, Dr Leslie Hunter, and to visit the church with a view to taking up my duties in the following January. But Providence had other views. On the eve of my departure the first severe air raid on Bristol occurred and parts of the city were devastated. I made my way to the station in the early morning, but the roads were blocked and the trains cancelled. Eventually I established contact with Dr Hunter and another date was fixed, but again I was to be frustrated, because my vicar and my fellow curate at St Matthew's had accepted other appointments in the meantime. As a result Dr Woodward sent for me to tell me that it was my duty to remain to provide continuity, and he wanted me to take over the whole parish of St Matthew Moorfields. It took me three months to make up my mind as I was so anxious to leave. Before accepting I made one condition: I must have a free hand to co-operate with the Free churches and to run the parish on an ecumenical basis. Permission was granted, though in retrospect I wonder on what grounds the Bishop gave it to me as not only was he breaking the law, but in so doing he was giving tacit consent to my illegal activities.

Shortly before my institution it seemed that once again there would be a fiasco. On the night of Good Friday, Bristol suffered its worst raid. Bombs hailed down on the parish, and especially on my mission district. I received a message that a member of our boys' club was wounded and dying. I hastened to the casualty station a mile away at the neighbouring parish of St Ambrose of which Frank Lee was the vicar. Fortunately Robert was still alive. While I was trying to comfort him another message came through to tell me that St Matthew Moorfields, like the Co-op funeral department opposite, was on fire. I hurried to the vicarage and asked Frank Lee to look after Robert while I ran at full speed to the church. As I was crossing St George's Park the Germans dropped a stick of bombs within a few yards. I picked myself up and in a dazed condition retraced my steps to Lee's vicarage. I was swaying at the balcony window when he and his wife caught hold of me and laid me on a sofa. Lee was an old fashioned Evangelical, was deeply concerned and after a prayer of thanksgiving said, "Stockwood, my wife and I are not imbibers but we always keep a little something for medical emergencies—not that we have ever had to use it." He came back to the room with an unopened bottle of whisky and poured out enough to fill a large tumbler. Never have I had a more generous libation. I set out a second time.

St Matthew's, as I approached it, was a macabre sight. The Co-op had been the first to catch fire. The staff had seized as many coffins as possible and stood them on their feet around the walls of the church. A man returning from night shift shouted to me as he passed, "Just like the Co-op ain't it? Buy your coffin now and get your 'divi' back."

Fortunately the fire squads managed to save the church without too much damage being done, apart from the roof which had to be covered with tarpaulin. The building, however, still smelt of charred wood when the Bishop instituted me to the living of St Matthew's on St George's Day, April 23rd 1941. Dr Woodward did not endear himself to the firewatchers when he said in his address that he hoped that during the course of my ministry the fire of the Holy Spirit would consume the church and that its flames would spread to every home in the parish. It was a thrill to be commissioned as a divine arsonist. I did my best to obey his orders.

3

Moorfields

Providence seemed determined that I should remain at Moorfields. When I expressed hesitation, Dr Woodward agreed that the appointment would not be confirmed unless I secured the services of two curates. I did; but after the appointment was announced, both withdrew. Their wives were unwilling to move to Bristol after the devastation of the Good Friday blitz.

I had to wait six months before my first assistant came to the parish. Patrick Fedden headed a list of gifted colleagues who included John Robinson, better known as the author of *Honest To God* and Bishop of Woolwich, and John Bickersteth, the present Bishop of Bath and Wells.

On the night of my institution I went with a fellow parson, John Ford, whose daughter, Anna, was to become famous on the television screen, to my boys' club camp on the Mendips near Cheddar. When we arrived shortly before midnight we found it had been dismantled by the army. We had to make do with a deserted hen house. As I lay on the boards, unable to sleep and hearing the bombs in the distance, I wondered how I should set about the task which, a few hours previously, the Bishop had committed to me.

I decided on a simple strategy with three prongs:

First, to gather together a small group for training.

Second, to introduce a simple 'People's Service' on Sunday evenings, while maintaining the official liturgical services for those who wanted them.

Third, to implement immediately the pact which had been agreed by Ronald Spivey, the Methodist minister, and myself, with the approval of the Bishop, to run the parish on an ecumenical basis.

There can be no short cuts in pastoral work. Gimmicks may attract the crowds for a few weeks, but they drift away. Nothing can be a substitute for the hard slog of establishing personal relationships. Day after day in those early months I gave much of my time to getting to know a few people. I went to their homes most days, we had picnics at weekends, we played tennis in the park. I continued to live in my slum-condemned house next to the mission hall and they helped me with the practicalities. The absence of a curate proved a blessing in disguise as I shared my work with them. For most it was the first time in their lives that they had been asked to accept responsibilities and the co-operation turned us into a team with a sense of mission. Later in the year others joined us, but we remained closely-knit.

When I became a bishop some clergy were inclined to complain that they did not know how to set about their task as parish priests. The sociological pundits encouraged them to have dialogues in depth with other pundits, to make charts and analytical graphs and to attend institutes of behavioural studies. All very impressive and sometimes necessary. I think, however, they might have been more successful if they had spent less time in conference halls in order to tread the streets and to knock on doors—systematically. In no walk of life which demands leadership can there be a substitute for personal relationships. A leader's task is to give himself so completely to a small group that the group learns to share with him in the leadership and to communicate it to others.

The unusual circumstances of the war were a help. As soon as I had accepted the living of Moorfields I was appointed to a responsible position in the civil defence service. I had to supervise the air raid precaution system for East Bristol with regard to shelters. I had a large area to cover with a paid staff of only a dozen but hundreds of volunteers. Apart from learning the art of administration and delegation, which were to prove invaluable, I had to inspect the accommodation, and to visit as many shelters as possible during raids. Inevitably I became well known. I listened to complaints, organised sing-songs, and was often asked to say prayers; though I suspect that as the bomb was heard to be reaching its destiny a popular petition to the Almighty would have been, "Please, Lord, alter the bomb's course and let it drop on the next shelter instead of this."

Another consequence of my involvement in civil defence was the necessity to move from the mission house to a more central position. I could not occupy the large vicarage, as it had been requisitioned for war purposes, so I lived on the main road above what had been a wine shop but which was temporarily closed. It now became my office, with my secretary's room behind. It was a boon. It was much easier for parishioners to walk through a shop door—virtually unnoticed—than to open the heavy iron gates and to walk along the vicarage drive, then knock on the door of a house which was markedly untypical of the other houses in the district, and which in this instance resembled a fortress. Even so, it was difficult for my old friends in the mission area to keep contact with me. They thought my elevation to the rank of shopkeeper implied a social apartheid which excluded them. I often think back to those early years in which I lived in two little rooms in what would now be regarded as a hovel, one of which contained a camp bed that I set up each night. In addition I had installed a bath in what had been a vestry behind the high altar, partly to benefit the football team but also to allow me to disinfect myself, morning and night, from creepy crawlies. Once the bishop, who had been preaching in the mission, had been caught in an air raid and had to take over my camp bed while I laid myself to rest on the floor of the side-chapel. I had become very fond of the people who had become so much part of my life—even to the extent of acting as a referee at a street fight on Christmas Eve, when a burly docker accused his neighbour of seducing his wife. I was sad to leave them and felt a bit of a traitor.

I now had to decide what I should do inside the church building. Because of my upbringing at All Saints', Clifton I maintained the pattern of daily Matins, Evensong and Holy Communion, but I knew that on Sunday something more was required if new people were to be brought into St Matthew's. I started the People's Service in the evening on Sunday evenings, after the official liturgy. It consisted of four hymns, a Bible reading, a few prayers and an address. The service, which I conducted from the pulpit in nothing more elaborate than a black gown, lasted less than an hour.

I took trouble over the planning of addresses. So many weeks were devoted to Christian doctrine, so many weeks to prayer and worship, and an equal number to the social implications of the Gospel. Some evenings were set aside for the consideration of contemporary happenings. The addresses were well advertised and the leaflets were professionally designed. It took six months to make an impact. During that period the congregation was in the region of thirty. Then things began to happen. One Sunday the numbers doubled, and a little later doubled again. We never looked back, and for the next fourteen years the church was usually packed, often with chairs in the aisle. Because of the size of the congregation I was able to invite well known preachers from many parts of the country and beyond, of all denominations, clerical and lay, men and women. I rarely preached more than once a month, except when I undertook an entire course on Church membership which I did every three years. Not many who occupied the pulpit are alive today, though some will be remembered, among them Walter Monckton, Stafford Cripps and the publisher Victor Gollancz. A few remain, Bishop Stephen Neill, Sir Richard Acland, George Thomas, later Speaker of the House of Commons, Lord George Macleod, former Moderator of the Church of Scotland, Sir Robert Birley, former headmaster of Eton, Stephen Spender, Bryan Green, Bishop George Reindorp, Canon John Collins, Bishop Simon Phipps. Although people came from other parts of Bristol when we had a star preacher, most were from the neighbourhood, because petrol rationing and the lack of public transport on Sundays made it difficult to travel. That was all to the good. I have never felt called to administer to an eclectic congregation. I was concerned with my parishioners. It was also my firm conviction that good and careful preaching did not necessarily require a West End congregation to appreciate it.

When the People's Service ended there was a short break before I administered Holy Communion to those who had been unable to receive the Sacrament at the main service in the morning. I have already referred to my contretemps with Father Stothert on the subject of fasting when I was a schoolboy. Now I had to endure it a second time. So outraged were the diehards, especially those in the locality, that they warned their congregations not to enter St Matthew's. One of them, who had been invited to preach before the rumpus occurred, used the occasion to denounce me from my own pulpit. Apparently it was better not to receive the Sacrament than to receive it, as did Our Lord on the first occasion, after breaking one's fast during the day. A trivial matter it may be thought, but it fired the hatred of petty ecclesiasticism and pharisaic legalism which was to be a characteristic of my episcopate.

Later on Sunday evenings in the summer months we had a series of concerts. Music lovers in East Bristol found their way to St Matthew's and although most of them rarely attended services it helped to create the impression of a community church. They felt it was 'home' and that they belonged to the family.

It is a sad reflection on the jealous attitude of the clergy that they tend to denigrate a brother priest who increases his congregations. He is dismissed as a stunt-merchant, or worse. In fact St Matthew's adhered to the Book of Common Prayer more closely than most churches. The main act of worship on Sunday mornings was Parish Communion and no alterations in the text of the authorised service were permitted. Tom Driberg, who visited us from time to time, and whose ecclesiastical affinities were as near to Rome as his political affinities were to Moscow, said he had difficulty in following the service because he had rarely encountered the Prayer Book in the churches in which he was accustomed to worship in the diocese of London.

It is my conviction that what matters is not so much the text of the liturgy, but the manner in which it is presented. Movement, colour, music and voice production are essential ingredients in a satisfactory act of worship, but too often they are dismissed as irrelevant. I took the line that the Holy Communion service was basically a passion play, a drama based on the birth, death and resurrection of Christ. For this reason the standards of production should not fall below those of the theatre and I insisted on rehearsals in the hope of near perfection. I had professionals to advise and train us and I kept watch on everything that happened, but as soon as the art of liturgical performance had been mastered I followed my custom of delegation. Within the congregation I found people, often in their late teens or early twenties, who proved themselves as masters of their craft.

Congregational involvement and shared responsibility were essential. The 'locals' read the Scriptures and administered the cup, practices in those days almost unknown at the Eucharist, and they occasionally preached. I invited them to suggest topics for addresses and choose the hymns. I was insistent that the church, a dreary Victorian building, should be beautifully decorated, while volunteers turned the hideous brown walls and pews into a riot of colour.

I dressed the choir girls, known as the 'Stockwood follies', in French-lavender purple and the altar servers in Richelieu crimson. On great festivals we had organ, piano and strings—and, for a short period, a harp. Every Eucharist is a festival of the Risen Christ and my motive was to make it what it ought to be, a victorious celebration.

My attitude towards ceremonial, though basically orthodox, is flexible. Too often our conception of worship has been limited to words, whereas our other senses ought to be involved as well. For instance, after the stark bareness of Good Friday every stop should be pulled out for Easter, including the one which appeals to the sense of colour and smell. We had a Midnight Mass at Christmas and Easter. For the latter we filled each nook and cranny of the building with primroses, daffodils, lilies and hyacinths, with the result that a sense of hope, cheerfulness, excitement and victory permeated the church even before the service had begun.

I had more difficulty with incense at Christmas. I had always liked incense not least for its liturgical historicity and symbolism. Nevertheless I knew that of all the 'High Church goings-on' it was apt to arouse irrational prejudices, coupled with the fear that the vicar was heading for Rome. So I played it carefully. I asked the parochial church council to agree to the use of incense on weekday festivals, but not on Sundays. They agreed. There were no problems until Christmas fell on a Friday. The leader of the anti-incense lobby was Charlie Hodder, a middle-aged railwayman with a large stomach. He was a splendid representative of the local population. I knew that if I could carry Charlie on any matter, I was virtually home and dry. Though I am not sure that dry is the appropriate adjective because his attentions were given in equal parts to St Matthew's and The Dove, a hostelry next door. These places of worship he visited twice a day, the church always being the first port of call.

On the Sunday before Christmas he arrived in the vestry to ask me whether we were to have incense at the Midnight Mass. I told him that he had been correctly informed and I could think of nothing more appropriate as incense was one of the birthday presents given to the infant Christ at Bethlehem. "But," said Charlie, "you promised not to use it on Sundays." "Agreed," I replied. "But Christmas is on Friday." "But it counts as a Sunday." So I argued with him and suggested we should talk things over. At the end of the day he was more or less convinced that I was playing fair. "But," he added as his parting shot, "if I goes out during the service its no disrespect to you, Vicar, but because that incense 'angs 'eavy-like on my stomach." "O.K., Charlie," I replied. "No offence taken if you have to leave, but we shall all miss you because you're such a part of the family and we all love you." On the actual night St Matthew's was crowded to overflowing. It was the war and our church was the only one in the area which was 'blacked out'. This meant that anybody who wanted a midnight service had to come to us. Ten minutes before we were due to begin, the churchwardens asked me to help them cope with the crowds who were surrounding the church in darkness. The moment I returned to the vestry, I told the clergy, the choir and the servers to take their places so that we could begin the Mass dead on time; I have always been a fanatic about punctuality. Off they went and, as I hurriedly vested, I remembered I had put no incense in the censer. It was too late. The man swinging the censer, a young soldier on Christmas leave, headed the procession and, determined not to let me down, went through the motions with the empty censer. I inwardly applauded his aplomb. By the time we had reached the third verse of "Once in Royal David's City", Charlie, who had probably spent most of the evening in the smoke-filled Dove, stumbled out of the church in a coughing cacophony and the leaderene of the Grandmothers' Union, Sophie Vowles, a superb character, had passed out in the aisle. The Midnight Mass once over and heading for the parish hall for a party and Christmas revels, Charlie took my arm. "Vicar, I wouldn't 'ave 'ad it 'appen for all the money in the world, what with our Albert back from the army and all, but what with the clouds of smoke getting right down in me stomach like, I 'ad to go." "That's all right, Charlie," I said. "You tell your tale to the church council and I'll tell them mine." We did. Afterwards we had incense every Sunday. I loved Charlie dearly. Like lots of men with Mount Everest stomachs, he was a great dancer.

Although we adhered to the official Prayer Book for the main services—Matins, Evensong, and Holy Communion—I decided to experiment with the occasional service as I thought that to many of my East Bristol people the prayer-book services were incomprehensible. I was particularly concerned with baptism. In those days most mothers brought their children to be christened. They would turn up on a weekday evening, perhaps without godparents, and expect the baby 'to be done'. It was a mixture of magic and superstition. I brought this misuse of the sacrament to an end immediately, although an unscrupulous parson in the neighbourhood advertised the fact that he would baptise any child, providing the parent bought a six-penny card of registration. Outside his church was a large notice: "The church with a thousand baptisms a year." I wrote a lampoon headed: "Being done for sixpence at St Noah's and St Jonah's." The vicar threatened to sue me, but the bishop intervened.

Having won half the battle I embarked on the next and more difficult half. I held a baptism service every three months, with a choir and full ceremonial, and I expected parents to attend preparation classes. Numbers dropped catastrophically. I realised I must produce a service that was more intelligible to my parishioners because the standard version was incomprehensible except to a theologically-trained mind. To east Bristol, and perhaps to Belgravia, it was mumbo-jumbo. I sent drafts of the service to Archbishop Temple and to the Bishop of Bristol. They congratulated me on my efforts, but insisted they could not officially approve a departure from the authorised service, though, once again, Dr Woodward reminded me that, like Nelson, his eyesight was somewhat limited. 'My' service went into several editions and hundreds of copies found their way into parishes throughout the country. Despite occasional episcopal explosions from the more conservative bishops, there was no serious trouble until I baptised the grandchild of the Prime Minister.

Janet Attlee, whose marriage service I had taken at Chequers, lived in Bristol. She attended St Matthew's. She asked me to christen her child and the Prime Minister and his wife came to the service. The press fastened on to the service and there was uproar, especially in Church newspapers. The Prime Minister expressed his views with the crisp brevity that was typical of him.

> 10 Downing Street
> Whitehall.
> 29. XI. 48

My dear Stockwood,

I am sorry that you should have been criticized on the christening service. We both thought it a great improvement on the more usual ritual.

Yours sincerely,

C. R. Attlee

The Archbishop of Canterbury, Dr Fisher, and the new Bishop of Bristol, Dr Cockin, were sent copies of the Prime Minister's letter and I heard no more. Some years later Dr Cockin used the service to baptise the child of one of my curates.

It was at the font in St. Matthew's that I met another member of the Labour Government, Nye Bevan. A friend of his wanted me to baptise his child with Nye as godfather. Although I had known his wife, Jennie Lee, for some years, having been chairman of her election committee when she contested Bristol Central in the war years, I had never met Nye. I was told he was an atheist with no liking for parsons. When his name was put forward to me as a possible godfather, I hesitated. Liberal as I was in these matters it seemed dishonest to accept an agnostic as a godfather, who necessarily promises to bring up the child in the Christian faith. While I was hesitating, Nye wrote to me. With characteristic integrity he asked me to send him a copy of the service in order that he might read for himself the promises he would be expected to make. A request I had never met before nor since. He told me in reply that while he could give no affirmative answer to the doctrinal questions, he would do what he could to encourage his godchild to reverence life and to reverence people. I compromised. I was moved by his honesty, but I felt it was inadequate. For this reason I suggested an additional godfather to make the orthodox answers, allowing Nye to remain silent at the appropriate moments. Thus began a friendship which was to endure and develop until many years later, as Bishop of Southwark, I preached his memorial sermon in Westminster Abbey.

It is one thing to bring a child into the Church through baptism; it is another to maintain his allegiance during childhood and adolescence. When I became vicar of St Matthew's it was still the custom for parents to send their children to Sunday School in the afternoon, if only to allow the home two hours of comparative calm. In view of the size of the families, a large audience was guaranteed, though audience is scarcely the right word. The children met in the parish hall under the tutelage of Mr James Clarke, who was well into his eighties and hard of hearing. Even so, when the babel reached a crescendo he repeatedly blew a football whistle and rang a handbell in the hope of restoring a measure of law and order. I was warned that if I interfered, the parents who had known Mr Clarke for generations would rise up in arms—and that the subscribers to the annual outing to Weston-super-Mare would cut off the supplies. I waited my time but when a few weeks later I found the hall in a state of siege with Mr Clarke blowing his whisle and waving his bell as though it was a continuous fire-alarm I thanked him for his services and took my leave of him. Octogenarian though he was, he still had plenty of fight in him. He sent a circular to the parents warning them I was a 'Rominiser', and advising the subscribers to withhold their donations.

The problem was now mine to solve. I knew I should lose those who had enjoyed the Sunday afternoon rough-house, just as their descendants would enjoy the Saturday afternoon riots on the football terraces, but I thought that I might gain the rest if only I could find ways and means of winning their interest and co-operation. And so it proved. Once again by the method of delegation and responsibility.

I revived the medieval custom of 'Boy Bishop'. In Cathedrals a boy was elected on St Nicholas' Day, December 6th, to assist the diocesan bishop at the main services until Holy Innocents' Day, December 28th, three days after Christmas. The purpose was to honour the boyhood of Christ. I adapted the custom to meet our needs. A boy was elected by the members of the Sunday School, now renamed 'the junior church', to serve as Boy Bishop for a year. To him I gave the responsibility of conducting the worship. Each week he submitted a draft service for comment and advice but so expert did they become that there was rarely need for alterations.

At Christmas the young people placed their vote on a plate on the altar and on the following Sunday there was an impressive 'enthrone-ment' service when the new 'bishop' was vested in cope and mitre with pectoral cross, staff and ring. He had a team to help him, assistants, choir and servers.

I was usually in the church on Sunday afternoons because one of the clergy gave the instructions, but the drill and the discipline was left to the Boy Bishop. A whistle was no longer required. The juniors enjoyed the service because they felt it was theirs. Of course the more rumbustious sometimes caused trouble, but the Boy Bishop was more effective as a silencer than I could have been; standing on the chancel step he pointed to the offender and commanded him to "Shut thee 'ole."

The ex-Boy Bishops, having become used to responsibility, usually continued to make a valuable contribution to St Matthew's. Often they served on the church council and became leaders of organisations. Most important, some, together with other members of the congregation, assisted me with confirmation instruction. I would speak on the main theme; for example the purpose of saying one's prayers, reading the Bible and receiving the Sacrament, while they would tell them what these things meant to them and how they set about them.

I left St Matthew's in 1955 and I was not to see most of the 'bishops' for a quarter of a century, until I asked fourteen of them to Bishop's House shortly before I resigned from Southwark in 1980. It was among the happiest of the hundreds of parties I had in my episcopate. All, including those who had started with few or no advantages, had a record of achievement. All received the Sacrament in my chapel. Such are the rewards in a priest's life.

The third prong of the fork with which to dig the ground was the 'ecumenical' one, though we did not use that grand word in those days. We were content to speak of co-operation between the Churches. I think the laity find it easier to understand and certainly to pronounce.

Ronald Spivey was the ideal Methodist with whom to co-operate. He had a good mind and wide sympathies. He was an arresting preacher and an even better teacher. He was basically a Wesleyan High Churchman with an affection for the Church of England. He had a pleasing sense of humour.

We decided to meet on Tuesday mornings for Holy Communion, breakfast and a staff meeting. Another decision, which typified my ministry, was the refusal to keep a minute book, coupled with the agreement to conclude our meetings within two hours whether or not we had completed our agenda. Committees, like church services, need to be conducted with devout despatch. If people like to know when business is due to begin, they are even keener to know when it will end.

The advantage of having no minute book lay in the encouragement it gave to flexibility. In those experimental days it was important that we should not feel bound by precedent. We dealt with each matter as it arose and in accordance with the immediate circumstances and not the circumstances of an earlier year. It was a pragmatic approach and we were not afraid to change our minds.

Within a few months we were joined by the neighbouring Anglican parish, three Methodist churches, one Baptist church and one Congregational church. In our hey-day there were twelve full-time workers, clergy and lay, persons. We called ourselves the Redfield United Front, Redfield being the area in which we worked.

It was not long before the protests began. The Free churchmen had their problems because of the fear of a take-over bid. Moreover for decades there had been an iron curtain between Church and Chapel. As with the Jews and the Samaritans there were no dealings between us. There were many reasons for it, but most can be placed under the headings of history, class, politics and doctrine.

Our problems arose from opponents outside the parishes rather than inside. There was anger because I asked the Free Church ministers to receive the Sacrament at the Tuesday morning Communion services and to preach from my pulpit. There was an attempt by one group to place St Matthew's on a black list and to break off relationships with my curates and myself.

The Bishop of Bristol, who had to contend with the condemnatory letters, was as usual a friend and guide. I knew I could not ask him to approve what was not specifically allowed, but I informed him of what I was doing and never disregarded his wishes.

Archbishop William Temple, who was still at York, showed a keen interest and when we started our united magazine, *The Redfield Review*, sent us this commendation:

I send my very best wishes for the success of the united magazine. This seems to be an admirable method of presenting to the world the united front which Christians ought to show. There are differences among Christians which loyalty to truth as we see it forbids us to deny; and loyalty to truth is a primary duty. Moreover some of these differences are of such a kind as to keep us apart in some most important ways. But when all is said the

51

differences between Christians are as nothing compared with the differences between all sincere Christians on one side and all non-Christians on the other. So even if we cannot yet unite in all things, let us show the world that in what matters most we are united, namely that in Jesus Christ 'God hath visited and redeemed His people'.

William Ebor

It was not long before the laity wanted to have the same opportunities to meet around the Lord's Table as did the staff. In fact they wished to go further. Whereas on Tuesday mornings we met at St Matthew's and only Anglican and episcopally-ordained priests celebrated the Communion (the Free Church ministers knew that I would become involved in an ecclesiastical hurricane if I invited them to do so), the laity wanted to have the Sacrament in each of their churches on an occasional weekday evening with their own minister as the celebrant. We tried to solve the problem by composing a Communion liturgy in which all the clergy, Anglican and Free Church, said the consecration prayer together. Although I had no scruples with regard to receiving the Sacrament in a Free Church and had occasionally done so, I had to respect the consciences of those who believed that only an episcopally-ordained priest might celebrate the Eucharist. Moreover, I knew the Bishop of Bristol would be unable to defend me. So I sent the draft service to William Temple, who had recently moved to Canterbury. He replied from Lambeth Palace on July 10th 1942.

My dear Stockwood,
  This is a purely personal comment on the form of service you have sent. First let me say personally that I welcome extremely this kind of experiment. I cannot officially approve it, if that means anything that can be quoted as equivalent to authorisation, but you understand all about that.
  I think there may be a real case for co-consecration in some of these experiments, though I feel pretty sure that our way through the difficulty is really to be found along the line of joint Ordination, with which the Americans are now occupying their minds. If that were agreed upon, of course we could have a real interchange in this sense, that while every man would himself celebrate according to the rite of the Church of the ministry in which he was ordained, we could all receive with full authorisation at one another's hands.

Now as regards the form of services: in the main I think it is good and probably contains as many elements as those uniting in the service would agree upon wishing to include. As I read it, it feels to me a little bit of a patchwork, but it is hard to judge this unless one has used it in actual worship.

I wonder whether you and your friends would like a little prayer that I often use as a vestry prayer after a Celebration, as follows:

Vouchsafe, O Lord, to dwell for evermore in the hearts of us thy servants, that we may be one with thee as thou art with the Father, God blessed for ever.

It is at least Johannine!

Yours very sincerely,

William Cantuar

Thus encouraged, I went ahead. The draft of the service was revised and the Bishop of Bristol, in his personal capacity, expressed his goodwill. The Anglo-Catholics, however, created trouble, especially those who knew neither Bristol, Redfield nor myself. They were convinced that the Free Churches were not true Churches and that their ministers were no better than laymen in dog collars. Hence our united Communion services were condemned. The fact that we were seeking to bring together Christians of all persuasions at the Lord's Table to bear witness to Christ in heavily-bombed East Bristol seemed to mean nothing to them. As there was a debate in Convocation a few months later on the general topic I wrote to William Temple again. He replied to me on June 11 1943:

My dear Stockwood,

I have not the least doubt that the debate in Convocation did harm: it was a quite abominable debate; but it represented the outlook that prevails among the older clergy, and on the whole Convocation represents the older rather than the younger. Of course the fact is the Anglo-Catholics cling to the view that though the Nonconformists are individually members of the Church if they are baptised, their bodies are religious societies like the S.P.C.K. or the Y.M.C.A., and are in no sense Churches. Also they hold they have no real ministries. We shall get nowhere in these matters if we are not perfectly candid, and so I thought it right to make my own position clear. That is that I fully recognise the reality of the Free Church ministries as authenticated by their

53

fruits—which seems to me a sound Scriptural principle to go by. But I am also convinced that they do not represent the permanent tradition of the Church, as our own does and moreover that as a result of their breaches in continuity, their sense of the one-ness of the Church throughout the generations suffers. As one distinguished Free Churchman put it to me, "We are hardly conscious of anything except the 1st century, the 16th and the 20th."

The upshot of this is that I do not feel able, except in special conditions, to make use for myself, or recommend Anglicans to make use of those ministries until a decision is reached which will effect unification of the ministries by adoption of the historic episcopate. But when that has been decided and before the actual union takes effect by the consecration of some leading Free Churchmen to the episcopate, I should think it right to signalise that the heart is now out of the division and to receive Holy Communion from representatives of those ministries before they were regularised in our sense of the word.

Yours sincerely

William Cantaur

In October 1944 the Redfield Synod was held. It consisted of clerical and lay representatives of the participating Churches. I gave the address, in which I put forward proposals to be discussed at the end of November at the Redfield General Assembly. Speaking in Bethesda Methodist Chapel I reminded the congregation of the progress that had been made since the turn of the century.

In 1898 a procession left this chapel of Bethesda and marched to the doors of the church of St Matthew Moorfields to greet a new vicar with criticisms, protests and abuse. Forty-six years later, a vicar of St Matthew Moorfields stands in the pulpit of Bethesda, at the invitation of the ministers of all denominations in Redfield, to preach a synodical sermon to the leaders of an affiliated group of Churches. There has been, to say the least, a re-orientation of ideas.

I spoke of the accomplishments during the past three years—a youth centre with its own vigorous 'parliament'; a street scheme to cover the needs of newcomers, the elderly and the war casualties; neighbourhood meetings to create a sense of community in the immediate locality; public discussions in St George's Park on Sunday evenings in the summer and in the local factories in the winter. Perhaps the most remarkable achievement was the permission given to us by the Bristol Educational Authority to teach in the schools.

Next I turned to the future and to the difficulties ahead.

First, there is the danger that ministers will move too far ahead of their people. The ministers, because they meet each week, tend to see things in a different light from those who sit in the pews, especially from those who have sat in one particular pew for forty or fifty years and whose concern for the worldwide Church is often limited by the walls of the building in which that pew is to be found. On the whole the ministers have received much encouragement from the senior members of their churches, but there are still some who have yet to learn something of the passion and the pain which Our Lord experienced when He uttered His prayer of yearning love, 'that they all may be one'.

A second difficulty arises from the attitude which we ought to adopt towards the practice of inter-Communion. Your ministers are not sure what is the wisest course to pursue in the immediate future, and one of the purposes of this Synod is to seek the advice of you who are the leading members of the laity.

A third difficulty, which if it is to be overcome will demand wise statesmanship and fearless vision, is this: at some point we must decide whether it is desirable to achieve a fuller measure of organic unity. At present it is not permissible for a minister who has not been ordained by a bishop to celebrate the Sacraments in an Anglican Church. Consequently, while the ministers can achieve equality of status in the pulpit, they cannot, so far as the Anglican Church is concerned, achieve it at the Lord's Table. It is no solution to suggest that we can ignore the rules and go our own way, because the result would be to create a schismatic Church in Redfield, which would not be recognised by the Church of England. Moreover, if an unconstitutional attempt were made, it would divide the Church in Redfield in two.

After considerable reflection, I believe that the Anglicans and the Methodists, who have so much in common, should seek to bridge the gulf by submitting to the appropriate authorities of the two denominations a scheme whereby the ministrations of the clergy should be acceptable to both Churches. To put it in a practical form, the Anglican clergy should receive some form of Commission from the Nonconformist authorities which would make it possible for them to take any service in a Nonconformist church, while the Nonconformist ministers should receive some form of episcopal Commission which would make it possible for them to take any service in an Anglican Church.

I concluded my address by putting forward a programme for dealing with the needs of the hundreds of servicemen who, at the conclusion of the war, would be returning to Redfield.

I sent a copy of my address to the Archbishop asking for his comments and advice. I received an acknowledgment from his secretary but, before he could reply, William Temple was dead.

I was thirty-one when the Redfield Synod was held and my ministry was in its spring. Now that I am retired I look back upon those fourteen years of co-operation as a golden age. There was rarely a day when I was not involved in the work of the United Front and with its ministers, while on many a Sunday we were in and out of one another's pulpits. Perhaps the happiest occasion in the year was the Midnight Mass when St Matthew's was packed with the representatives of all the congregations while the Free Church ministers joined with the Anglicans in administering the Christmas Sacrament. Such a depth of ecumenical experience was never experienced by me after I left Bristol in 1955. On my appointment to the University Church at Cambridge, the Bishop of Ely told me that Free Church ministers might occasionally preach, but nothing more. When I moved to Southwark the clergy rarely availed themselves of the liberty I gave them, while the Free Church ministers were slow to respond. Perhaps the trouble was due to 'bureaucratisation'. The ecumenical movement had become an end in itself with an octopus of vested interests, subsidised committees, hair-splitting theologians and ecclesiastical politicians. Our background was different and less sophisticated. As I said in the Redfield Synod address, "Three and a half years ago the ministers of the churches and chapels in Redfield met one Tuesday morning for the sacrament of Holy Communion at St Matthew's. They subsequently discussed the work which they could jointly undertake. They had no plans. They set up no committees. They made no rules, they elected no chairman. Instead they laid all before God and waited for His guiding Spirit to lead them step by step."

4

The Market Place

I worked hard in the parish, but I did not allow it to absorb my energies. I knew that my responsibilities were not confined to the church building and to what happened within it. While I had a special care for the congregation, I was as concerned for the thousands who never set foot inside St Matthew's, especially for those who were the victims of the social system. Of course I did what I could to poultice the sores by helping those in immediate need, but I was more concerned to remove the cancer which produced the sores. This was the flash point. The Church of England had reason to be proud of its record as a major distributor of charity. It knew better than most organisations how to remove the extra crumbs from the rich man's table to give to the poor, but it was careful to impose no threat upon the rich, still less to suggest that the poor should sit as equals at his table. In short, a priest, while distributing charity to the poorest, was expected to support the class-stratified society and the economic status quo. It was Charles Kingsley not Karl Marx who first spoke of religion as the opiate of the people. He was partly right. If there had been no Lady Bountifuls, no crumbs from the rich man's table, no talk about a happy land above the bright blue sky when we die, there might have been a revolution long ago. In the last century the vicar of St Matthew's, living in his iron fortress, had a carriage and horses. He and his four curates wore top hats and frock coats. On Sundays they distributed sixteen dinners to the hungry. What is more, at the evening service a bread ticket was placed in every tenth Prayer Book. A celestial bingo sesson!

As a young man I assessed the situation in terms of black and white. I believed that the capitalist system with its unscrupulous drive for profits was responsible for national and international distempers. The basis of British society as constituted in the Chamberlain era was greed, not need. To maintain the basis, the appeasement of Hitler abroad and the dole queues at home were requisites. Of course it was a simplification and, as I grew older, I knew other factors had to be taken into consideration.

57

The war having started, there was a political truce. The three main parties agreed not to contest by-elections. The supporters of Sir Stafford Cripps in his Bristol constituency were not so easily silenced. We had been content to be expelled with him when he tried to establish a united front to rid the country of Chamberlain, in order to overthrow Hitler, and now we were happy to remain in the political wilderness.

In January 1941 a new organisation called People's Convention met in London to challenge the Government and to determine peace aims. There were 2,234 delegates, representing 1,200,000 people in 1,304 organisations. On the morning it began, in the Royal Hotel in London, queues stretched more than half a mile along the pavement. I was impressed. At last there was a vigorous movement to bring about a better ordering of society. I was on the point of joining. But I was disturbed. The leaders were members of the Communist party, most of whom had supported the Stalin-Hitler pact. Although I had become keenly interested in the Soviet system, had studied Marx and had read widely, I had come to be suspicious of a political party which appeared to rate obedience to the Kremlin as of more importance than loyalty to one's country, and at a time when we were alone and our future existence was in doubt.

When the Convention was first suggested in the previous autumn I wrote to Sir Stafford Cripps, now our Ambassador in Moscow, for his advice. He wrote to me from the British Embassy on December 7th 1940.

My dear Stockwood,

I have only just received your letter of the 11th October asking my views as to the People's Convention. My own view is that it is too early for any such convention. An exploratory commission will only accept the cut and dried Communist programme, which will be laid before it no doubt, and I don't feel that that is wise or worthwhile. A great deal of thought and hard work by genuinely flexible minds is required to find the way out of our difficulties. I would not if I were you take part in the Convention otherwise than as an observer. If you do please write and let me have a detailed account of it!

All good wishes,

Yours very sincerely,

R. Stafford Cripps

58

Cripps returned to London in May to report to Winston Churchill. He made a visit to his constituency and spoke in St Matthew's hall. He told us something of the hideousness of Stalin's tyranny and estimated that there were fifteen million political prisoners. In his judgment the Soviet dictator had betrayed socialism and there was little to choose between his régime and Hitler's.

Cripps had dropped a political bomb. Criticisms of the Russian experiment were attributed to the partisanship and malevolence of the capitalist press, and there is no doubt that it had overplayed its hand for political reasons; but now the respected leader of the extreme Left was wrecking the hopes and dreams of many socialists who had risked much to support Russia and to further the Soviet ideal in Britain.

People in the hall reacted in different ways—disbelief, anger, sadness and "I told you so." I asked Cripps if there were any signs of hope that the abuses of Stalin's régime could be overcome and the way to true socialism restored. "It all depends," he said, "whether or not you believe in the triumph of the human spirit. I do, but it may take five hundred years."

Because I had always had my suspicions, I was disappointed but not surprised. The Church press had consistently reported the persecution of Christians and the butchering of priests. No matter what the weaknesses of the Russian Orthodox Church may have been, I was sure that a political philosophy that was committed to the violent extirpation of religion and to the widescale murdering of believers was evil. I had hoped, however, that with the passage of time, a change would come. Religious persecution was not a new phenomenon. Our own record both in Britain and in Ireland was enough to make us bow our heads in shame. And, of course, there were the Crusades.

Within a month everything changed. Germany attacked the Soviet Union. The Communist party substituted the Union Jack for the Red Flag and became enthusiastic supporters of the Churchill Government. They wanted England to win the war in order to save Russia from defeat. The People's Convention was forgotten.

These events raised in my mind the issue of patriotism in relation to political conduct. Crimes innumerable have been committed in the interests of 'my country, right or wrong'. Hitler and Stalin are recent examples. Henry VIII is one of many in England. A man must do as the State commands whether or not his conscience approves. That is why I have reservations when it comes to singing

59

the popular hymn, "I vow to thee, my country." In the first verse we affirm a love and service for our country that 'asks no question'. For a Christian such an affirmation can be incompatible with his allegiance to Christ. It is true that in the second verse the author, Cecil Spring-Rice, writes of "another country, I've heard of long ago, most dear to them that love her, most great to them that know," but he does not indicate what happens when loyalties to these two countries come into conflict; perhaps he never envisaged that they would.

The fact is, when a person is baptised he becomes a member of the Church, whose primary, if not its only, purpose is to further the Kingdom of God. "Your kingdom come, your will be done, on earth as in heaven." Hence a Christian is a member of a supra-national community and his first loyalty is to the Kingdom of God. And there can be no doubt as to where he should stand if there is a conflict between the lesser loyalty to his country and the greater loyalty to God's Kingdom. After all, that is what was expected by most of us of German Christians. We applauded them when they resisted Hitler and, because of their Christian commitment, were put into concentration camps and incinerators. We assumed there could be no alternative. True enough, but what we expected to determine the conduct of German Christians should determine the conduct of Christians everywhere.

A Christian will strive to be a good patriot and to give of his best to his country, but he should question everything, supporting what he believes to be compatible with the will of God, and opposing what he believes to be incompatible, even though his opposition may be regarded as treachery by those who fail to understand his motives, as has often happened.

For some Christians the choice was not an easy one. We were asked to support a Government that appeased fascism abroad and condoned appalling social conditons at home, and a Prime Minister about whom Stafford Cripps said in a speech in Birmingham, Chamberlain's home town, in March 1938: "The puny son of one who could at least be called courageous, however mistaken his views, has disgraced not only his native city of Birmingham, but his country and the whole civilised world as well . . . The people of Birmingham have a specially heavy responsibility, for they have given the world the curse of the present British Prime Minister." But when war came the issue was clear to me, although I detested the Chamberlain Government and longed for something better to take its place. I knew there could be no future for our country nor for the world until Hitler had been destroyed. Hence my duty as a Christian and a patriot presented no difficulties.

For communists it was different. To dismiss them as traitors is an over-simplification, though judged by normal standards many were. But it is worth looking at the situation from their point of view, a view which the leaders of the People's Convention hoped would win my support, but which I decisively rejected.

Communists then believed that their first loyalty was to the Soviet Union because, they assumed, it was the architect of world brotherhood and justice. Just as the Kingdom of God demands the primary loyalty of Christians, so does the Soviet Union make a similar demand on those who believe in the Marxist Utopia. It is difficult for a later generation that has become familiar with the horrors of the communist régimes, and of the prostitution of socialism in the Soviet Union, to treat seriously the reaction of the Communist parties in the 1930s, but of their sincerity I have no doubt. They were utterly committed to the Soviet experiment in so far as they believed it was the harbinger of a new age. When Hitler made a pact with Stalin in August 1939, they supported the pact because they believed it would save Russia. The Nazis might temporarily triumph, but eventually the defeated countries would become Soviet republics and enjoy the blessings that had been denied to them under their capitalist rulers. If it be incomprehensible to us that men once not only believed that patriotism meant loyalty to Marxism and to its Russian agents but made great sacrifices for their beliefs, then it is even more incomprehensible today when the Utopian illusions have been dispelled and we know the brutal facts. Traitors some of them certainly were, but they considered themselves to be super-patriots, evangelists of a new gospel that would bring hope, justice and brotherhood to mankind. Their activities might bring chaos and defeat to a nation and individuals might be sent to their deaths, but it was the price that had to be paid for the realisation of a glorious ideal.

I do not regret my association with members of the Communist party at the time of the People's Convention. They were dedicated people, dedicated to the ideal of the classless Utopia. Of course they were mistaken, but they had a zeal which was rarely found in the Church. If Christians had believed as passionately in the Kingdom of God, post-war Europe might be different from what it is today.

Why were they mistaken? For the reason that most political parties are mistaken: the failure to come to terms with original sin.

Whether we like to admit it or not, man is selfish and prone to evil. No matter what his philosophy may be, he puts himself at the centre of his universe. He will make common cause to defeat his enemy, but as soon as he is in authority he is tempted to use his position to maintain his rank and privilege. It is true of our country, no matter what Government is in power; it is true of the communist countries. In fact the position is worse in the communist countries because in the absence of free elections the party officials have privileges which can be retained indefinitely.

This gloomy diagnosis, which was a constant theme in my sermons during the war, did not lessen my interest in the political scene. As Archbishop Temple frequently reminded us, politics cannot turn bad men into good, but the society for which politics is responsible can encourage men to be good or bad. If a person is born in an over-crowded slum and grows up ill-educated with no prospect of a job, he is unlikely to become a useful member of society, but if he is given the environment which had been reserved for the privileged classes he might achieve his potentialities to the satisfaction of himself and for the benefit of his country. The tragedy of pre-war Britain was the appalling environment in which millions had to live. My desire was to be associated with a programme of change. I had no faith in revolution, and even less in the ability of the Tory party to achieve a better Britain. I could not work for the Labour party because Stafford Cripps and his followers in East Bristol were expelled. We were isolated, but free to do as we liked. As one who has always found it difficult to treat party allegiance too seriously and has preferred independence, this suited me.

An unexpected opportunity came when Stephen Spender asked me early in 1942 to write an article for the March edition of *Horizon*, which described itself as a review of literature and art, with Cyril Connolly as Editor. I was surprised and flattered because the magazine was widely read in thoughtful circles. I wrote the article in William Temple's cottage on Exmoor, and it was published under the heading of "The Church and post-war reconstruction." It attracted more notice than it deserved and launched me on a wider political scene. I found myself asked to address meetings in places as wide apart as Edinburgh, London, Cardiff and Exeter. These opportunities increased when in July of the same year, Sir Richard Acland, a crusading Liberal with a keen Christian conscience, and with the determination to awaken the nation to the problems that would need to be faced in post-war Britain, founded the Common Wealth party. It was an amalgamation of forward-looking groups including those which had been politically affected by J. B. Priestley's Postscripts to the Sunday nine o'clock news. Its immediate campaign was to stimulate the fight on both fronts against Hitler and the Tory reactionaries. As there was an electoral truce between the main parties, Common Wealth enabled dissidents to campaign, especially those with Left convictions. I became an active member. We won three by-elections. The response was surprising because the proposals for common ownership were far to the Left of the Labour party's and they were not primarily in the interests of greater efficiency but in the interests of a more generous and satisfying way of life. William Temple said of the movement, "This is significant: this is the first time the middle classes have listened to a moral argument for more than a hundred years."

In 1942 the Member for Bristol Central, Lord Apsley, was killed in action. His widow, a cripple for whom there was much sympathy, was nominated as his successor. The Labour party was not allowed to challenge her, but others did. Jennie Lee was asked to be Common Wealth candidate. She refused, but agreed to stand as an Independent with Common Wealth Support. I was chairman of her election committee. In her book, *My Life With Nye*, Jennie writes: "That was the most enjoyable election I ever fought. Against me I had a Tory candidate and an I.L.P. candidate. For me I had Dick Acland's idealistic troops and also the great majority of the Bristol Central Labour party. They knew perfectly well that although Nye, Stafford Cripps and quite a few other Labour MPs could not support me openly, they were entirely on my side."

It was an exciting campaign. Speakers included Michael Foot, Tom Wintringham, Victor Gollancz, Hannen Swaffer, Dick Acland and Tom Driberg. I acted as host and many stayed with me in my rooms over the shop. Thus began my personal association with politicians who were playing an active part in national life. All of us had one thing in common: when the war was ended the pattern of society was to be changed. We had too many memories of the 'hard-faced business men', the war-time profiteers, the sycophants on the Lloyd George honours' list, who had prostituted the ideal of 'a land fit for heroes' and had brought misery, unemployment, and degradation to millions of the working classes. Bristol Central had been heavily bombed. The register was out of date. Voters were scattered. It was not surprising that Jennie lost the election. The businessmen cast their double vote for the Tory candidate. At the count in the City Council chamber I approached the chairman of the Conservative Election Committee and, as an act of normal courtesy,

extended my hand saying, "I believe you are my opposite number."
Refusing my hand, he replied, "Reverend Sir, to be opposite to you
in all things is my one wish." Illustratively he turned his back,
adding, "You are a disgrace to the Church."

The Labour hierarchy gave us no sympathy. We were rebels who
had defied the party line. They expelled us again. We were not too
much dismayed. I remained an Independent, giving what help I
could to Dick Acland and Common Wealth.

As the war approached its end, efforts were made to bring us back
into the fold as the official party did not want to have rival 'Labour'
candidates in the Bristol East constituency, especially as they knew
that Cripps was likely to be the winner. I was asked to put out feelers
to Sir Stafford. They wanted him to meet a respected Bristol Labour
leader, Bill Wilkins. I did as I was asked. The reply came on
December 8th 1943.

My dear Mervyn,
    Thank you for your letter. As to the meeting with Wilkins I am
afraid it is out of the question my going back into the Labour
Party under existing circumstances. If those circumstances change
I am always open to reconsider the position. A great deal *may*
happen before an election—I only hope it does so far as the
Labour Party is concerned! I don't think it is the slightest use my
discussing the situation with Wilkins or any of the others as we
should simply reach an impasse which would merely make the
situation more difficult. Thank you for your good office. I still
hope a solution may eventually be found.

Yours ever,

Stafford.

A year later there was a reconciliation and, a few days before
Christmas, Attlee wrote to Cripps, "It is a very real joy to me that
we shall be again together in the party in the New Year."

This created a difficulty for Cripps. The Government was evenly
balanced and Churchill appointed him as an Independent. He
thought that his re-admission would be a problem for the Prime
Minister, and he offered to resign. Churchill replied immediately:
"I have always considered you a socialist and as belonging to the
socialist representation in the Government. Your decision to re-
establish your formal position as a member of the Labour party
raises no question affecting the balance of power in the Government,

except of course that you will henceforth count as a socialist instead of something even worse."

Cripps told me that Churchill puckishly regretted that he had been brought back into the fold because the Prime Minister was looking forward to being asked to speak for him as an Independent candidate at the forthcoming election. Stafford assured him of his appreciation, but wished to be spared the kiss of death.

During his negotiations with the National Executive, Cripps insisted that those who had stood with him in Bristol should be accepted back into the party. So back we went, and I became deeply involved. Between January and May, Cripps made speech after speech on the post-war world. He insisted that while we should fight hard to improve material conditions at home and abroad we should do so as Christians who followed the teaching of their Master. He concluded an address to the students of the University of Glasgow on February 9th 1945 with these words: "If we can become more whole-hearted followers of Christ and so make our Churches more alive and active in their leadership, we can instil a moral purpose into the world, without which it will drift from war to war and decline into chaos. That is the job we are given as Christians. I pray that you and I may have the courage to carry it through."

Bristol East saw little of Cripps during the election campaign. He was sufficiently confident of his position to consider himself to be better employed touring the country. His message rarely varied: "The Labour party does not picture this post-war period as a sort of Utopia into which we invite you to step. Far from it—it is going to be one of the most difficult and trying periods in the history of our country."

When the results were declared on July 26th, Cripps had a majority over his Conservative opponent of nearly eighteen thousand.

It had been his intention to tour the constituency to thank his helpers, but, as it poured with rain throughout the day, he remained in my study over the shop to await the outcome. The ensuing four hours were as fascinating as they were memorable.

Cripps had told me that Churchill would remain Prime Minister until he failed to get a vote of confidence in the New Parliament. Meanwhile the Parliamentary Labour party would meet early in the following week to choose their leader who would eventually be summoned by the King to form a Government. It was unlikely to be Attlee as he was considered to be too weak. Although Cripps' opinion has been disputed it is confirmed in the memoirs of Anthony Eden:

> July 25th 1945. It is evident we are out. Rang up Winston and said what I could. Mr Churchill's mood at that moment was not to resign, but to meet Parliament as a Government and let Labour turn us out. I counselled no decision until more returns were in . . . The Prime Minister grunted and asked me to get back to London as soon as I could . . . When I went to see the Prime Minister at the Annexe on my arrival in London, he told me that he had already resigned.*

As soon as it seemed likely that Labour was winning, telephone calls came through to my study thick and fast as Stafford had sent my number to the party headquarters in London. Herbert Morrison fancied his own chances and sought Stafford's support against Ernie Bevin. Bevin was as opposed to Morrison but would not have been adverse to his own occupation of Downing Street. Both agreed on the unsuitability of Attlee. Hugh Dalton seemed content with the role of mischief-maker and suggested to Stafford that he, Stafford, might be the most suitable candidate, though I suspect he said the same to each in turn, hoping perhaps that he might become the compromise choice. The intrigue, the back-biting, the ambitious scheming continued until Morrison phoned to say, "The old man has done it. He's gone to the Palace and the King will have to send for Attlee." As Cripps said, it was Churchill, a Tory, who chose his successor, not the Parliamentary Labour party.

I did not see much of Cripps in the months immediately following the election as he was busy with Indian problems, but he came to St Matthew's on the Sundays he was in Bristol. It was his hope that when the British withdrew Hindu and Muslim would work together in a united India. But it was not to be. When he was in Simla in May 1946, he sent me this poem:

> Rimming the distant circle of the pale blue sky
> In never-changing whiteness stand the Himalayan heights.
> The lesser hills fill the foreground, range on range,
> Folding their tree-clad slopes into the deep valleys.
> High above, weaving in endless circles, soar the kites.
> In the cool and silent event at Igaza, the Psalmist's words
> Lingering in my memory, rise to my lips: "I will turn
> Mine eyes unto the hills from whence cometh my strength."

* *The Eden Memoirs The Reckoning* Page 549

The snow-capped mountains stand unchangeable
Mooted in timeless grandeur, their unsullied peaks
Flood the frail human mind with majesty eternal,
Symbol of that strength which comes from God alone.
That purity of purpose, divine and everlasting patience
And endless courage which are the very hallmark of His love
Surrounding all who seek His help and guidance.
So it was the Psalmist saw those other hills to which
   he turns his eyes
And from them drew His courage and His strength.

R.S.C.

I joined the Bristol City Council in 1946 as member for the St George West ward in which my parish was situated. I was neither the first nor the last priest to stand for election, but it was looked upon with disfavour when a priest stood in the Labour interest. He was guilty of bringing politics into religion. For a Conservative it was different. He was a public-spirited member of the community without political affiliations, except for his accidental connection with the Tory party. I had no qualms. In the pulpit I had said time and again that it was my duty to proclaim the principles on which politics should be based, but Christians, including the clergy, had to decide for themselves which of the existing parties was the most likely to implement a programme based on the principles. There could never be a wholly satisfactory choice, but choice there had to be. For me it meant working within the Labour party for the well-being of my area and for Bristol.

The Bristol City Council had attracted some of the best men and women on both sides of the political divide. I have had contacts with many borough councils, and when I moved to Cambridge nearly ten years later I served on its council; but Bristol stood head and shoulders above them. I think the main reason was the strong Christian influence that had permeated the parties for years. When in 1948, we started the Christian Group with a short church service before the monthly council meeting, we usually had a third of the councillors present. During Lent the Bishop of Bristol presided over discussions on civic affairs in the Mayor's parlour, and twice a year there was a Communion service in the lovely Lord Mayor's Chapel, built by John of Gaunt in the fourteenth century. The Conservatives tended to be active Anglicans with Sir John Inskip as their leader, while the Labour party had several Methodist lay preachers. They had joined the party as a group, as young men in the earlier part of the century, a result of a gospel mission. Instead of becoming ministers they decided to educate themselves in order to serve the poorer classes as their representatives on the City Council. Among them was George Shallard, who collected books and had a sizeable private library, while Whit Burgess was an authority on Scandinavian literature. In those days as there were neither emoluments nor expenses, a person who served on the council was out of pocket. For some members it meant real sacrifice. Robert Lyne, the deputy leader of the Tory party, made it his business to learn of councillors who were in need or ill and he often called at their homes with gifts of fruit, flowers and vegetables from his garden. He never patronised. He was liked by all as a quiet unassuming friend.

I loved my work. I felt that at last I was able to do something other than talk for the poor and underprivileged. In addition to my 'surgery', where I dealt with individual cases of hardship, I served on the Health Committee and the Cemeteries' Committee. I took the line that if I could not cure my clients, at least I could give them a good burial! In due course I became chairman of Health and vice-chairman of Cemeteries. The work on the Health Committee was fascinating and we were fortunate to have an outstanding chief officer in Dr Robert Parry, a Welsh visionary with the ability to get things done.

One of my first efforts was to fulfil my intention to establish a birth-control clinic, having been appalled by the size of the families which I had found on my arrival at the Blundell's mission. Squalor and poverty were inevitable, and for the woman it was a slave existence. Worse still were the back-street abortions. I encountered opposition from the local Roman Catholic church, St Patrick's. When I was standing for re-election the priest sent a four-man deputation to ask me to give an undertaking that I would desist from my family planning activities. "Gentlemen," I said, "before I reply to your questions, will you answer mine? How many of you use contraceptives?" There was silence.

Another venture was the William Budd Health Centre. As it was about the first of its kind in the country it attracted attention and caused controversy, especially in the medical profession. When the centre was opened officially, Iain Macleod, as Health Minister, who had disapproved from the outset, said to me at luncheon before the ceremony: "It's just like you socialists, Mervyn, you waste money upon useless projects and white elephants like this William Budd Centre. I bet you there will never be another. The doctors don't want them. Nor do the patients." I wish I had accepted the challenge.

My experience as chairman was to prove a great help for my subsequent work in Southwark. It taught me the art of administration and, as important, of delegation. It was a large organisation with several committees employing hundreds of people. On Dr Parry's advice, I chaired only the main committee. The sub-committees had their own chairmen, though I read the papers, was available for consultation, and would attend if I was asked for a particular occasion.

We began our meetings on the dot and ended on the dot, whether or not we had completed the agenda. It was not only the officials who welcomed the despatch with which business was conducted. The mothers who had their eye on the clock knew at what time they would be home to attend the needs of the family.

My mentor was Arthur Parish, the leader of the Labour group. I have served on many committees and have sat under as many chairmen; I put Arthur Parish at the top of the list. He was efficient, courteous, brief, and a careful listener. In addition he had two special qualities. He knew how to get to the heart of the matter that was being discussed and how to explain complicated subjects in simple words. And he knew when to intervene. It was an uncanny knack. If he had used his powers as chairman to stop a talkative person in full flood he would have been accused of dictatorial interference, he never did; but he knew instinctively the moment that the speaker had lost the sympathy of the audience and had become an irritating bore. Years later I often wished that Arthur Parish had been appointed as full-time chairman of the General Synod.

In May 1953 I was in trouble with the Labour party as I disobeyed the whip and voted with the other side. Usually the two parties had good relationships. There was a gentleman's agreement with regard to the annual appointment of the Lord Mayor. It alternated. Similarly with the sheriffs. On this occasion the Labour party wanted to push ahead with comprehensive education, but was hindered by the smallness of its majority on the education committee. In order to obtain control it decided to appoint a Labour alderman, although under the agreement a Conservative should have been chosen. All these years later it may seem a storm in a teacup but at the time it made headline news in the Bristol press.

Sir John Inskip, who had been a stern critic when I first became involved in politics, sent me a kindly letter in which he wrote: "On the surface the dispute may have seemed a small one but it struck deep. I am sure that you have greatly strengthened the influence of

69

the Christian Group on the Council. A complete stranger spoke to me on the steps of the Commercial Rooms this morning and said 'I shall never again say that parsons should keep out of politics'!"

It was not easy to stand out against the party, but I have always believed that what is morally wrong can never be politically right. In fact some colleagues told me they wished they had taken an independent line too. A few were angry, and wanted the whip to be withdrawn, but Arthur Parish poured oil on troubled waters with his customary skill. I told him that I would not vote against the party line again—unless conscience was involved. Friendship was repaired, and I still treasure a pair of silver candlesticks which the Labour group gave me when I left for Cambridge two years later.

The incident was not without importance for my future career. Sir Walter Monckton, who had become a close personal friend since his election for Bristol West in 1951 and was now in the Cabinet, knew the facts. It enabled him, so he told me later, to assure those of his persuasion who were concerned with appointments in which I might be involved that, although I had definite views, I was more than a card-carrying politician.

Since the last months of the war I had been increasingly involved on the wider political front. I was asked by Archbishop Fisher to serve as a member of the British Council of Churches which concerned itself, *inter alia*, with the social matters, particularly with post-war problems and relationships with Germany. I joined the Central Religious Advisory Committee of the BBC that dealt with religious broadcasting. John Heenan, years later to be the Cardinal Archbishop of Westminster, used to share a taxi with me. I was elected by the Bristol diocese as a Proctor in Convocation, which in simple language means becoming a member of the parliament of the Church of England. I believe I was the youngest. These additional duties necessitated frequent visits to London. Sir Stafford Cripps, who had succeeded Hugh Dalton as Chancellor of the Exchequer in November 1947, knowing that my stipend was small, allowed me to use a room on the top floor of 11 Downing Street. It became a second home. Although I was careful to behave as a private family guest, I often met members of the Government. In particular I remember the evening visits along a corridor to the Attlees next door. It was the practice of the Prime Minister to join his wife for an hour at nine o'clock. Often Clem would hold a skein of wool in his hand while Vi did the winding. The Prime Minister was not the most talkative of persons. His conversation consisted of clipped monosyllables accompanied by pensive drawings upon his pipe. But he was like a man reborn when the conversation turned to cricket or to history. On his seventieth birthday I went with a schoolboy to dinner. Having warned David Tankard of the possible silences, I urged him to learn the biographies of the best-known cricketers and the details of test matches. David did his homework so well that Clem was enthralled and was reluctant to leave the table for the theatre. On another occasion I foolishly initiated a discussion on Oliver Cromwell, whose acts, attitudes and dictatorial methods I have always disliked. I told Clem that had I been alive during the Civil War I should have been a supporter of King Charles, in spite of his shortcomings. For good measure I added that I could not understand how a man who had suppressed Parliament could be regarded by people like himself and Isaac Foot as a great parliament-arian. Clem trounced me, quoting incident after incident, speech after speech, to prove me wrong. That was not all. A week later I was sent on loan two history books from the Downing Street Library dealing with the seventeenth century, with the request that I should carefully read the Cromwellian chapters.

Occasionally Stafford and Isobel Cripps had an informal supper with Clem and Vi Attlee in their private flat and I joined them. Food was scarce and rationing was strictly observed, but no matter how small the portions, they were served on impressive silver dishes. Stafford was a vegetarian so there were separate dishes for himself and his wife. When the cover was removed there could be seen a concoction of scraped carrots and the like.

Stafford was known by Churchill as 'Misery Cripps', but the title was unfair. Cripps had never fully recovered from his physical disabilities in the First World War, and on medical advice he had observed strict dietary rules with regard to food and drink. It appeared to those who did not know him to be a dreary, puritanical and frugal way of life. His guests understood the position. For them there was good food and wine. He never imposed his austerity upon other people and he was a charming and witty host. Of course when rationing was introduced his guests had meat only if they brought their coupons with them. I used to stay with him and Isobel at their home in Gloucestershire at Christmas and Easter and for longer periods in the summer. As I am not 'a yoga and yoghurt merchant' I sometimes slipped down to the local hostelry for a couponless steak and kidney pie.

The Labour Government did not live up to expectations and there was much criticism of Attlee. The position worsened when he became ill. It was said he had lost his grip, and some colleagues shared these views and wanted him to be replaced. Herbert Morrison was supposed, rightly or wrongly, to have had dreams of a ride to the Palace to kiss hands. Whatever the truth of that may be, I remember walking up the stairs at Downing Street as members of the Government were assembling for a meeting. I was making for my bedroom. Cripps was in front of me and Morrison in front of him. As both men paused on the landing I heard Cripps say, "My dear Herbert, the idea that you could be Prime Minister is ridiculous." Morrison moved silently to the next flight of stairs.

Cripps was to have his own problems of loyalty. Bristol East, by which I mean the party caucus, which like any caucus is a small group of extremists, unrepresentative of the generality of voters, had regarded their Member as their Left Wing hero and revolutionary. They had become disillusioned. They thought that as Chancellor of the Exchequer he should have broken with the capitalist world and have established a socialist basis. Instead he appeared to them to have moved to the Right.

I wrote to Cripps and warned him of this intrigue. I told him that there were suggestions that he should not be chosen to stand for the constituency at the next election. I suggested he should come to Bristol to put his cards on the table. Lady Cripps replied on her husband's behalf on April 29th 1948: "There is only one way to approach this and that is by digging down into the deepest roots of humility, as far as one can understand it. I only wish they could be as loyal to Stafford as he is to them, but how can one expect them to be in the lives they have to lead? I feel I could burst into tears. They need a shepherd and it is a reflection on us if we fail to meet the challenge. The personal hurt just does not matter if we mean anything by a Christian profession."

The intrigue grew worse during the summer and on September 29th Stafford wrote from the Treasury to tell me that he had appeared unexpectedly at the selection committee in Bristol on the previous evening, much to the embarrassment of his detractors. "I took the opportunity of saying that I knew the gossip that was going about. I said I was not prepared to accept the candidature unless all this sort of thing stopped completely."

That was the end of the matter. The caucus liked to believe that it represented the Labour voters in Bristol East. It did not. And it knew the likely consequences of Cripps expelling them, rather than vice versa.

The years passed and my friendship with the two families deepened. I rarely talked politics with Attlee or Cripps as I knew that when I was with them they wanted to escape from the burdens of office. I used to act as 'chaplain' when a priest was required for a family occasion and Attlee gave me his private telephone number. I rarely used it, but I remember an occasion in 1949 when Cripps and Bevin had concluded a successful piece of economic business with the United States, and I phoned Clem to tell him that Stafford had told me that Ernie, who was still in the United States, was deeply hurt that he had received no congratulatory message from the Prime Minister. Clem seemed surprised. "Would Ernie like a message do you think? I'll send it now." It was typical of Attlee's modesty and perhaps his insensitivity. It was typical too of Stafford's thoughtfulness to ask me to approach the Prime Minister.

One night about this time I was walking with Stafford from a meeting to Downing Street. Big Ben was striking midnight as we passed the Cenotaph. "A totalitarian dictatorship," he said, "is a pathetic short cut to Utopia. It cannot give men the full life. Only a democracy based on an inner spiritual discipline can do that." And then he added somewhat sadly, "I wonder whether we have a sufficient faith in God in this country for that spiritual discipline." In his later speeches this theme was uppermost in his mind. Life makes sense, life offers hope, only when men find their fulfilment in God.

Cripps had struggled against ill health for years. In 1950 he knew he was exhausted and had no alternative but to resign. The few of us who knew the facts were pledged to secrecy until he came to Bristol in October to meet his committee. He stayed at my vicarage. While we were at the meeting a press reporter broke into the house and hid behind a sofa, hoping to record our private conversation. Stafford discovered him and led him to the front door in withering silence.

As we walked up the stairs to our bedrooms he said to me, "Be sure to call me early in the morning. I want my last engagement in Bristol to be at the Communion Table."

A few hours later, after receiving the Sacrament, he said so simply, almost in an undertone, "I *have* handed in my seals of office to the King."

Stafford went to a clinic in Zurich. In June 1951 the position was desperate owing to a grave spinal infection. His wife sent for me and I went to Zurich, taking with me roses from Churchill and orchids from Attlee to be placed upon the table in his bedroom at which I celebrated the Communion. He had a temporary recovery and returned to Gloucestershire. I spent the day with him on which many who had just been appointed to Churchill's first post-war administration wrote to him in reply to his messages of congratulations. I remember Walter Monckton's note, "My very dear Stafford, I shall always try to find my inspiration and guidance where you have always found yours."

Cripps returned to Zurich. For months he lay in a plaster shell, immovable. He died on April 21st 1952. I buried his ashes in a remote cemetery in the Cotswolds, near to the village of Sapperton.

I first met Walter Monckton in the Lord Mayor's chapel in February 1951. I had arranged a service taken by the Bishop of Bristol for the candidates standing in the by-election for Bristol West. Oliver Stanley had died and Monckton was the Conservative choice, perhaps because it was the specific wish of Winston Churchill. In his papers he wrote of his introduction to the House of Commons: "As we started on our journey up the Chamber, Mr Churchill said that he had never done this before, and we must lean inwards as he was no longer very secure on his legs."

As Monckton left the chapel he came to me and, offering his hand, said, "I believe you and I have a mutual friend in Stafford Cripps." Thus began a friendship between Walter, Biddy and myself that became for me a major factor in my life, and I like to think for them too.

Monckton, although different in temperament from Cripps, had been influenced by him. He shared his Anglican faith and his social concern. He was not a natural politician and he disliked party vendettas. Indeed he could have been a member of any party, though loosely attached. He was basically a middle-of-the-road man. Churchill, who rightly guessed that the Conservatives would win the next election, was keen to benefit from Monckton's brains and his skills as a negotiator.

When Churchill formed his Cabinet he asked Monckton to become Minister of Labour. Monckton dithered as he had little experience of industrial relations. That, said Churchill, was why he wanted him. The fact that he was without a political past was his strong card: "Yes," Monckton is reputed to have said, "no political past, and no political future!"

I think Monckton had hoped for a legal appointment. Attorney-General perhaps with the hope that he might eventually become Lord Chancellor. But it was not to be. Churchill was determined. "Oh my dear, I cannot spare you for that . . . I have the worst job in the Cabinet for you." And a hard job it certainly was. The economy in the post-war years was in a parlous condition and there was constant industrial strife. The Minister was under severe pressure. However, although the trade unions were suspicious of the Tory

Government he won their respect, often their trust, and sometimes their affection.

Walter and Biddy, when not in London, lived at Priors Court in Worcestershire, a lovely black-and-white house with a beautiful garden. I often stayed with them, and a visit to the Shakespeare Theatre at Stratford was a regular item on the programme. I usually slept in the haunted wing, but to my disappointment I never saw the ghost.

Monckton had been a practising High Churchman but on account of his divorce he had been banned from the Sacraments. I had always been appalled by this vindictive religious ostracism and, with his permission, I referred the matter to the Bishop of Bristol. Dr Cockin immediately removed the ban and encouraged me to hold a private service of blessing on their marriage. This brought the three of us close to each other and whenever they were in Bristol on Sundays they came to St Matthew's for Communion. After the service he came to the hall for coffee where there were large numbers of young people. They were devoted to Walter, who got to know many of them by their Christian names. Although most were on the other side of the political fence they looked upon him and Biddy as part of the parish family. It had been Stafford's custom to read the Scriptures at the Communion service and when he died Walter took his place. There is still at St Matthew's a chalice which Walter gave in memory of Stafford.

In 1953 I asked Monckton and Attlee if they could get me a visa to visit the Soviet Union. For several years I had spent my summer holidays looking after Swiss chaplaincies. It had been a great experience. In those days the presence of a British chaplain was thought to lend tone, and I, in common with others, stayed at five-star hotels free of charge. It was a widening experience. Interlaken, Zermatt, Geneva, Zurich were among the places I served. I met people who would not ordinarily have come my way and I made many friends from other countries. This meant that I started to travel widely and had invitations to visit Lutheran, Calvinist and Old Catholic parishes.

During the week there was little to do and I spent hours on the mountains, usually alone. However when I was in Zermatt I met a colonel who asked me to prepare him for confirmation. This I did after dinner. The instruction over, we went to a night club. On the final evening we ran out of money. We were determined not to be defeated so went to the club and offered to put on a show, the colonel to play his guitar and I to sing. Although my singing voice is appalling, it had the desired effect. The audience stormed me with francs to shut me up.

Now I had had my fill of chaplaincies and wanted to spend my holidays differently. The bishop gave me leave of absence to go to Russia to write a book. Monckton did his best. He even prevailed on Churchill and Eden to intercede on my behalf, but to no effect. In those days it was virtually impossible for a priest to be admitted except for the Red Dean, Hewlett Johnson of Canterbury, who had an uncritical approach to the Soviet régime and was a leading propagandist for its alleged superiority over the West. Then Attlee advised me to approach Harold Wilson who, after the collapse of the Labour Government, had joined a timber firm which did business with the Soviet Union. Wilson was successful. Shortly before my departure I went to his office to be briefed. Apart from more serious matters he told me to take a supply of toilet paper and soap, and a stopper for the wash basin. He suggested that if the hotel service became too incompetent I should sit in my bedroom chair and complain loudly in the certain knowledge that my angry monologue would be bugged.

I wrote a book on my experiences called *I Went to Moscow*. It was an interesting period as Stalin had just died and Malenkov took his place. Nobody knew what might happen next. It was good to see the Soviet system at close quarters. There were few surprises, as Stafford Cripps had often talked to me about the country as he knew it when he was Ambassador. There were good features and I was impressed by the determination to rebuild the cities which had been destroyed to a degree that was beyond the imagination of most of us in the West. But I was glad to leave. It was a servile state ruled by terror and corruption. A prostitution of socialism; an affront to human dignity.

My enthusiasm for a genuine socialist society remained un-diminished. In spite of my friendship with Walter Monckton and, through him, with other members of the Churchill Government, I believed that Labour was more likely to implement the ideals on which a just society should be based. I remained loyal to the party. On Stafford's resignation Tony Benn succeeded him as member for Bristol East, and, as a member of the selection committee, I voted for him. I had taken soundings of Roy Jenkins and Tony Crosland and others who had known him or about him at Oxford. He had the socialist vision and it was clear that he was committed to it. Although his inspiration was broadly Christian, he lacked Stafford's burning personal faith, and he had understandable reservations about the Anglican Establishment, many of which I shared.

However I remember telling him, on the steps of St Matthew's, that I thought the major difference between us was his weak hold on the doctrine of original sin. I suspect that he believes man is basically good, whereas I think he is prone to evil. This is more than theological hair-splitting as it has political implications. If man is good he will presumably sacrifice himself for the well-being of society. If he is prone to evil he is motivated by selfishness. We are likely to achieve our political goals, even if they constitute something less than Utopia, if we make a realistic valuation of human nature. If we fail to do that either our dreams are shattered, or else we are driven to use dictatorial and repressive methods to achieve our ends. The most that politics can do is to increase the opportunities for establishing a better or a worse society. But the basic problem remains MAN, who usually places himself at the centre of his small universe. Until we accept that truth, politics remains the science of deferred repentence.

5

Move to Cambridge

I was happy in my work in Bristol and had no wish to move. The end of the war meant that thousands were returning to civilian life and the Redfield United Front was involved in helping them to adjust. The chief problem was housing. Many had got married on the spur of the moment and when they came back, if their wives had not already left them, they needed accommodation. There had been virtually no buillding in the war, but hundreds of buildings had been bombed. The position was serious and sometimes we had to use the church for makeshift accommodation. Rarely a day went by without a small procession coming to my home asking me to help and expecting an immediate solution.

Employment was another problem. While employers did their best to take back those who had been called up, many had never had jobs. So we acted as an unofficial exchange.

The men who had been away several years found it difficult to settle to civilian life and sometimes those with families found their children resented their appearance. So we ran simple courses on marriage and home-building, and rented a community house where they could meet couples with similar problems. The unmarried were as welcome and some found partners.

Church life moved at a quicker pace. The end of the black-out meant an increase in evening activities and many came forward for instruction. We usually had a full house at the Parish Communion on Sunday mornings, while the simple evening service attracted the enquirers.

For these reasons I was not enthusiastic when the Bishop of Bristol, Dr Cockin, encouraged me to respond favourably to a letter I received in 1947 from the patrons of St Mary's, Oxford, the University Church, requesting me to allow my name to be considered. It was true that I had been at St Matthew's for eleven years, but I felt there was still much to be done. Moreover I was a little more than a new boy on Bristol City Council. But Dr Cockin was adamant. He had been vicar of St Mary's before the war and he was anxious that I should follow in his steps. He was kind enough to say that while he valued my ministry in Bristol he thought I might have a particular ministry for the undergraduates at Oxford, most of whom were men with war service.

Although I had sat lightly to rules and regulations, I had a High Church view of episcopacy and had always respected the Bishop's wishes. So to Oxford I went to be vetted by the patrons, Oriel College and the churchwardens of St Mary's. I dined in hall and was warmly received. In fact the reception was such that I felt I was likely to be appointed. I was still uncertain in my mind. As I wandered along the streets I felt that I did not belong to Oxford and never would. Whereas Cambridge was, is and always will be one of the great loves of my life, Oxford leaves me cold. As I lay in bed that night I wondered what I would do if the decision was left to me. I need not have worried. My hosts spoke of my suitability in generous terms, but then got down to business—politics. I knew from the inquisitorial questions they put to me that while they would never admit to political prejudice they had no intention of appointing me. And I suspect that the churchwardens who had to be consulted agreed with them. I returned to Bristol and the inevitable letter arrived. It was almost the right job, but there were 'problems'. Dr Cockin was more disappointed than I. He told me that one of the 'problems' was the Bishop of Oxford, Kenneth Kirk, who was renowned for his rigidity. Apparently he said to Cockin, "We had enough trouble at St Mary's in the last century with Newman, without inviting further trouble in this century with Mervyn Stockwood." It was nice, though a little sacrilegious I thought, to be put in the same category as the great Cardinal, though I realised that in the eyes of the Establishment we had one thing in common—both of us were nuisances and threats to peaceful academic life.

I remained contentedly in Bristol, though I frequently preached in universities and public schools. Among them was Eton. The headmaster, Robert Birley, was an old friend who had preached at St Matthew's and had sent boys to live in the parish to learn about life in the inner city. We enjoyed one another's minds and I remember an occasion when we talked through the night and found, when I pulled the curtains, that it was daylight. In 1951 he told me he would like me to go to Eton as chaplain. But this put me in a quandary. I felt that as I had been at St Matthew's for fifteen years and as I had found schoolboys responsive when I had addressed them, it might be right to accept, especially as I was fond of Birley and had a respect

79

for him. But I thought that such a move would be misunderstood and that my parishioners and Labour friends might feel betrayed.

I asked Birley to hold his hand while I sought advice. After consulting Dr Cockin I wrote to Cripps, who was in hospital in Zurich. He sent a message to the effect that as so many Eton Boys eventually held positions of influence it was important that they should associate the chapel with a lively Christianity and leave the school with a definite faith!

I also wrote to Attlee, who had recently said to me that if only Archbishop Fisher had been prepared to take risks by having a Nye Bevan on the episcopal bench he would have liked to submit my name to the King. Here is his letter:

> 10 Downing Street,
> Whitehall.
> 2. 3. 51

My dear Mervyn,

I do not know what scope there is for a chaplain in a school. Probably more at Eton than elsewhere as I understand they encourage individuality more than in newer foundations.

I am sure you are right to contemplate a change of work and I am hoping some time to see you in a wider sphere than that of a parish.

I shall not regard you as in any way stepping out of the fight by taking on the Eton appointment but I don't think I can advise one way or the other. I have no doubt that the Eton boys would benefit greatly.

Yours ever,

Clement Attlee.

I sent a copy of the letter to Robert Birley, who wrote: "It was good of the P.M. to write as he did. He came down to Eton on Friday and spoke to the Political society. He made a very good impression. I think we do encourage individuality here. But what really matters here is, I think, this. There is a real chance at Eton to have a school where Christianity is the essence of the place." He added that he was writing to the Bishop who was to discuss the matter with me when he came to St Matthew's on the following Sunday. Another factor that had to be taken into consideration was a bout of ill health. My doctor favoured a school job because of the longer vacations. So everything combined to suggest I should accept. I did. But on Good Friday Birley wrote: "This is a very difficult letter to write. I feel that we had better give up the idea of you coming to Eton." He explained that the appointment had to be confirmed by the Provost and that he was doubtful: "The reason for this doubt is I imagine clear enough, your close association with the Labour party. I hope this will make no difference to our friendship, which I greatly value." It did not. Moreover I visited Eton frequently during the next thirty years under successive headmasters and was once graciously entertained by the Provost, who warmly complimented me on my address and said how greatly the boys had appreciated my visits. The Provost who had vetoed my appointment!

While the negotiations with Eton were continuing the Bishop of Birmingham, Dr E.W. Barnes, asked me to visit him as he had a proposition to put to me. Barnes had been involved in controversy for a quarter of a century. He was an outspoken 'modernist' who appeared to sit lightly on the creeds and was regarded by the more rigid as a heretic, unfit to hold episcopal office, or indeed any office in the Church. Coupled with his radical views was a detestation of magic and superstition. He considererd it his duty to bring the Anglo-Catholics in his diocese to heel, especially those who reserved the Sacrament in their churches. The situation in Birmingham had national coverage and on one occasion he was publicly denounced in St Paul's Cathedral when he was asked to preach. He crossed swords with successive Archbishops and Dr Fisher, rebuking him in Convocation, said that were he himself to hold such doctrinal views he would not feel it right to retain his bishopric.

Barnes was an ardent pacifist with socialist sympathies. During the war he had asked me to address his diocesan conference on "The future of the Church of England." In his introduction he said, "You will have observed that Mr Stockwood is a young man. He may therefore be forgiven for believing that the Church of England has a future."

Although the Bishop had not mentioned any job in his letter I knew that the Provostship of his cathedral was vacant. I hoped it was not that because I felt that I was temperamentally better suited to serve in a parish than on a cathedral chapter. Moreover, Bryan Green, an outstanding preacher and evangelist, was filling St Martin's in the Bull Ring, which was a short distance from the cathedral. There was not room for the two of us! But it was the Provostship. After dinner, Barnes took me into his study and sat in a rocking chair. He began the conversation by telling me of the salary and the apartments of the Provost. Before going on to the more serious aspects he said, "Mr Stockwood, if you were to come to this diocese may I be assured that you would not seek to reserve the consecrated bread and wine?" As I had introduced reservation of the Sacrament in my church in Bristol it was not an easy question to dodge, but as I had already made up my mind that I had no intention of accepting the post I gave him an ambiguous answer. He realised that I was not reacting as he had hoped, so he stood up and said, "With your permission, Mr Stockwood, I will withdraw and ask my wife to take my place as she is better at explaining the situation." Mrs Barnes was a charming woman and if anybody could have persuaded me she would have done so.

The next morning the Bishop insisted that I should visit the cathedral. I remember little, except that outside was a statue of one of his predecessors, the High Churchman, Charles Gore. Barnes looked up at Gore's face and after a short silence, smiled before turning to me: "How curious that such a gifted man should have thought it necessary to defend the indefensible, the doctrine of the Virgin Birth."

The Bishop asked me to reconsider the matter. I did, but my own bishop was sure I should not go to Birmingham. Barnes, in a generous letter, told me he was disappointed. I was glad of the encounter because in his few remaining years I used to meet him and I enjoyed his conversation. Beneath the controversial exterior and the doctrinal polemics was a simple and prayerful piety.

In 1954 the BBC began to look for a successor to Francis House, the head of religious broadcasting. Dr Cockin, who had been involved in the affairs of the department for several years, suggested I should be considered. He told me that his proposal had the good wishes of the Archbishop of Canterbury. I was interested but not too hopeful. A few years previously I had had difficulties. I had been asked to give a radio talk on the meaning of baptism. The arrangements were made and I wrote my address. Then a General Election was called. I was told I must stand down. I was astonished. I said to the head of religious programmes in Bristol that I would send my address to the department and that if anything in it was thought to be of a party political nature I would remove it. That, however, was not the point. It was not the address but the fact that a Labour member of the Bristol City Council was to give it. I referred this matter to the Bishop. Cockin was indignant. He threatened to raise the matter publicly and to disassociate himself from the decision and to express his confidence in me. He prevailed, but I knew there would be people in the BBC who would be glad of an opportunity to pay off old scores.

The Director-General, Sir Ian Jacob, sent for me and we talked in general terms about religious broadcasting over a glass of sherry. Then he asked me about my friendship with Sir Stafford Cripps, for whom he had small regard, though he was careful to point out that in his position he was above party politics. We broke for lunch, and as we went to his club in a taxi he asked me whether it was true that I was a friend of Aneurin Bevan. I said he had become a great friend. Not so Sir Ian. I remember him saying that when Bevan was kicked down the steps of a West End club he had got what he deserved. The conversation over the table continued agreeably. Sir Ian said he had been favourably impressed by what he had been told of my work in Bristol, but that my known political affiliations created problems. That was that. Roy McKay, chaplain of a public school, was appointed. Presumably he had no embarrassing political affiliations.

Twenty years later when the Queen was opening the new Covent Garden market in Battersea I found myself sitting near to Sir Ian. "Do you remember the day you came to see me at the BBC?" he asked. "I knew I was right. It was not a big enough job for you. You were cut out to be a bishop." A case of being wise after the event; I am sure that neither he nor I thought in those terms.

In May 1954 Dr Fisher asked me to address his clergy at a residential conference in a holiday camp. The Archbishop was kindness itself, but it scarcely compensated for the primitive conditions which prevailed in a small and grotty collection of huts. On the final evening, Fisher said, "Stockwood, you are a great problem to me. Everybody seems to like you, but nobody wants you." I was in no state to continue the conversation as it was clear I had picked up a bug in the camp, and was feeling ill. The next morning I started back for Bristol. I knew I must have had a high temperature and when I reached the vicarage I collapsed. I had Streptococcus fever which in those days could be dangerous, if not fatal. It was several weeks before I was fully restored, and the doctor urged me to move to less demanding work. Once again it seemed that a suitable opportunity had come. The Mastership of the Temple church had become vacant and Walter Monckton was keen that I should be appointed. I warmed to the idea as it meant that I could have concentrated on a ministry of preaching without being subjected to the heavy pressures of parochial life. And for the first time I should live in London. Monckton did his best. He persuaded one of the Inns of Court but not the other. From what he told me it seemed that my membership of the Labour party rendered me unacceptable.

I suspect that in their eyes I was a parsonic tort who would condemn them to liability to ecclesiastical damages.

In fact as things turned out I am glad of these misadventures, because had I been successful I should not have been free to accept the post that was eventually to be offered to me.

In the Lent term of 1954, Michael Ramsey, then Bishop of Durham, conducted a teaching mission in Cambridge. I was among the assistant missioners. I stayed at Corpus Christi College. It was a happy occasion and memorable for many reasons, not least the weather. There was brilliant sunshine each day without a cloud in the sky, but it was bitterly cold. The Granta was frozen and became a promenade. It was possible to skate to Ely. The college made me most welcome and I was asked to stay as a guest during my summer holiday. One afternoon I was having tea with one of the dons, Garth Moore, when the telephone rang to inform Garth that the vicar of Great St Mary's, the University Church, was resigning. "I wonder," said the informant, "who will take his place." Jokingly Garth Moore said, "Mervyn Stockwood. He's sitting here now." Later that afternoon I said to Garth that if a serious proposition were to be made I should be interested. I heard nothing for months. The patrons of the living were Trinity College, Cambridge, and they had always appointed a don who continued to live in college, or a retired priest, with private means, preferably a Trinity man, who happened to live in Cambridge. There was no vicarage and the stipend was negligible, little more than £200 a year. The patrons approached Canon Charles Raven, the former Master of Christ's College and Vice-Chancellor. He had married a wealthy American widow, who had died on their honeymoon. Raven was outraged. He thought it disgraceful that a man in his seventies should be asked to hold such a responsible position. The patrons continued their pursuit but the number of retired wealthy Trinity clergyman had sadly dwindled. Eventually it dawned upon Trinity that it might be necessary to acquire a vicarage and to appoint a run-of-the-mill parson. My name was put forward to the livings' committee. I am told there was a split vote and that one of the opponents complained that if I were to go to Great St Mary's, "things might begin to happen"—the last thing that he wanted. At some point it was decided that the Master of Trinity, Lord Adrian, should resolve the problem. Was I or was I not a suitable candidate? I was taken to Lord Adrian's room by Professor Burnaby, the Regius Professor of Divinity, with strict instructions that I was not to detain the Master, a convinced agnostic, for more than ten minutes. In addition I was warned that the Master was as shy as he was brilliant, and that conversation might be difficult. Shy he was, and brilliant he was, but I fell for him immediately. After a few awkward interjections and silences he said, "I understand that you went to the Soviet Union last year." My heart sank. I saw myself back in Ian Jacob's room and all the other rooms in which I had been subjected to political inquisition. But I should not have worried as Adrian was too big a man. "Hester, my wife," he continued, "is very interested in hospitals and asked me to be sure to ask you about post-war development in Russia." Fortunately my Soviet hosts, knowing I was chairman of the Bristol Health Committee, had taken me to several hospitals, and I was well briefed. The Master appeared to be fascinated. His shyness left him and he plied me with questions. There was a knock on the door. It was Professor Burnaby, who feared I had outstayed my welcome. "Thank you," said the Master, "but it would be very kind of Canon Stockwood to stay a little longer if he can afford the time; we are having a most interesting discussion on medical resources and tuberculosis."

Burnaby knocked a second time. The Master switched the conversation. "Ah yes, Canon Stockwood, Great St Mary's. I wonder what you would find to do there if you were to be appointed." The conversation came to an end. Although we had scarcely mentioned the University Church I knew that this charming, clever, humble man had chosen his own way to size me up.

Burnaby took me into hall for dinner and I was placed next to a senior don who was a strong Tory and deeply suspicious of me. I think he was expecting an unshaven roughneck in a Red tie. We got on well. On the news of my appointment he is alleged to have said, "At least he knows how to hold a knife and fork. And he's quite well informed on wines."

The letter from the Master came to me in January 1955. It was a happy coincidence that on the following Sunday I had a long-standing engagement to preach in Trinity Chapel. The Adrians also asked the Lodge representatives of 'town and gown', people that I was likely to meet when I took up my duties. However, at the reception in the evening a young man arrived who had not been invited. He was an official of the extreme evangelical society, the Cambridge Inter-Collegiate Christian Union, usually known as the CICCU. He made straight for me. "I understand you are the new vicar of the University Church. My committee would be glad if you would let them use Great St Mary's for a Billy Graham mission next November." It had been arranged that I should be instituted in June, just before the long vacation, so that I should have four months in which to take stock without being involved in the pressures of university life. I knew that the Billy Graham mission had been proposed and that it had already aroused strong feelings. I had no wish to express an opinion myself until I had had careful consultations with the Bishop, the Vice-Chancellor and the deans and chaplains. Fortunately the Master overheard the conversation and he conducted the intruder to the door. But the matter would not be brushed under the carpet. I was plunged into the fray and within days of the announcement of my appointment I was at the heart of the controversy. The CICCU wanted to take possession of the church for a week and during that week to exclude the Bishop of Ely and myself from their services. The majority view was to refuse the request as it was thought that it would not be appropriate to hold a hot-gospel mission within the precincts of the University Church. The Bishop and the Vice-Chancellor took a different view. If I was in Great St Mary's each evening and if all the arrangements were approved by me, the evangelistic temperature might be reduced and the gospel became less 'hot'. I did as they required and the CICCU grudgingly accepted the compromise. It was a relief to turn from their committee, most of whom were narrow-minded enthusiasts, to Billy Graham himself. He was invariably co-operative and gracious. It was a joy to work with him and although our view points are different we remain friends to this day.

I was sad to leave Bristol. I had nineteen happy years at St Matthew's. The actual parting seemed like a divorce because I felt I was deserting the family I loved. In spite of all the problems, there are few jobs more rewarding than that of the parish priest.

Whereas St Matthew's had become highly organised and, thanks to a vigorous team of clergy with a lively church council and an efficient secretariat, it more or less ran itself without requiring much attention from me, Great St Mary's needed a major reconstruction. It was not the fault of my predecessors. As the Master of Trinity told me, nobody seemed to know what the role of the University Church was. On Sunday afternoons there was an official sermon by a distinguished theologian but the vicar was not expected to be present. Even if he had turned up he would have found the Vice-Chancellor in his stall. On University occasions the building, apart from the sanctuary, came under the jurisdiction of the Vice-Chancellor and the incumbent had no status. On Ash Wednesday, for example, the Vice-Chancellor was obliged to say the litany. I was present as a member of the congregation when Lord

Adrian, in an academic cope, read it beautifully, agnostic though he was.

Great St Mary's, being within a few yards of the Guildhall, was also the civic church and for centuries the Mayor and Corporation had attended in state for special celebrations. Apart from these two uses, the church building was little attended. There was virtually no parish, and what there was consisted of shops, the market place and the Roman Catholic chaplaincy. Perhaps it was for this reason that the small congregation could be shepherded by one of its dons or a retired priest. Moreover as there were six churches within three minutes of Great St Mary's there seemed little point in building up yet one more congregation.

I arrived in June and spent the first weeks cleaning the church, turning out the cupboards and getting windows repaired to prevent the pigeons from leaving their white remembrances. One of my finds in an old chest was a deed, yellow with age, giving us a title to land in Madingley, not far from where Churchill College now stands. These activities attracted the notice of the press and the curious started to come to church. Particularly did they comment on the text of my first sermon from the book of Isaiah: "If you must bore men, well and good; but must you bore your God also?" I chose it because it was compulsory for a new incumbent to wade through the Thirty-Nine Articles in full on his first Sunday. At St Matthew's I had read only the first and the last, having said to the churchwardens beforehand, "As for the remaining thirty-seven, let's call it a day and regard them as good as read." But it could not be at Great St Mary's. I had been told that Dr Newton Flew, a distinguished Methodist who had examined me in the theological tripos, intended to arrive at the church at twelve noon with other theological worthies to hear me 'read myself in'.

As the weeks went by, plans for the future began to germinate in my mind. One summer's evening, as I was walking along King's Parade, I was suddenly struck by the geography of Great St Mary's. The University began in it, not the present building but an earlier one, parts of which survive in the chancel. It was opposite the Senate House. It was part and parcel of the inheritance of Cambridge men. It was a witness in stone of the relationship between faith and thought. But it was also situated in the market place next to the Guildhall and therefore a symbol of the relationship between religion and life. My job was to proclaim the Christmas message, "Glory be to God in the highest," and then without the 'e', "Glory be to God in the High St."

For those who are unfamiliar with Cambridge it may be worth pointing out that the religious life of the university centres on the college chapels, and communicants are expected to receive the Sacrament at college altars. It was necessary, therefore, that I should be careful not to offend the deans and chaplains by giving the impression that I regarded the University Church as an alternative. Past experience had already taught me the dire consequences of clerical jealousy. For this reason I decided that the sacramental services, together with evensong, should be for the town; matins for town and gown, and the late evening service for the University.

In October I embarked on my plan, having previously sent to each undergraduate a beautifully designed card with the programme for the Michaelmas term. It was well received, though one dean of a college threw his five hundred copies into the furnace.

For the town I started a Parish Communion at 9.45 a.m. We had our difficulties. The choir I had inherited, which included three men between the ages of seventy and eighty, refused to attend. Anything but matins was popery. Fortunately I had been joined by Norman Hill: neither the best administrator nor preacher, but a loving and lovable man, a saintly character and the most loyal of colleagues—a superb pastor. Norman and I did our best, though I think that in those early months we rarely had a congregation of more than two dozen at the Eucharist. I decided to resort to the tactics I had employed at St Matthew's years before. I spent hours and hours with young boys and girls until the day came when they enlisted as servers or choristers. Slowly our numbers grew, but it was not until after I had moved to Southwark that my successors established a breakthrough. I am glad to think, however, that it was during my incumbency that for the first time since the Reformation the Eucharist became the principal service on Sundays and vestments were worn, while on weekdays there was a daily Mass. In the side-chapel, the Sacrament was reserved, the sick were anointed and confessions were heard.

It was not just my upbringing at All Saints' Clifton that was responsible for a pattern of spirituality that is associated with High Anglicanism. I knew that I intended to include 'fringe' elements that would be adversely criticised by the more conventional. I was determined they should not dismiss Great St Mary's as a circus or concert hall. It was first and foremost a house of prayer. Moreover in addition to the public services there were always two sessions each day, lasting half an hour, for silent contemplation. I made it my duty never to be absent from any of these activities during term time.

I wondered about matins. I had thought to discuss it because it was 'stuffy' and so few attended. The Bishop of Ely, Dr Edward Wynn, who had been my confessor in my undergraduate days, urged me to retain it so long as there was a demand. Rather than let it die, I decided to increase the demand by 'brightening' it up. There were no stunts, but I invited first-class preachers to take part in interesting courses, with the request they restrict themselves to twenty minutes. The service followed the Prayer Book but it was kept short—four popular hymns, one well known psalm, two brief lessons, read in modern English and related to the sermon, and, after the creed and the collects, four prayers concluding with a period of silence. I guaranteed that the service would be over in less than an hour.

There was an immediate response. Even before the undergraduates returned the congregation had doubled. We had started to attract the visitors who swarmed on Cambridge during the long vacation, while the old-stagers did not object. On the contrary as one elderly woman said, "How kind of you to curtail the length of the service. Not every man understands how difficult it is for some of us, advanced in years and with bladder problems, to last out." The students were spared such problems.

To my surprise, the service was popular with the undergraduates. It suited those who had become accustomed to matins at school, especially as it was rarely found in their college chapels, except as an introduction to the Communion service before breakfast. And it appealed to those who had not reached the age of commitment which is expected of those who take the Sacrament.

The congregation grew steadily but the breakthrough came in the following year on Remembrance Sunday. The Mayor and Council were due to attend but as the country was in the midst of the Suez crisis the leader of the Conservative party, who strongly disapproved of my views, urged his followers and all loyal citizens to boycott the service. He could not have done me a better turn. There were queues in King's Parade and Petty Cury, while the market place was thronged. Two thousand found their way into the church and hundreds were turned away. We never looked back. I suppose it became part of the done thing to go to Great St Mary's on Sunday mornings. A quarter of a century later, I looked at the attendance records and found that in term time we averaged in my first year about two hundred and in my last term over a thousand. Of course, as soon as it became known that the students were flocking to church the townspeople became interested, especially the young married couples. It was a splendid mixture of town and gown and because of the size of the congregations it was reasonable for me to invite preachers from all parts of the country and beyond.

I regretted I could not ask Free Churchmen, but that was the ruling of the Bishop. Nevertheless, although he would not permit them to take part in a liturgical service, he allowed them to preach at the informal service we held on Sunday evenings at 8.30 p.m. Again these drew large audiences and they were followed by a question and answer session, which we called Mars' Hill. It was given the name because the preacher stood at the top of the wide staircase that led to the gallery, while the mob, or Areopagites, hurled questions at him from below. I remember that a frequent leader of the mob was David Owen, the future Foreign Secretary.

On weekdays I encouraged the university to use the building for concerts, exhibitions and conferences, and once a year we had a series of lectures on Wednesday evenings. Of course the politicians came, Nye Bevan among them. Even the 'top brass' came, because no political party in Cambridge could provide an audience, let alone as uncommitted audience, of a thousand.

Another year we had the Ambassadors of the leading countries including the United States and the Soviet Union, but not on the same night.

The course of lectures I remember best, because it was printed, was called 'Religion and the Scientists'. The purpose of the course was to encourage dons and students who were accustomed to different academic disciplines to understand one another's language. Instead of staging a debate between scientists and theologians I thought it more fruitful to invite the scientists to explain their interpretation of some of the facts of existence; and it was made clear to them they would be free to say exactly what they wished. One thing became quickly apparent. Although the dispute between religion and science was less strident than it had been, and neutrality had taken the place of cocksure hostility, the gulf between the two had not been bridged. Theology, so far from being the queen of sciences, was regarded as a peripheral Cinderella. At Cambridge and elsewhere there was no real communication between the theologians and the scientists. The theological faculty dealt adequately with the small group of undergraduates who, because they intended to be ordained, were encouraged to read for a theological degree, even though much of the information they acquired was useless and of no avail; but little was done by the faculty to convince those of other faculties of the relevance of theology, and even less to encourage its students to wrestle with the intellectual tensions experienced by those whose approach to life had been rooted in scientific concepts. I readily agreed that while Christianity is a revealed religion, and reason, by itself, cannot get us more than part of the way, theologians should help students to understand the thought patterns of a contemporary world. The university had a tradition, going back hundreds of years, of discussing matters of intellectual moment, and it had never feared robust disputation. Anything that helped men to pursue Truth was recognised to be of God.

It was at this point that I was grateful for the occasional visits with my mother to Dr Beckh's Unitarian church in Bristol. I realised they had made an indelible mark upon me, a mark which questing undergraduates quickly recognised. When they asked me to what extent I was a committed believer, I usually replied: "For two seconds out of three." In any case the scientists agreed with me that like St Paul we could never expect in this world to do more than see through a glass darkly, though not all would have continued to agree with the apostle when he claimed that one day we should see face to face.

I insisted on the element of agnosticism in a lecture that I gave at the invitation of Dr N. F. Mott, the Cavendish Professor of Experimental Physics, to his students. I based my talk on J. B. Phillips' translation of the Greek: "At present we were men looking at puzzling reflections in a mirror. The time will come when we shall see reality whole and face to face. At present all I know is a little fraction of the truth, but the time will come when I shall know it as fully as God now knows me."

Professor Mott occasionally came to Great St Mary's, and more often was to be found alone in a pew on weekdays. I once asked him the reason for his attachment to the building and he told me that while his religious convictions were few he regarded the University Church as the place where men had pursued Truth for centuries and that he was engaged in that pursuit. I was glad he and many more felt like that, because it indicated precisely one of the roles of Great St Mary's. Had I remained longer at Cambridge I should have painted on the church notice board these words of A. J. Balfour, not only because of their aptness, but because they sum up my own theological attitudes:

Our highest truths are but half-truths,
Think not to settle down for ever in any truth.
Make use of it as a tent in which to pass a summer's night,
But build no house in it, or it will be your tomb.

91

When you first have an inkling of its insufficiency
And begin to descry a dim counter-truth coming up
                                                    beyond
Then weep not, but give thanks:
It is the Lord's voice whispering, "Take up thy bed
                                              and walk."

If I were to have an epitaph, I hope it would be this.

It was estimated that at some times of the year between two and three thousand undergraduates a week passed through the doors of Great St Mary's for one reason or another, but I was careful to maintain my distance. I agreed with the deans and chaplains of colleges that, while the University Church should fulfil its function as a forum, I should not concern myself with the pastoral affairs of the undergraduates unless the clergy asked me to do so. In return they were glad to let me know of senior members of the university who had difficulties, because it could be easier for somebody not associated with a college to help. I think the students were glad to have it this way because they knew they could come to Great St Mary's anonymously without any fear of being 'button-holed'! Of course I met them socially. I frequently went to their parties, and on Sunday afternoons I kept 'open house' at the vicarage. Once a term I had a party for the captains of the university clubs—rowing, rugby, football, cricket—the chairmen of the Union and the main political and cultural committees. I was particularly attached to the Scots. They were forbidden to play their bagpipes in the market place on St Andrew's Day because the Sassenachs objected to the cacophony. I invited them to climb the steps of the tower to play on the top, where they were free from the insults of the Cambridge citizens and could claim that the University Church was temporarily under Presbyterian domination. It was usually bitterly cold and, on their descent, as they were in their kilts, I met them in the belfry with bottles of Scotch.

Much of my time was devoted to visiting my town parishioners. As the congregation grew I asked people to let me have their names and their birthdays so that I could put them in a book which was placed on the altar. We remembered them at the early Communion service and called on them in their homes later. As at St Matthew's I made it a rule that I would make no less than three visits a day.

In 1956 I stood as the Labour candidate for the Romsey Ward in Cambridge and came at the head of the poll. In my election address I said:

When I first went to my Bristol parish I was confronted with the problems of acute unemployment and distress, and I tried to do what I could to help people who often lacked some of the basic essentials of life. During the war many houses were bombed, and after the war whole streets were condemned under slum clearance orders. This meant I was frequently dealing with the housing problems of people, and I handled personally more than two thousand cases.

Cambridge is, of course, different from Bristol and the problems are not identical. At the same time each city has to provide adequate health, education, housing, welfare and recreational amenities for its people. This means that the City Council should have on it men and women who realise what the needs are and will take practical steps to meet the needs.

As a person I have always held the view that the Church as an official institution should stand outside party politics, yet the individual Churchman as a private citizen in a democratic country has the right and duty to decide for himself which of the existing parties is most likely to further the sort of society in which he believes. It is for this reason that, as a private citizen, I have been identified with the Labour party for the last twenty years and have tried to further its aims in the interests of all sections of the community.

I enjoyed my short period of service, but the Cambridge Council was no match for the Bristol Council. Labour was perpetually in the minority and the Tories tended to be small businessmen who could not make up their minds whether the major evil was socialism or the university. They disliked both and, as I had a foot in each camp, Alderman James and his bandwagon were bothered and pothered. I wish I could have remained longer, as I should like to have launched broadsides at the infamous Planning Committee which brought ruin to Petty Cury and rendered hideous parts of the city that were dear to generations of Cambridge men.

When I came to Great St Mary's in 1955 I wondered how I would cope with the senior members of the University. I made no claims to academic pretensions and I had had little to do with the intellectual world during my years in Bristol. I had read widely but was in no sense a scholar. I need not have worried. I quickly discovered that dons were of the same species as my former parishioners. They expressed themselves differently. They were less demonstrative, but their malice and invective more subtle.

On my first evening I was asked by F. A. Simpson, an eccentric historian who had been at Trinity since the early years of the century, and who, apart from writing two distinguished books on Napoleon III, was given to idleness and gardening, to dine with him at high table. As we waited for the Latin grace to be said by a scholar, he pointed to a colleague immediately opposite, whom he had hated for decades, and in an audible voice said, "It was not until I met Gow that I realised the sin of gluttony was something more than a theological concept."

Simpson was a character who had become a fellow of his college long before there were rules with regard to retirement. Although he was in holy orders he rarely practised them and his ideas were unusual. He had a great reverence for Our Lord, to whom he referred in lowered voice, but Jesus of Nazareth he disliked because, "He was rude to his mother and cursed a fig tree." As for life after death he feared it though he thought it improbable. When discussing the subject over a glass of sherry—good Spanish, the South African being kept for the young men from "grammar schools and humble backgrounds"—he said, "The idea that I should survive indefinitely, in light perpetual, with my colleagues at high table is a lamentable possibility that fills me with dismay."

Simpson came to Great St Mary's on most Sundays, but for parts of the service only; he spent the rest of the time making short sallies into neighbouring churches to find out what was going on and, if he thought fit, to clip their hedges with his secateurs. Sometimes on his return to Great St Mary's he would stand at the door, groan at the preacher, turn off the lights and walk out. He had strong dislikes, both parsonic and electrical.

Although there were eccentrics like Simpson, most dons were little different from their less academic contemporaries. Whether or not Sir Henry Willink, the Master of Magdalene, who had been indirectly involved in my appointment, had told his colleagues of my arrival I do not know, but I think somebody must have alerted them because during my short stay in Cambridge I received an invitation from every college to dine, and many came to informal parties at the vicarage. Dinner in hall, with wine and fruit in the common room afterwards, is a leisurely affair, which gave me opportunity to meet many interesting people and to make friends with their families. It was a broadening experience and I often recall those lovely evenings of gracious living in beautiful surroundings.

Although Henry Willink was a good friend, we clashed in the press. He had been a Cabinet Minister and, on his appointment to

Magdalene, became the chairman of the Cambridge Conservative party. He used to send me angry letters about things I had said or done and foolishly I would reply as angrily, instead of remaining silent. Our relationship became strained for a few weeks and we avoided one another, but soon everything was forgotten and forgiven until the next time. When I returned to Cambridge after my appointment to Southwark I invariably went to see him in his retirement and illness, and I was moved when his family asked me to take part in his funeral. Yet another example of the power of genuine friendship to rise above political differences. We were fond of one another.

Because of the Bishop's ruling I saw a little of Free Churchmen, either in the town or in the university. It seemed strange after years of almost daily co-operation. Occasionally I received invitations to preach, but it could not be reciprocated. Of course there were no joint staff meetings and no sharing at the Communion Table. Perhaps it was just as well because this lack of ecumenical activity prepared me for Southwark.

It was unexpectedly different with the Roman Catholics. Monsignor Gilbey had moved into Fisher House as Chaplain in 1932, the same year as I had been admitted as an undergraduate. He was a distinguished-looking man who attracted immediate attention. Immaculately dressed in a frock coat, a shovel hat and black gloves, he became a personality in Cambridge life. Anglicans were encouraged to regard him as an *éminence grise* as it was thought that his generous hospitality and exquisite courtesy coupled with unusual charm might divert their steps from Canterbury to Rome. During my student days I never met him, though I have a vivid recollection of sitting at a table next to his at a riverside inn by the little village of Over Cote when he drank chablis from a lily glass while the landlord expelled some rowdy students from the rooms, throwing the cutlery after them.

Soon after my institution to Great St Mary's I met the Monsignor in the market place. He introduced himself and, on learning that the new vicarage was some distance away in Madingley Road, asked me to treat Fisher House, one of the few occupied houses in the parish, as a second home. Today such an invitation might not be surprising, but then it was. In Bristol I had no dealings with Roman Catholics, as both denominations treated one another with dislike, if not worse. There was an iron curtain between us. I took the Monsignor at his word and on most Sunday mornings I went to Fisher House for breakfast between the two early services. That was not all. We often met for luncheon, and sometimes when I was tired and had not time to return to the vicarage I rested at the Chaplaincy. In the long vacation we spent a day together touring Essex or Suffolk. Gilbey knew more about architecture than I did, and his knowledge of the Church of England was inexhaustible. He was a charming and informed companion and he never lost his poise, not even when on one of these occasions he arrived earlier than expected at our point of meeting in Great St Mary's to find me receiving a Roman Catholic priest into the Church of England.

Through him I became friendly not only with the students who seemed to enjoy his limitless hospitality but also with priests who came for the weekend to preach. Best of all was the annual dinner he gave to F. A. Simpson on his birthday in November. Simpson expected us to be in full dress though he himself would be in a suit which looked as if he had bought it at a pre-war jumble sale. Infinite trouble was taken with the menu, but the meal would be interrupted by Simpson because he decided either that the lights were too strong and had to be switched off, or that the room was too hot and his waistcoat had to be removed. These birthday celebrations continued long after the Monsignor and I had left Cambridge, though both of us returned for the occasion. When Simpson was in his nineties the dinner took place in a suite of rooms in Trinity College to which there was a lift, as Simpson was now too feeble to climb the stairs. In the lift he collapsed and appeared to be dying. He was lifted out bodily, sighing and groaning with his eyes shut, and placed on a sofa; Gilbey and I both eyed one another thinking no doubt as to which of us should administer the last rites. After all it was a moot point, as he was Simpson's host and I the co-religionist. We need not have bothered. As soon as Simpson heard that caviar, pheasant and cheese soufflé were on the menu he enacted a resurrection, in which he professed not to believe, and regaled us with reminiscences well into the night.

Although Cambridge was not without its problems I was supremely happy. It seemed that the job was tailor-made. I had no desire to move. It was, therefore, with mixed feelings that I had a letter in November 1959 from the Prime Minister, Harold Macmillan, asking me to let my name go forward to the Queen for nomination to the bishopric of Southwark. In my reply I dithered: "The suggestion raises several issues and I should be grateful if you would allow me to postpone my answer some days. In particular I have to decide whether or not I ought to leave the University Church."

I consulted friends; most advised me to stay. I had a letter from Professor Nevill Mott of the Cavendish which almost determined the issue:

I will try to put in writing some of my feelings about Great St Mary's, particularly as it affects senior members of the university. You are a born teacher. You can put, or cause to be put, the pros and cons of Christianity, of Suez or of Wolfenden, to our young men, and to older men too, in a way which leads them to think the matter out for themselves. In this you are *very* much part of the university—a man who knows how to put ethical issues before us without hiding any aspect of their intellectual content. I think it important for those of us who teach in university that there should be a focus for our aims and aspirations such as your church provides. We are divided in Cambridge into our inward-looking colleges, our ambitious departments and our various cliques. Apart from some devoted administrators and our ceremonial in the Senate House, what is there to remind us that we are a university with a purpose in the world? Your church does that—a perpetual reminder that values matter and that our job is to teach men to think about them. I know this is valuable to me and I am not the only one who thinks so.

Mott's letter, while too generous in his estimate of my work, caused me to write to Archbishop Fisher to tell him that I thought I should remain in Cambridge. He asked me to Lambeth to talk. "Now Stockwood," he said, "sit down and tell me your reasons for not going to Southwark. There is no hurry; take as long as you like. Then I'll tell you why you're wrong."

I felt so pulled in all directions that I asked those whom I had consulted personally to meet together in the room of Hugh Montefiore in Caius on the following Sunday night to help me make up my mind. Before the meeting I had an opportunity to talk over the matter with Michael Ramsey, the Archbishop of York, who happened to be in Cambridge. He was reluctant to commit himself, but in his inimitable way he said, "*If* you decide to become a bishop I shall be glad to welcome to the bench a man who when all of us, like sheep, are saying 'Yes, yes, yes,' will have the courage to say, 'No, no, no, no, no.'"

At the meeting all except Ken Carey, Principal of my old theological college, had changed their minds and told me I should go to Southwark. Years later I asked Carey the reason for his advice and he told me that in my Westcott House file there was a note to the effect that I suffered from such indifferent health it was unlikely that I should reach the age of thirty. Knowing this, he thought Southwark would kill me. When in my early years as a bishop I had several operations and spent weeks in hospital he must have thought he was justified.

I wrote to Fisher to inform him of my acceptance. He replied,

I am glad you have got the decision off your chest. It is not surprising it left you tired. You may comfort yourself that your decision accords with the earnest desires of the Archbishops, the Prime Minister and many others; and you may therefore conclude that to the utmost of your ability you are following a call of the Holy Spirit.

I do not know what fortunes await you as a bishop. Of one thing I am pretty certain and that is that daily throughout your career your conviction will grow that the Holy Spirit has put you into this office, and that if anything goes wrong it is not a misreading of His will, but human failings in carrying it out.

This is all I need to say at the moment. May I add that so long as I am in this office I shall always be at your disposal to give any advice or help that I possibly can. No doubt there will be plenty of things of which I shall want to give you advice, and on which, arising out of the experience and practice of the Church, you will want violently to think otherwise.

The evening before the announcement in the press I broke the news in Fisher House at Monsignor Gilbey's dinner table, as once again we were celebrating Simpson's birthday.

Simpson stood up, took off his shredded Oxfam pullover and groaned.

6

Chanctonbury Ring

I dreaded the thought of leaving Cambridge where I had felt fulfilled and I was apprehensive. Fisher had told me that Southwark was the Cinderella of the dioceses and no bishop should remain for more than twelve or thirteen years, as otherwise he would go out of his mind. A remark that caused Montgomery-Campbell, the Bishop of London, who was renowned as an amusing and caustic wag, to remark: "My dear Mervyn, I never knew you had a mind to go out of."

On New Year's Eve I walked on the Sussex Downs to Chanctonbury Ring. Since my undergraduate days it had been a favourite haunt of mine and I try never to make a decision of importance without turning matters over in my mind as I wander around the Ring. There was a particularly beautiful sunset, a flaming red sky. As I looked at it spellbound, deep black storm clouds suddenly appeared. I took it for an augury.

My last service at Great St Mary's was on Easter Day. Garth Moore, anxious to spare me hundreds of farewells, whisked me off to his college, Corpus Christi, for hall. Later that night I returned to the church and sat in a pew thinking not only of my own ministry and of the thousands who had flocked there, but of the preceding generations and the famous theologians that had met within its walls ever since the university started on the site centuries before. I never surrendered my key of the vestry door, as I thought that one night I might like to return unbeknown to anybody. I never did.

As I had arranged to have a short break before taking up my duties in Southwark, I went to Capri. Julian Grenfell, whose fianceé lived in Florence, joined me in Rome on my return journey. Before leaving Cambridge I had told Monsignor Gilbey of my plans and he insisted that he should try to get tickets for Julian and myself to attend a papal audience. Nothing happened until, on an afternoon when we were visiting the Lateran, a Vatican official appeared with an impressive card of admission. How he knew we were there I had no idea, the Lateran being only one of many places on our list. I then remembered to my dismay that I had no clerical collar, so Julian, with his smattering of Italian, and I, in sign language which suggested that I was about to slash my throat, enquired of passers-by the way to the local Moss Bros. Next morning we took our place in a long queue before finding seats at the back of a large audience hall. We were glad to be in a remote place because we had no idea what we ought to do when Pope John arrived and we did not want to give offence. His Holiness was late and we thought that the public audience might have been cancelled. Suddenly, to our astonishment, an official in uniform called out, "Dr Stockwood." Julian and I were thunderstruck. We pushed through the staring crowds, wondering what was to happen to us. Julian suspected that our denominational allegiance had been discovered and we would be expelled. We walked at a brisk pace along interminable corridors, into lifts, up staircases and along corridors. Julian said to me, "Do you think we are heading for a dungeon?" Instead we arrived at the door of the private study of Pope John.

To this day I have no idea who was responsible, nor has Monsignor Gilbey. It was one of the greatest moments of my life, and every detail is vividly printed on my memory. Monsignor Cardinale, now the Papal Nuncio in Brussels, acted as interpreter. Through him the Pope told me that he had given me this privilege because he knew of my deep concern for Christian unity and he shared my longings and prayers. He gave me a message for the Archbishop of Canterbury in which he expressed the hope that the two of them would meet. It was Easter week when one of the scripture lessons was the story of the walk of the two disciples to Emmaus. The Pope led me to the window, from which we looked down on two fountains, and then said, "Two souls can meet in prayer though distances divide them. Just as on the road to Emmaus the two disciples found their separate and individual problems solved because of Him who walked in their midst, so in the Spirit of Emmaus we walk together." He then blessed us and as he gave me the Kiss of Peace at his study door he asked me to write to him and said, "Next time you come to Rome, you must see me."

A few days later I was at Lambeth Palace to stay the night with the Fishers before my consecration on the following day. May 1st was chosen by the Archbishop, though he had forgotten it was Labour Day. After dinner I told the Archbishop of my visit to the Vatican. He was not pleased. "When you are older, Stockwood, you will be careful before allowing these Roman Catholics to pull the wool over your eyes." I mentioned the Pope's hope that they might meet. I do not think it registered because in his retirement, when our relationship had become sadly soured, he denied that I had been the bearer of an invitation. However Monsignor Cardinale has confirmed that it was made and that I was commissioned by the Pope to be the bearer. The details are unimportant; what matters is that Fisher eventually went to the Vatican and the wool began to be removed from his eyes, and from the eyes of thousands, on both sides of the divide.

I had a bad night. I was ill and could not sleep, I expect it was nerves. And I was worried about dress. The Archbishop insisted that bishops should wear gaiters and aprons. I was determined not to do so. It seemed foolish for a twentieth-century pastor to wear the hunting-rig of a seventeenth-century squire. Apparently there had been an explosion at a recent bishops' meeting at which the Bishop of Birmingham, then the brave Leonard Wilson who had been tortured in a Japanese camp, had been rebuked for being improperly dressed. He returned in his gaiters. I did not wish to be discourteous but I let it be known that it was a matter of conscience and nothing would change my mind. As I waited in the corridor outside the breakfast room, Fisher came downstairs whistling. I noticed he was wearing trousers. It was typical of him not to quarrel with me on my consecration day.

As I could not eat anything, Mrs Fisher said, "Mervyn, you do look unwell. I wonder what I can do for you. It's such a long service and Geoff won't shorten it." And Geoff wouldn't. Then Mrs Fisher remembered that some years ago they had been given a present of brandy and it had not been opened. She filled a small bottle and I put it in my pocket. "Just in case," she said. Fortunately I survived the service, but when I reached the retro-choir two hours later I was feeling faint. I put the bottle to my lips, choked, gasped with horror and spat. Mrs Fisher had put the brandy into a TCP bottle.

A bishop cannot embark upon his duties until he has taken his oath of allegiance to the monarch. As the Queen was out of London, I had to wait for a few days. I remember that when the moment came, my car broke down and I had to call on a curate to drive me to the Palace in a Mini. When I had kissed hands I was offered a cup of chocolate. I think I was the first bishop to appear before Her Majesty without gaiters.

A few days later was the service of enthronement. I spent the previous night in the Cathedral in solitary prayer, while my chaplain slept on a camp bed in the vestry until he joined me for the early Mass. I decided to make the enthronement service as simple, short, colourful and congregational as possible. We disposed of the ludicrous legal paraphernalia in the morning when nobody but the officials were present, instead of boring the diocese by incorporating it into the main service, as is customary. Among the hymns I chose, "The day Thou gavest Lord is ended," because it was a favourite of mine and of Walter Monckton; another was, "Guide me O Thou great Redeemer," to the famous Welsh tune, again because I liked it and so did Aneurin Bevan. As Walter and Nye were sitting next to one another, I thought it right that although politically divided they should sing in unison. The Cathedral organist was not best pleased. He wrote to remind me that an enthronement service was not a cup final. Presumably he wished for hymns that would satisfy his pride, give the choir its head and bore everybody else. It was a valuable lesson. For the next twenty years I always informed him and his successors with regard to hymns and musical settings whenever I attended the Cathedral. We established a reasonable compromise.

I went to Cambridge to the Master's Lodge at Christ's to find the quiet to write my enthronement sermon. My text came from the Book of Proverbs: "Where there is no vision the people perish." I made several points:

1. The Church exists to further the Kingdom of God. The primary unit designated for this purpose is the parish. The one question I ask of a parish is "What impact is your parish making upon the locality?" That is the question that is the acid test when it comes to judging the quality of Churchmanship.
2. The Church must consider whether the parochial system is adequate to its tasks. I should like to see cautious experiments with a new type of priesthood and a new type of organisation. Is it possible, for instance, that an ordained man who works in industry may be in a better position to understand the needs and outlooks of his associates than a parochial clergyman, who is inevitably segregated?
3. If we are to evangelise the country we must not be content to think in narrow denominational terms. It so happens that the mitre I am wearing was given to me by twenty Methodist ministers with whom I worked and worshipped in Bristol. And the head which wears the mitre was less than a month ago blessed by His Holiness, the Pope. The Bible which I have here in the pulpit was inscribed and given to me by Alexis, the Patriarch of the Russian Orthodox Church.
4. We must reconsider the relationship between dogma and Truth.

102

What do we mean by faith? The problem is not solved with answers such as, "The Church says," or "The Bible says." The anthropologist, for instance, finds it difficult to understand what we mean by original sin; the biochemist cannot easily make a nice distinction between nature and grace; the physiologist is not sure of the relationship between mind and brain; the sociologist has questions to ask with regard to the determining influences of environment; and the psychologist may be doubtful of some of our moral categories.

5. The strength of the Christian Church depends upon the calibre of its members. We need men whose minds and energies are dedicated to God in prayer and sacrament; above all, we need men who are personally converted, who can say of the Living Christ, "He is my Lord and my Saviour".

The storm clouds that gathered over Chanctonbury did not take long before releasing their downpour. Within a few weeks I was involved in the defence of a mother who was sentenced to prison, unjustly I thought. I fiercely attacked the magistrate. There were headlines in the press. Within a few days the magistrate died of a heart attack. I received hundreds of abusive letters accusing me of being the cause of his death, although the coroner said that it had nothing to do with the incident. Even so it was wrong of me to have jumped to conclusions without first listening to the other side. As I had agreed some months previously to appear on a radio question programme (with Lady Barnett who was to die so tragically), I was asked the inevitable question. I did not attempt to defend myself. I said I had done wrong, and apologised. That has always been my line—rather than try to defend the indefensible—to say, "Sorry."

A few days later I was in trouble with the Apostolic Delegate, Archbishop O'Hara. I had spoken on the radio in aid of the week's good cause, birth control clinics. The Delegate was furious. Questions were asked in the House of Lords. At a charity luncheon at the Savoy at which the late Duke of Gloucester was presiding, proceedings were held up while the Delegate, who had been placed next to me, insisted that the seating arrangements should be changed. He maintained that had Pope John known my views on contraceptives he would never have received me at the Vatican. I doubt it.

Next came Carshalton. All Saints' had had as its rector for many years an erudite priest who had assumed that the Reformation had never taken place and that it was his duty to adhere to the practices and liturgy of the Church of Rome. My predecessor, Bishop

Simpson, had recently persuaded the patron to appoint as the new rector a High Churchman who was loyal to the Church of England. While I was still at Cambridge I received letters and protests from both sides. Matters came to a head in August 1959 when the elderly curate of the daughter church of St Andrew, Father Harris, refused to obey the rector and continued to use the liturgy of the Roman Catholic Church. Leigh Edwards, the rector, appealed to me. I spent hours with Father Harris, reminding him of his promises to use the Church of England prayer book and of his duty to carry out his rector's instructions. My efforts were useless. Harris told me he knew he would have to suffer the fate of a martyr for what he believed to be the Catholic Church. I had no alternative but to support the rector. There was a massive explosion. Harris resigned, but after consultation with his friends, withdrew his resignation. I refused to accept the withdrawal. I have often wondered if I could have played my cards differently. I do not think so. As when I tried to argue with the CICCU with regard to the use of the University Church by Billy Graham, I was dealing with an inflexible bigot. Years later he returned to the diocese to live in an old people's home in Coulsdon. I called on him on Christmas Eve and we were reconciled.

Inevitably the Archbishop was alarmed by reports he was receiving, and, unbeknown to me, sent for a few of the top brass critics. He wrote to tell me what he had done, addressing me for the first time by my Christian name. In his letter he wrote:

(a) You have jumped into your tasks with both feet, and no doubt will jump into others. The great thing is that the objectives are first class: less courageous men have dodged them for a long time. It is worth putting up with your mistakes and your precipitances for the sake of the thing in the future.
(b) As you know well, some are gossips. I told them this very bluntly and it shook them.
(c) You are doing a great job, though very often doing things in the wrong way. Fortunately you learn from experience and you listen to criticism gladly and openly. You must be more careful to consult them before you act, even in small things.

At the bottom of the page was a postscript: "I spent part of my time explaining how dull, wooden-headed, and unimaginative quite a lot of my clergy are, almost incapable of facing a new idea without panic."

The Archbishop urged me to rest, so I spent some weeks in Florence with Simon Phipps and Julian Grenfell in charge of the American Church, with a free pass to the galleries in the evening when the doors were closed to the public. That is the way to look at the paintings in the Uffizi. My hosts, who included three ex-wives of famous toothpaste manufacturers, were most hospitable, though unfamiliar with English titles, so I found myself addressed as the Lord Mayor of Southwark in the speech of welcome.

As the Carshalton affair was still occupying the correspondence columns, I feared that the links I had established with the Vatican might be impaired. I took the opportunity of contacting Monsignor Cardinale who had acted as interpreter in the Pope's study. He told me that the Pope had been informed and that he sympathised with me. A priest, he said, should be loyal to his Church and obey its rules, or leave it and join another.

When I called on Cardinale he was living in a co-operative block of flats. Although he was a member of the Vatican staff and engaged in diplomatic activities he was anxious to remain rooted in the lives of the people and to engage in evangelistic work. He told me that the citizens of Rome were little different from the citizens of London in so far as church-going was concerned. They were outside organised religion, and were unlikely to return. For that reason he and another priest had taken apartments in the block in the hope of getting to know their neighbours. An important factor was a common room on the ground floor where the tenants could meet. He was encouraged by the response, and already a few had met for instruction and a house Mass. He believed that in many city areas, not only the inner city, the way forward for the Church was the informal local group, rather than the parish unit.

I was fascinated by what Cardinale told me because I was keen to implement the plans I had suggested in my enthronement sermon with regard to auxiliary priests. I wanted to train men for the ministry while they were still in secular employment and to encourage some to remain in their employment after ordination. I was increasingly sceptical about the value of the traditional theological college training, for two reasons. First, it required a student to spend months studying subjects that would be of little use to him when he found himself in a parish; as someone put it, "learning to answer questions no sensible man asks." Second, it removed many students from the social milieu and made it difficult for them to return to it. There were not many ordinands from the working classes as I had known them in Bristol, but the few that came forward tended to become 'gentrified' with the result they were strangers in their homes. They had moved to a different culture; they had assumed what they considered to be more respectable accents; they were no longer accepted by their contemporaries whom they used to meet at street corners, in the pub and on the football stands.

I put my plans to the meeting of bishops. They were not enthusiastically received, least of all by those who had been principals of theological colleges and who found it difficult to believe there could be an alternative method of training. The Archbishop was the exception. Geoffrey Fisher gave me guarded support and urged me to go ahead. It was typical of the man. The Archbishop was basically a liberal traditionalist who, like Gamaliel, took the line that "if this movement is merely human it will collapse of its own accord. But if it should be from God you cannot defeat them, and you might actually find yourself to be fighting against God."

After consultation with John Robinson, the Bishop of Woolwich, who was the driving force, I appointed Canon Stanley Evans as Principal of the Southwark Ordination Course. He was an unusual man with an unusual history. As a member of the Communist party he had denounced me as a fascist because of my criticism of the Soviet Union. Like Hewlett Johnson, the Dean of Canterbury, he had never questioned the official party line. It astonished me, as he had a first-class mind and a memory which I can only describe as fantastic. He was a walking encyclopaedia. Then came the Russian invasion of Hungary. His eyes were opened and he went into the wilderness, severing many friendships that had become precious to him. The invitation to join me in Southwark in order to launch the scheme gave him a new lease of life.

The headquarters of the Southwark Ordination Course was at Bletchingley in the Surrey hills. The men had a residential weekend once a month and a fortnight during their summer holidays. Apart from that they attended lectures on weekday evenings in the Chapter House near London Bridge. From the start I insisted that there should be no lowering of standards. The men had to take the same exams as their contemporaries at the traditional colleges. I knew that if we didn't stick to this rule the critics would dismiss our men as second-class intellects for a second-class priesthood. Of course it meant hard work. As soon as the men returned from the office or factory they had to get down to their studies. And for three years, weekends and annual holidays were bespoken. But they triumphed, and I remember the thrill when I ordained the first batch

106

in Southwark Cathedral at Michaelmas 1963. Twenty years have passed since its inception and the Southwark Ordination Course has gone from strength to strength. What is important, similar courses are to be found in other dioceses. As I reflect on the course it had four basic merits.

1. The course accepted men of different persuasions, whereas most theological colleges cater for a single point of view, Anglo-Catholic or Evangelical.
2. The men did not learn their theology in a vacuum. Each day they had to live it out in the secular world and to be subjected to questioning by their fellows and their families.
3. It taught men to work hard. There are too many clergy in the Church of England who are acquainted with only one verse in the Holy Scripture, namely, how "to be at ease in Zion". Such men would have fallen by the wayside as their idle dispositions could not have coped with the pressures.
4. It was sound economics. It saved the Church thousands of pounds. The residential fees for weekends and summer schools were minimal and most lecturers were paid by the secular authorities.

I was less successful with the other goals I had set before the diocese in my enthronement sermon. While there is much to be said for the parochial system it is not necessarily the best organisational unit in the inner city. A single-handed clergyman with pastoral responsibility for thousands of people is likely to be overwhelmed with the chores of the job, and to give up. I had many parishes in which men had been for years and were virtually useless. In one instance there were four adjoining parishes with a total congregation of less than fifty. I longed to hand the area over to a team of missionaries. But there was nothing I could do. A parish priest has a freehold and, providing he does not commit a crime, he cannot be removed. Adultery, like drunkenness within the sanctuary, is a grave ecclesiastical offence, but neither idleness nor incompetence is. There can be few professions that provide greater opportunities for a man who has drive, initiative and pastoral zeal, but—alas—the reverse is also true. As a priest is unaccountable to anybody for the use of his time he can treat his stipend as unemployment pay and his vicarage as an almshouse. Today the situation is changing. The reduction in the number of clergy, coupled with the effects of inflation, has led to a diminution in the number of parishes and an increase in team ministries.

The failures were in a minority, and some of them were not culpable. They had set out with high hopes, but, unable to cope with the situation, had lost heart.

I decided my primary duty was to encourage the clergy by getting to know them personally. During the first year I called at every vicarage, about three hundred in a diocese which stretches from Woolwich to Kingston and from Lambeth to Gatwick and has a population of over two million.

There were amusing moments. When I knocked on the rectory door in a village in the Reigate area wearing a collar and tie, the wife said I could not see her husband as he was awaiting the arrival of His Lordship the Bishop. Another wife, who, like her husband, was well on in her eighties, said, "Good afternoon, Dr Garbett, I'll tell the vicar you've come." Garbett had been the Bishop forty years before, and had died as Archbishop of York. Incidentally, the vicar in his young days had crossed swords with Garbett. He was an enthusiastic supporter of the local football club and held an annual service for them. The sanctuary was decorated with goal posts, the sidesmen wore shorts and the team colours, while he himself started the service by blowing a whistle. Garbett did not approve. Here are some verses from hymns. The service began thus:

> Keep thyself pure! God calls you for His glory,
> From sinful lusts and thoughts impure to flee;
> And in your life to live the wondrous story,
> The power of Christ Who died has made me free.
> Keep thyself pure! "But can I in my weakness
> Conquer desires that gain so firm a hold?"
> Coming to Christ in humble, lowly meekness,
> Weakness is strength, His power can make thee bold,
> Glory to Jesus!

It ended thus;

The Footballers' Hymn

Tune: Wessex "Mine eyes have seen the glory."

As you line up for the whistle, with the ball about your feet,
And you face the team opposing, which you know you're out to
  beat.
Then the Lord of Life is calling, 'mid the friendly cries which
  greet,
  "Play up and play the game"!

If you try to be unselfish (since the part must serve the whole),
Though the 'ha'pence be another's and the 'kicks' your only toll,
And you care not who may score it, if your team can gain the goal,
    Well done! You've played the game.

For this Law of Combination is the Law of God above,
And his team can only prosper when men learn to play and move
In an unison as comrades, in the harmony of Love—
    —The Secret of the game.

Then followed the National Anthem and the Last Post.

The vicar of Petersham, Parson Mills, had held on to his living for longer than most people could remember. "Good afternoon, my Lord," he said. "I know why you've come. The same reason as your predecessor and his predecessor came—to ask me to resign. Well, I am staying." And stay he did. I was fond of old Parson Mills. What he believed I do not know, and there were few people in his exquisite church with its double-decker pulpit to find out, but he was an erudite scholar with a particular interest in Georgian architecture, of which there were splendid examples in Petersham. Once when he was lunching with me I said jokingly, "Is it true that you preached a series of sermons on Georgian architecture on the Sundays in Lent?" "No," he replied. Then after a brief silence with a mischievous twinkle in his eye, he added, "It was the Sundays after Easter."

Once a week I had a lunch party for three of the clergy and their wives, and less often a stand-up buffet lunch for twenty curates. It took me seven years to cover the diocese, but it was well worthwhile. I think my guests enjoyed coming to the house to meet me informally rather than to talk business in my study as the clergy normally had to do. As I knew how hard most of them worked and how rarely they had anybody prepare food for them, I saw to it they were well wined and dined. And the meal was never hurried. I set aside two and a half hours for the occasion.

"To be given to hospitality" is a Scriptural injunction which is laid upon all Christians, but I found it particularly necessary as I believe that a man in a position of leadership must devote immense care to the cultivation of personal relationships. I am thinking not only of the clergy, but of people in many walks of life with whom I had to be concerned, teachers, politicians, ambassadors, businessmen, trade unionists, students, actors, visitors from overseas, and many more. When I left Southwark my chaplain told me that our visitors' books had more than nine thousand signatures. If a vote of thanks is to be proposed it should be to my faithful Arab chauffeur, Munir, who although not employed as a cook accepted the responsibility, and did it superbly, chiefly I think by instinct. Now that I am retired and have to look after myself I often wish that Munir and his family lived nearer to Bath, as I am sure do my guests!

As important as giving hospitality to the clergy is the readiness to receive it from them. The occasions that a bishop is able to visit a particular parish are few and far between. It means much to the parson and his wife if he will sit down at the table with the family rather than drive off as soon as the proceedings in the church are over.

I tried to meet all the clergy and full-time helpers once a year in a four-year circle. In years one and three I, or the Suffragan Bishop, visited them in their deaneries for Holy Communion and breakfast before addressing them. In year two I held twenty-one house parties at our headquarters in the Surrey hills. The parties lasted two days and, although we worshipped and studied together, I encouraged a relaxed atmosphere with plenty of free time. In year four all clergy under the age of sixty went to a Butlins camp—Bognor, Clacton, Minehead—from a Monday to Friday in the summer. There were usually about four hundred of us. There were five Butlins during my episcopate. They were approached with apprehension, but enjoyed in retrospect. It was my hope that this four-year cycle would knit us together as a diocesan family. On three occasions out of four the unit was the deanery, perhaps fifteen parishes. The deanery cannot come alive unless the clergy are known to one another. Alas, they are often strangers and critics. I constantly reminded them of their duty in this matter and I expected all to call on a newcomer and to be present at the annual deanery party.

Of course I saw the clergy on other occasions. I, like all bishops, was in and out of parishes and there was a regular routine with regard to men who went to a new parish. After six months they sent me back a report and then I would go through it with them.

The most demanding and the most valuable chore I set myself was the official Visitation of all the parishes in the diocese. For those who are unaccustomed to Anglican practice let me explain that the bishop is the chief pastor of all the parishes in his diocese. His vicars, as the name implies, are vice-pastors, who see to the day-to-day running of the parish in the absence of the bishop. However, if the bishop decides to hold an official Visitation he is both bishop and parish priest. I made clear that the purpose of a Visitation was not to impose my authority but to live in the parish as a pastor and to get to know the people whether or not they went to church. Above all I wanted to come alongside the parson and encourage him. It was a mammoth undertaking and took seventeen years to complete. I arrived on a Sunday and remained until the Monday night. Apart from services and meeting the church council to discuss their answers to an exhaustive questionnaire, I spent the time visiting homes, factories, hospitals, schools, town halls, farms, police headquarters, inter-racial clubs. I remember going with one rector to a vast high block of eighteen storeys in Woolwich to call on a family that had recently arrived on the top floor. Because the power-workers were on strike, and the lifts were out of action we had to climb interminable stairs. I suggested to the rector that he should not say I was the bishop as it would be shock enough for them to be confronted by the parish priest. A woman opened the door. Suspicions evaporated after a few minutes' chit-chat and the rector was asked inside. I was standing in the background so he pointed to me, saying, "I've got a friend here, may he come in as well?" For me that summed up the purpose of these Visitations. This particular incident made a deep impression on me. It helped me to understand the problems of high-rise living. As we made the return journey, a mother with a baby in a pram and two small children and the groceries was making the ascent. She was exhausted. I said, "She must be praying for the end of the strike." "Yes," said the rector, "but it won't make all that difference. They often have to wait ages for a lift and lots of them give up in despair and leg it."

The following week I was in Bermondsey and the lights went out. It was winter and a dark evening. There was a ring at the vicarage door and an enchanting urchin said, "Our Mum told I to go to the Catholick to ask the priest for some candles they put in front of them images, but the Catholick ain't got no more 'cos the father says them be pinched and 'e told I to come 'ere." Fortunately the church was High and as it had been wisely locked there were still a few candles at Our Lady's Shrine. So I gave him a couple to take back to our Mum. "Thanks, Mister. Do you want the money? Cheerio."

To devote so much time to the clergy and their parishes meant withdrawing from other things. Aneurin Bevan never tired of saying that politics is the language of priorities; and so is the Christian religion and all that appertains to it, including a bishop's job. Where do his priorities lie? I refuse to believe that he needs to desert his diocese for days on end to attend committees. It appals me that at a time when the clergy are in short supply bishops are increasingly asking for additional suffragans to help them—even in the smaller

111

dioceses. The reason given by one bishop with a very small population was that he had to spend nearly a hundred days a year in London. The primary task of a bishop is to be a shepherd of his flock. I sometimes wonder whether the reason is that some bishops prefer to be in London listening to one another's speeches, drawing up reports and serving on commissions rather than engaging in the hard slog of personal pastoral work, knowing their people and being known by them.

Be that as it may, I realised in my early months in Southwark I must be determined not to be engulfed in the bureaucratic machine which, like an octopus, was suffocating the Church of England. Of course a bishop must accept his share of basic general responsibilities along with his colleagues, and this I gladly did. For years I was on the governing body of the Church Commissioners and I was punctilious in my duties in the House of Lords, and from time to time I would undertake particular missions if asked to do so by the Archbishop; but I think that nine-tenths of my time was spent inside my diocese doing my pastoral job.

I do not want to suggest that I confined myself to the people who belonged to the churches. I was as concerned for those who, whether or not they were practising Christians, were involved in the life of the community. Each May I had a party at Bishop's House for those who were about to become Mayors, their wives and the executive officers. There would be about sixty people. The purpose was to show the concern of the Church and to establish contact with the chief officers. It meant that when difficult problems occurred concerning the fabric of society—housing, race, education, unemployment, health services—I had direct access to the departments. More important, I was able to put the clergy, who understood the local difficulties better than I did, into contact with people I knew would be keen to help.

The summer party was an interesting political mixture. The boroughs nearest the river, Greenwich, Lewisham, Southwark, Lambeth and Wandsworth were usually Labour, whereas the Wimbledon, Richmond, Kingston, Reigate and Godstone areas were Tory. In the early years I had my problems because the Tory councils wondered whether it was safe to sup with the devil unless it were with a long spoon, and some councillors berated me at their meetings; but as the months passed they knew that although I had strong political views, I tried to remain above party loyalties when dealing officially with the boroughs.

I had hoped that the troublesome period through which I went in

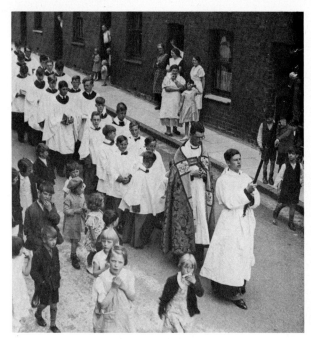

Above left: Procession in the streets of the Blundell's School Mission.

Above right: John Robinson, later Bishop of Woolwich and author of *Honest to God*, with the author on St Matthew Moorfields' outing to Weston-super-Mare, c1947.

Sir Stafford and Lady Cripps with the author, c1944.

Great St Mary's, the University Church, Cambridge, 1958.

Above left: The Prime Minister, Mr Harold Macmillan, walking in procession with the author to receive honorary degrees from Lord Monckton, Chancellor of Sussex University, 1963.

Above right: The Archbishop of Canterbury, Dr Geoffrey Fisher, after the consecration of the Bishop of Southwark (left) and the Bishop of Barking (right), May 1st 1959.

The author sitting at his consistory court, 1964.

The author visits the Patriarch of Moscow while on a parliamentary mission to the Soviet Union, 1977.

Above left: Lord Longford with the author at a party given by David Frost at Alexandra Palace.

Above right: The author speaking at a Foyle's luncheon at the Dorchester Hotel, with Barbara Cartland, in honour of the publication of *I Seek the Miraculous* by Barbara Cartland, 1979.

The author with the Bluebell Girls.

The Archbishop of Canterbury, Dr Michael Ramsey, with the author after the consecration of David Sheppard as Bishop of Woolwich, 1969.

Sir John Betjeman with the author in the out-of-door pulpit of Christchurch, North Brixton, c1973.

Diocesan Eucharist on Wimbledon Centre Court, 1980.

At a staff meeting.

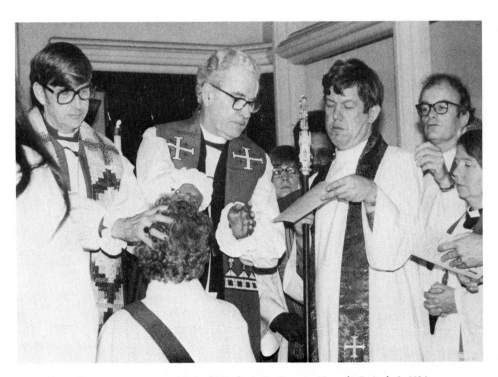

The ordination to the priesthood of Elizabeth Canham in Newark Cathedral, USA, 1981.

Swan song in Bath.

With Malcolm Muggeridge at Chanctonbury Ring, 1982.

my early months would give way to more peaceful times and leave me free for my pastoral work. But I seemed to be accident prone. Two incidents occurred, neither of which was of my choosing, that were to hit the headlines. The first, a brush with the Freemasons, was of little importance except that it eventually disrupted the happy relations that I had with Archbishop Fisher; the second, a consistory court case concerning Dr Bryn Thomas, the vicar of Balham, was a near calamity and brought me more unhappiness than any other incident in my episcopate.

I had had friends who were Masons but I was never attracted to the craft itself. I knew they were benefactors and did much good work, but I could not understand why a Churchman should need to join a semi-religious society. But that was not all. Many bishops were Masons and it was thought, probably quite wrongly, that they tended to bestow favours on clergy who 'stood on the square'. Some of my contemporaries at Cambridge openly told me they had signed on in order to climb the preferment ladder. In particular it was a pity, it seemed to me, that there should be a division among the bishops. We were supposed to be a brotherhood but here was a secret society within the brotherhood. I noticed that it was the Low Church bishops who tended to be Masons, like Geoffrey Fisher. Disapproving of ritual and ceremonial in church, they wore sartorial dress at Masonic meetings and performed elaborate rites, some of which seemed a near parody of the sacraments of Baptism and Holy Communion.

Curiously enough when I was engaged in a contretemps with Geoffrey Fisher in 1967 he appeared to endorse my view. I have a letter in his own handwriting in which he said: "The ritual is glorified nonsense based on a legend of sort. Why not? We all *like* that kind of play-acting if it is in a friendly atmosphere and even more if it poses as a secret! We could get some features in the ritual made less ridiculous. But when all is said and done the ritual sets out to glorify craftsmanship."

The occasion of the row in 1959 was the request by the relatives of a Freemason to hold a Masonic funeral in a church in the diocese. I carefully studied the proposed service and I found that the words 'Jesus Christ' were omitted from the prayers and the word 'Architect' substituted. Worse still, the cross was to be removed from the altar and an additional non-Christian ceremony was to take place at the graveside. I informed the vicar that while people must be free to bury their dead in their own way, I thought that in this case it would be better for the service to take place in a Masonic temple. A bishop, when he is consecrated, promises to banish strange doctrines; therefore I could not allow the doctrine of the divinity of Christ to be treated as peripheral. Moreover every church was dedicated in the name of the Holy Trinity and not in the name of the Architect.

The line I took stirred up a hornets' nest. I was warned that I had offended important benefactors and that the diocese would suffer financially. It may have done so.

Unfortunately when I had another difficulty with Masons some years later and had to take a firm line, I had an angry letter from Geoffrey Fisher, now in retirement. He rebuked me for arrogance in not having consulted my brother bishops. In fact I had consulted the Archbishop of Canterbury who warmly supported me in the action I had taken. I sent a copy of the Archbishop's letter to his predecessor. Alas, it strained our relationships to breaking point. I was sad because Geoffrey Fisher had been a good friend and adviser. Moreover, during my first year in Southwark, when I had no home of my own, I had lived at Lambeth Palace for several months and became very fond of the Archbishop and his wife. What grieved me especially was the fact that it was the Masonic issue that led to the point of no return. It more than confirmed my view that it was unhelpful for some bishops to belong to a secret society which demanded an absolute loyalty. It was calculated to divide us into two groups and could lead to conflict.

A Freemason was also at the centre of the scandal that was to overtake the diocese and bring me so much misery. I do not hold the Freemasons in any way responsible since Bryn Thomas's membership may have been no more than a cover. He was also a member of the Communist party, or a fellow traveller—so he told me.

Thomas had been the vicar of Kemble in Gloucestershire and when I was at St Matthew's we exchanged visits. I enjoyed preaching for him as he was a good host and an interesting conversationalist. Although both of us were socialists he was further to the Left than I and I had no sympathy with his views on the Soviet Union. I lost contact with him when he moved, and I was surprised and pleased when I received a telegram from him on my appointment to Southwark telling me that he was the vicar of Balham. Within days I had a letter asking me to preach on a Sunday evening and to have supper afterwards. A date was fixed several months ahead. However, before this engagement it was arranged by the rural dean that I should meet the clergy of his deanery for the first time in Balham at his parish hall, and that Bryn Thomas would act as host. I was somewhat surprised when I found on the table in his hall a note informing me that he could not be present as he was attending a Masonic meeting.

During the next months I had complaints about Thomas, but few could be substantiated. I was particularly worried by his proneness to litigation, especially when it came to matters of real estate in which it was said he was involved. I referred the tenants to their lawyers, taking the line that it was a secular matter beyond my competence. But in December 1960 I had a formal complaint with regard to sexual offences. It was neither simple nor straightforward; nor was it an occasional lapse that could be overlooked. A woman concerned, having been to the lawyers, laid the complaint with the request that the case be tried in the consistory court. For those who are not familiar with the facts, the consistory court is one of the courts of the land. It is the court of the bishop of the diocese, but the bishop usually delegates his responsibilities to his chancellor, who is a barrister. My chancellor was Garth Moore. When complaints are referred to the bishop he allows the case to go forward unless he chooses to use his veto. I hoped that the matter could be settled out of court. As the evidence appeared to be so damning, I urged Bryn Thomas to resign. He refused and told me he would ruin me if I proceeded. I thought a possible way out would be to allow him to resign his Orders. I consulted Archbishop Fisher. He insisted that resignation was intended for those who wished to leave the ministry for honourable reasons. Thomas must be tried in court and, if found guilty, be deposed. I sent intermediaries, one after the other, to the vicarage, but to no purpose. I was in despair because, unlike divorce cases which only publish the grounds of complaint, and the judgment, the consistory court cases are published in detail. I assume Bryn Thomas thought that rather than bring such a fate upon the Church of England I would give way to what was virtually blackmail.

On the evening before the case was to begin a letter from him was left at my house. Instead of abuse and blackmail it was a friendly and respectful letter asking whether I would allow him to resign his Orders and call off the case. It was too late. I prefer not to refer to the sequel except to mention that the case dragged on for days, from the beginning of Passion week to Maundy Thursday. The press made a carnival of it, relishing their opportunity to print the sordid details. Bryn Thomas and some of his associates were guilty of unbelievable perjury. I cried myself to sleep most nights. The verdict was inevitable. Having deprived him of his living, I had to allow some weeks for him to appeal to a higher court before I deposed or unfrocked him. Charles Claxton, my friend from Bristol days, now

Bishop of Blackburn, insisted I should recover my nerve during the interval by going with him to Jersey. It had to be called off as Bryn Thomas, prompted by a Sunday newspaper, decided he too would go to Jersey. Charles and I went to North Wales and climbed Snowdon, while Megan Lloyd George did what she could to cheer me up in Criccieth.

Bryn Thomas did not appeal. I then had to proceed with the grisly business of unfrocking or deposing him in his absence. Garth Moore told me it had to be done within the context of a service in the Cathedral. The suggestion was abhorrent to me. I had hoped that I could have done whatever the law required of me in my private chapel. However, in fairness to Garth Moore, he was doing no more than telling me that I should follow precedent. As I had been a bishop for less than two years I assumed I had to accept his advice. Had I been more experienced I should have refused and dared the consequences. I used the service based upon one that my predecessor, Bishop Simpson, the kindest and most gentle of men, had used on a similar occasion. I was castigated in the press for acting as a mediaeval prelate and for kicking a man when he was down. The letters of abuse poured into Bishop's House. Even Tom Driberg interviewed me on behalf of the *New Statesman*.

The case cost the Church thousands of pounds in legal fees. What Bryn Thomas had to pay I do not know but he was signed on by a Sunday newspaper, the *People*, for a series of articles under the heading, "And now the vicar confesses. I foundered on the desires of the frustrated women of Balham." I understand he was well rewarded. Years later he returned to a hospital nearby with a terminal disease. I sent a priest to see him. He was refused admission on the grounds that the patient had registered himself as an atheist.

There are black sheep in every profession and the priesthood is no exception. Most years there were difficult cases, but never again did I allow one to go to the consistory court. Sometimes I succeeded in persuading a man to move to secular employment or to sign a legal deed of resignation from holy orders, but if he refused I thought it better to leave him to do his worst than to play into the hands of the media. I do not blame the press because it is accepted that it will stop at nothing to boost circulation. Whether or not the press destroys reputations and brings calumny upon the Church is not its concern. It publishes what is calculated to lead to financial gain.

Today more is done to deal sympathetically with the clergy when they find themselves in difficulties. Breakdowns and lapses are usually due to pressures of work, domestic unhappiness or feelings of failure. In particular the 'home scene' is different from what it was. A parson was accustomed to have his wife at his side. It was a shared ministry. Today she has a job, either because she has been trained and does not feel fulfilled unless she is employed, or because she must contribute to the family exchequer. Often she is paid better than her husband. She may leave home in the early morning and it is left to him to get breakfast for the family, and to take them to school and do the shopping. Whereas married couples in other professions can look forward to weekends, it is not so in their case. Saturday is a favourite for weddings and parochial activities, while Sunday is taken up with services. Tension leading to estrangement may follow. Both become lonely and may seek sympathy elsewhere, or, as is more likely, turn their backs upon their problems by becoming 'workaholics' and strangers to one another. I set up a pastoral unit which consisted of trained counsellors, aided by professional psychiatrists. In addition to dealing with individual cases they ran courses for the clergy to help them to understand the needs of themselves and their parishioners. I hoped the clergy knew that providing they were frank with me and would seek help they had nothing to fear. There were times when I had to take a strong line for the sake of the parish or the family; but these cases distressed me. I found it difficult not to make allowances, except in the case of the idle and incompetent.

It was this desire to deal gently with the clergy that led to a head-on collision with the chancellor of the diocesan consistory court, Garth Moore. At Great St Mary's he had been a good friend and I was looking forward to working with him in Southwark. Of course I had had no experience of him in his official capacity, and I knew little about his work, except that during my last weeks in Cambridge he told me that the Southwark diocese had become lax under Bishop Simpson's fatherly care and that he hoped I would insist on faculty jurisdiction being observed, a faculty being legally necessary for any alteration in a church. I held my peace because I thought I had few qualifications for not doing so. Both at St Matthew's and at Great St Mary's I had never bothered about faculties unless we were contemplating a major alteration in the fabric of the building. On one occasion as Bishop Woodward was walking up the aisle of St Matthew's, he said, "I always have to play Nelson here as I never know what illegalities you and your young curates have been up to!" Again at Great St Mary's a gifted wood carver gave us a beautiful mace to be carried in procession. It attracted attention in journals for its artistic merit. It never occurred to me to waste time and money on applying for a faculty. The Bishop of Ely, Noel Hudson, was due to preach on Psalm Sunday. A neighbouring parson, who concerned himself with faculties, wrote to Hudson suggesting that he should defer his visit until I had applied for a faculty. Hudson did not welcome impertinent suggestions that impinged upon his authority. He came.

In the circumstances it was unlikely that on my arrival in Southwark the poacher would turn gamekeeper. My desire was to help the clergy with their tasks and not to worry them about faculties unless they planned to do things that might be a cause of serious controversy. Moreover I had an instinctive suspicion of the legal departments of all religious faiths. I remember all too well the part they played in leading the opposition to Jesus and bringing him to the Cross. Their record in the Church of England left much to be desired. In the last century they had helped to send faithful priests to prison because they had used incense or worn vestments, or had introduced into their churches trivial matters of ceremonial, like adding a little water to the wine at the Holy Communion service.

For these reasons I was disturbed, on my arrival in Southwark, to learn of the hostility that some clergy felt for the chancellor.

In September 1963 matters became serious when a vicar in Camberwell found himself in trouble with the chancellor with regard to railings he had erected to protect his church from hooligans. I decided to write to Sir Henry Willink, the Master of Magdalene College, as he was a senior ecclesiastical lawyer and judge or dean of the appeal court, known as the Arches.

September 30, 1963

My dear Henry,

I do not think there is need to tell you of my regard for my Chancellor, Garth Moore. Not only were we good friends in my Cambridge days but I can never be too grateful for his support and loyalty during the dark days of the Bryn Thomas affair.

For these reasons and for others I much regret the deterioration in relationships between him and my diocese. Rightly or wrongly an increasing number of clergy and laity regard him as unnecessarily exacting or difficult. Instead of approaching the clergy with tolerance and sympathy and settling matters where possible outside court, he appears to some of them to favour the role of police officer.

I have a case in which a Camberwell incumbent applied for a

118

faculty for some outdoor railings to protect his church from hooligans. The application was approved by the Diocesan Advisory Committee and by the Archdeacon, and in good faith the incumbent commenced the work in order to save a certain amount of money before the faculty was actually granted and to protect his church. Garth is now insisting that the matter be heard in open court. The incumbent feels that he is being unreasonably treated in this respect, and I have asked Garth to deal with the matter without referring to a Consistory Court.

Garth, in his present mood, seems determined to go ahead. Meanwhile the incumbent has spent so much time and energy on the matter that he may decide to ignore further citations from the Chancellor. The consequences could be serious for the reputation and discipline of the Church, and, if the incumbent were to be prosecuted for non-appearance, the affair would become a *cause célèbre* and an occasion for ridicule in the national press.

I am fully aware that the law cannot be rightly disregarded, but it does seem to me that in Church courts it is necessary to strike a fair balance between the enforcement of the letter of the law and the understanding of the problems which incumbents face.

I have given you one example, but I could give others. You know South London. You know the difficulties that confront the Church. The clergy have frustrations and disappointments enough without being harried. What causes me disquiet is the pastoral aspect of legal administration.

I am anxious not to be involved in public dispute with Garth over his authority, but I have received sufficient complaints in recent months to suggest that I could find myself in a position of embarrassment. I wonder if it would be possible for you to bring your good offices in play. Perhaps you meet the Chancellor from time to time for general discussion. If so there might be an opportunity.

Yours ever,

Mervyn

The public dispute came quickly enough. St John's Peckham was destroyed in the war. The new building was dedicated by me soon after my arrival in the diocese. For whatever reason this new church proved to be an architectural disaster and the district surveyor was of the opinion that "there is a very dangerous risk in leaving this structure standing for even one day longer than is absolutely

119

necessary." The church was demolished as soon as possible for safety's sake and a confirmatory faculty was sought. I thought no more about it until January, 1964, when I was at Syracuse in Sicily awaiting an operation, I read in *The Times* that Garth Moore had criticised the diocese for its handling of the matter. And if the report is to be believed, the chancellor said, "In this present case, the court was far from satisfied that if any application to authorise the destruction of this church had been duly made it would have been granted. This had been the sort of church which ought to have been preserved."

Then followed a long correspondence and a series of interviews involving the Archbishop of Canterbury, Sir Henry Willink, lawyers, diocesan officials and many more. I had had enough. I found that Southwark was one of the few dioceses in which the diocesan bishop could sit in his own court, instead of the chancellor, if he was asked to do so. And that is how it remained for the next sixteen years. When petitions came to me, I settled them privately in my study unless I was compelled to hear them in open court. The few I did hear I enjoyed, and I took much care in writing judgments. I think my legal background may have been a help and I was fortunate in knowing lawyers who, appreciating the problems, allowed me to turn to them for advice.

I am sad that my friendship with Garth Moore came to an end. I am sure he acted from what he considered to be high motives, believing that every jot and tittle of the law should be scrupulously observed. I was as convinced that the Sabbath was made for man and not man for the Sabbath.

7

Wanderings

As a student I became interested in the Eastern Orthodox Church. I was impressed by its historicity, the splendour of its liturgy, and its distinctive qualities. It was unlike anything I had experienced in the West, either Catholic or Protestant. At my theological college when the Patriarch of Rumania came on an official visit it fell to me to look after him and his brother bishops. I remember cleaning his shoes, an incident which delighted my audience when I mentioned it forty years later on the occasion that I received an honorary degree in Bucharest.

As I was keen to experience the ceremonies of Holy Week with the Orthodox in Jerusalem, I set off in 1963, partly to recover from an operation. I broke my journey in Rome as Pope John had let me know through Monsignor Cardinale that he would receive me. I was deeply touched, especially as there were rumours that his days were numbered.

On the day before I went to the Vatican I read in the local press that a senior divine of the Church of Scotland had given His Holiness a stone from the Dead Sea. Whether the nature of the present was due to a canny sense of economy or whether it was to remind the Pope that the Presbyterians also claimed to be a rock-based Church, I do not know, but I thought it might create a happier impression if the Church of England adopted a more generous and appetising attitude. So I went to what I might call the local Harrods and ordered the largest Easter egg in the shop to be decorated in the papal colours.

I set off with my offering, forgetting that I ought to have obtained official permission as custom demands when dealing with Heads of State. I drove past the sentry posts and was received by officials who immediately wanted to know what was in the box. Monsignor Cardinale came to the rescue and the box was passed to a little man in velvet and lace, who carried it with difficulty as we walked through long corridors and magnificent reception rooms, with soldiers and chamberlains saluting me and the Swiss guards coming smartly to attention. In the ante-room to the Pope's study a young American chaplain with a merry twinkle asked me what was in the box; I replied, "The head of John the Baptist. Fetch me a charger." The egg was unpacked and preceded me on a silver plate as the Holy Father in his white cassock, skull cap and scarlet slippers came forward to welcome me.

We had an informal conversation. He asked me about my work, my diocese, of the condition of religion in England. I told him that in Southwark communicants on Easter Day numbered less than three per cent. I sighed sadly, but he understood our problems and with a laugh and a characteristic tapping of his feet on the ground added, "That is why God makes young men bishops; they have the courage to surmount disappointment. He wants you to find the solution." He was particularly interested in the Southwark Ordination Scheme and asked me to let him have full details. Another matter that concerned him was the syllabus in our schools: "What are you doing for your young students to help them relate Christian dogma to scientific thought?" he asked. The minutes hurried by and the ante-chambers were filling with people from all parts of the world for a public audience. I rose to go but the Pope kept me for a few minutes to ask me about my visit to Palestine, cheerfully reminding me that he had first gone to Palestine before I had been born, a fact I found difficult to accept because, although he was over eighty, he was amazingly young in mind and vigorous, rising early in the morning and working late at night. We walked towards the door and he pointed to the Easter egg and said with a chuckle, "It's still the Lenten fast. I must keep it till Easter Day." "Yes," I replied, "but one day the shell will be broken and new life will come from it, just as on the first Easter. Our Lord broke out of the tomb." And I think that both of us knew in our hearts that we longed for the day when all who acknowledged the Risen Christ would find themselves members of the same Church.

I knelt to receive his blessing and then he raised me to give me the Kiss of Peace.

Two days later I was in Nazareth. I asked a monk for a drink of water and he let down a bucket into a well. It was an ancient one and it must have been the same as Jesus used when, as a boy, he went to fetch water for the family. As I put the cup to my lips I felt nearer to the Bible story than when I visited the more famous shrines and elaborate churches with heavy, expensive and hideous decorations.

Nazareth reminded me of Shrewsbury, a strange mixture of new and old. The outskirts reflect the benefits of modern civilisation—petrol stations, radios, pneumatic drills, hurry and noise. The old consists of squat houses and narrow streets, along which no car can go, but only mules. And the shops are so huddled together that a customer on one side of the road can shake hands with a customer on the other. In fact, as I watched, a housewife at the fruiterer's turned round to chat with a neighbour at the butcher's opposite. A mule, laden with vegetables, banged them both in the back. It must have been much the same when Mary did her shopping.

Nazareth is among the mountains and as Jesus must have spent years of his life in the open countryside alone with his thoughts, I spent some time in the hills hoping that I was walking along some of the same paths.

My companion was an Israeli who had escaped from Berlin. His parents, brothers and sisters, uncles and aunts had been exterminated in Hitler's gas chambers. He had carved out a life for himself in a kibbutz, a settlement which is run on a voluntary communal basis. Apart from a tenement, the members have no possessions and what they earn goes into a common pool. Although a foreigner is well advised to refrain from involving himself in arguments on the political situation, the fact remains that in Israel there is a spirit of determination that is turning deserts into towns, swamp waste-lands into fertile valleys and stony hillsides into orange groves. But, as I said to my friend, I wish his people would show to the Arabs the consideration which they themselves had been denied. I went to several Arab refugee camps in the Jericho district, and I crossed the Jordan to meet King Hussein. I came to the conclusion, which I still hold, that the Israelis are arrogant in victory and lacking in compassion. If they continue along the same path one fears there may be a day of reckoning.

When I reached Jerusalem it was filling up with pilgrims from all parts of the world. The goal was the Church of the Holy Sepulchre, which is a conglomeration of chapels, caves and tunnels built over the traditional sites of Calvary where Jesus was crucified and the garden tomb where he was buried. Within a few hours of reaching the city I joined a procession that was assembling in Herod's Court, where Jesus was condemned to death. It was scheduled to march along the road where he had carried the cross and to finish in the Holy Sepulchre. But I had little hope of getting into the church. I was surrounded by hundreds of people of every language and costume. All had a similar aim. But it was my lucky day. A Franciscan friar had had a copy of an Italian paper in his hand in which there was an account of my visit to Pope John, and my photograph. He looked hard at me as I stood helplessly in my purple cassock in the crowd

123

and then ran towards me and greeted me like a long-lost brother. He told me to follow him. We hurried down the narrow streets, did zig-zags around the mules, souvenir stalls and bazaars, and dived through a small doorway into the Holy Sepulchre. It was dark as we groped our way along passages and flights of steps. I clutched the cord of his cassock. In a matter of moments I found myself unexpectedly kneeling at the marble slab in a small narrow cave where the body of Jesus is said to have lain after it was taken down from the cross. It was a moving experience as the slab in the tiny dark cavern is the foundation on which the Christian structure depends. If the body had remained to rot in the tomb, there would be neither Christianity nor Church today.

Because of the unique importance of that empty tomb, Christians of different brands have staked their claims in the Holy Sepulchre. It is as though Westminster Abbey belonged to the Church of England, the Roman Catholics and the Nonconformists, each having its own chapel but all holding their services at the same time. Worse still, the Eastern Churches have a different calendar from ours, so when I was invited by the Roman Catholic Patriarch to sit next to him at High Mass on Easter Day, others were celebrating Palm Sunday. The words of the liturgy were drowned by the wailing of the Egyptians and the chanting of the Greeks.

The ceremonies during Holy Week were so many and varied that it would require another book to describe them, but there were three that stand out in my memory.

On Maundy Thursday the Armenian Patriarch, in a packed church, washed the feet of twelve people in a moving ceremony. Afterwards I called on him. He was an astute politician who had been imposed upon his people by the King of Jordan, who had deposed his saintly predecessor at bayonet point.

On Easter eve the Ethiopians, who have a chapel on the roof of the Holy Sepulchre, search for the body of Jesus by the light of the moon. The Abbot, under an umbrella of green and gold, read the story of the burial and the empty tomb while his monks did a ritual dance to the accompaniment of tom-toms and drums.

Earlier in the day the Greek Orthodox had the dramatic ceremony of the Easter Fire. The Patriarch struck a light on the slab of the tomb to signify that Christ had risen from the dead, the more superstitious believing that the light had descended miraculously from heaven. The thousands of worshippers thrust their candles into the tomb or thereabouts and then snuffed them to take them back to their homes to be relighted on their deathbeds. There were a few young men who put the candles into glass containers and took them on their motor-bikes to the villages, with the result that within a few hours a light blazed from the front window of every Christian home in the country. It was an impressive ceremony, but the incendiary risks constituted a hazard. Thanks to the good offices of the British consul I was allowed a seat on the Jerusalem fire-engine, which had taken up its position within feet of the tomb.

Impressive as these services were, I treasured most my visit to the Sea of Galilee in the highlands of Palestine. It was the place, according to Scripture, to which Jesus returned after his resurrection to discuss future plans with his followers. I remember especially the little bay at the edge of the lake where I celebrated the Holy Communion under a palm tree. It was the place where the disciples had breakfasted with the risen Lord after they had spent the night fruitlessly fishing.

A fascinating experience was my expedition to the summit of Mount Gerizim to witness the Samaritan Passover sacrifice to which the High Priest had invited me. The Samaritans have lived in Palestine for more than two thousand and five hundred years, and are one of the oldest racial sects in the world. They hate the Jews and instead of worshipping with them in the temple at Jerusalem they have their own altar of sacrifice on Mount Gerizim. When, in the first century, the Jewish temple was destroyed by the Romans and the Jewish sacrifices came to an end, the Samaritans continued alone. Every year the ancient ceremonies of the Passover, which commemorate the escape of the Israelites from slavery in Egypt, are carried out in full.

The Samaritans have dwindled to about four hundred and are scattered over the country, but all of them make their way to the top of the mountain where tents for each family are set around a rough altar of unhewn stone. The High Priest entertained me in his tent. The office, or rather the business, goes from father to son. Business it was. Having been warned of my arrival he had put together a collection of sham Dead Sea Scrolls which he was prepared to sell me at a cut price, a few hundred pounds. Next he asked me if I would ask the Queen of England to send him a donation to repair his synagogue. When he found I was not as forthcoming as he hoped, he turned his attentions to an American businessman, informing him that he had had a vision of him on the previous evening handing over a million dollar bill to pave his synagogue in gold. These transactions finished, the High Priest moved to the altar and read the story of the Passover. At the appropriate moment the lambs were slaughtered and the blood smeared on the tent doors. Then came the actual sacrifice. It was like the climax of a cup final. There was not a suggestion of reverence. It was din, laughter and mob yelling. Special bits of the lamb were put on the altar, the fire was kindled and all was burned as an offering to Jehovah. But the carcasses were put on a spit and, after they had been roasted, the meat was distributed and eaten with unleavened bread and bitter herbs; the High Priest having first had a massive helping, which he ate like a melon, grasping it in his hands with the grease dropping down his robes. And so the grim events of the first Passover were recalled. How different from the crude happenings on Mount Gerizim was the message of Jesus. He said that God wanted not the sacrifices of animals but the voluntary offering of men's life in union with his own sacrifice. An attitude that is incarnated each day in thousands of places in the sacrifice of the Mass.

Graft is not restricted to the Samaritans. The well at Samaria where Jesus asked a woman to give him a drink is hired out each year to the Greek priest who makes the highest bid. He charges the pilgrims what he can. I was keen to celebrate the Holy Communion in the garden in which the well is set, but I knew the priest would refuse. So I and my friends sat at a table and produced a picnic lunch. Included in the basket were the bread and the wine that were necessary for the Sacrament. We spread the packets of sandwiches and the thermos flasks and had our service.

Cana of Galilee is a squalid little village. Perhaps it was more attractive when Jesus went there to grace a wedding feast with his presence and change water into wine. The priest who, by his appearance would seem to have been a stranger to water, insisted that the wine was descended from the original vintage. He gave me a sample in the hope I would place an order—I took a sip and handing the glass back remarked, "Much better if it had remained water!"

I often returned to the Holy Land. Once in four years I led a diocesan pilgrimage, feeling that a visit to the famous biblical sites could be an immense help to the clergy, especially with their preaching. I had some unusual and alarming experiences, such as, for instance, when I was in Damascus. There several of our party had to give up their hotel bedrooms because members of the Government wanted to witness a public execution from them. On my last visit, shortly before I left Southwark, a bomb exploded in the courtyard of a hotel where I had been visiting a friend. I had been in the courtyard less than two minutes previously.

Another memory I cherish is the Muslim dinner given to leaders of our party by Muslim friends in Jericho, a fantastic town, hundreds of feet below sea level and always warm even in mid-winter. As is customary, our Arab hosts stood throughout the meal and lavished goodies upon us. The main dish was a roasted sheep and, as the chief guest, I was presented with the eyes of the poor creature. Fortunately, Joe Fison, who had succeeded me at Great St Mary's and had recently become the Bishop of Salisbury, was present. We had travelled by ship on what was billed as "A Voyage of a Lifetime", which indeed it proved to be. We stopped at the usual places in the Mediterranean, beginning at Rome, where we were received by Pope Paul VI. At all the receptions I had had red-carpet treatment, not because I was senior in age, but on account of my ceremonial status as leader. This provided me with my cue. I told my host that the Christian religion attached importance to the virtue of humility and that too many privileges had been showered upon me during the voyage. If it persisted I should be guilty of the sin of pride. But poor Bishop Fison had had nothing. He had always been in the back seat. For this reason I must forego this signal honour and allow the Bishop of Salisbury to receive the distinctive platter. Those who knew Joe Fison can imagine the piercing yell that filled the room seconds later. He subsequently disposed of the sheep's eye in an aspidistra.

Stanley Evans, the ex-communist Principal of the Southwark Ordination Course, was on the voyage. He was not best pleased when it was suggested in the brochure that the ladies should wear long dresses and the men black ties at dinner on board ship. He subsequently published an account of our pilgrimage in a book entitled, *To Calvary in Evening Dress*.

The voyage included a visit to Mount Athos, a semi-independent monastic state but under the surveillance of Greece. The ancient monasteries and the scenario have a beauty to which words cannot do justice. It is famous for its sexual discrimination—nothing female, human or animal, is allowed to set foot on its soil. When we put into the small harbour, the captain told the women pilgrims they had to remain aboard.

Within minutes there was a second batch of pilgrims led by Robert Stopford, the Bishop of London. The captain of this ship gave similar instructions. However he met his match in Kathleen Stopford, a somewhat unusual bishop's wife who spoke her mind with no inhibitions. "What?" said Kathleen, "I've never heard such nonsense. Of course I'm going ashore with Robert. He's the Bishop of London."

"I'm afraid it makes no difference."

"Do you mean to tell me that while the men have fun on the island we women are to remain cooped up on this ship?"

"Yes."

"Indeed we shall not. If the men are going by themselves to Athos, you, captain, can take the women to Lesbos."

My first pilgrimage which had started with my audience with Pope John, ended with a meeting with Athenagoras, the Patriarch of Constantinople and presiding bishop of the Eastern Orthodox Church. Whoever holds this position is not to be envied. The Patriarch is viewed with suspicion by the Turkish authorities and by the Muslim population. Christians are few and far between, as their forebears changed allegiance to Mohammed centuries ago and their cathedrals became mosques. The situation is as difficult ecclesiastically. The Russian Orthodox Church, for political reasons, has to maintain its distance, while the Greeks tend to be quarrelsome. The Patriarch needs diplomatic skill, saintliness and patience. All three qualities were to be found in Athenagoras, a man who was in his middle seventies, well over six feet tall, with a flowing white beard and piercing eyes.

It was Easter Monday. The Patriarch had observed the Lenten fast with an asceticism unknown to us in the West, and today he and his colleagues were to eat meat and to be indulged for the first time for several weeks.

The residence of the Patriarch is the Phanar, a modest building, unlike the Vatican or Lambeth Palace, in the poor quarter of Istanbul. It had been damaged by fire some years previously and not repaired. On arrival I talked with bishops and priests who had come from afar for the Easter feast. To my surprise they came to the house in collar and ties, and then went to a changing room to put on their robes. The reason for this is the rule of the Turkish Government which forbids clerical dress in the streets. The Patriarch was still in his mini-cathedral distributing coloured, hard-boiled eggs to the faithful. On his return to his reception room his bishops gathered around him in a circle and I was valiantly kissed by each of them on both cheeks. I had no idea how long I was intended to stay. I thought it would be a short audience. Instead he asked me to stay to the feast and to a private audience afterwards. It was an excellent meal. I made a note of the menu: soup, rice sprinkled with yoghourt, Easter lamb and roast potatoes, almond-paste tarts, eggs, fruit and cheese, all washed down with admirable wine. But I noticed that Athenagoras, though frequently telling the waiter to replenish my plate and glass, ate sparingly. He added water to his wine.

The Patriarch moved from one language to another and when I asked him how he learnt to speak such fluent English, he told me that after being Bishop of Corfu he had moved to America.

After luncheon he took me to his study and we discussed relationships between the Orthodox Church and the Church of England. He asked me about my recent visit to Rome, my talk with the Pope and my views on the approaching Vatican Council. He was especially glad to receive the message that Pope John had asked me to convey to him. He was keen that when I broke my journey in Greece I should call on the Primate in Athens. This I did. I felt I was back in the Middle Ages and was not impressed. The Greek Church needed a massive reformation, and still does.

Upon my leaving the Phanar, the police, dressed in civilian clothes, cross-examined me about my talk with the Patriarch. I was non-communicative as I had been warned that our conversation would be bugged and was therefore already known to them. On the following morning an emissary from the Patriarch arrived at the airport with bottles of wine and, which I found moving, boxes of Turkish Delight for my aged mother.

The Orthodox Church with which I was to have the closest ties was the Rumanian. I have visited the country for many years since the early 70s and I hope to preserve my contacts. Although there are many things about Rumania's communist régime that are abhorrent to me, I love the country, its people and above all its Church. As in Poland, the Church is in a strong position. It is said to be as well supported as is the Roman Catholic Church in Ireland. During the Stalinist occupation it was viciously persecuted and a veil is now drawn over the murders and imprisonments. Fortunately the nominal President was a Christian. When he was on the run from the fascists he was given refuge in the roof of a country priest's house in the mountains. This priest became the Patriarch Justinian. For some years the West wrote him off as a political stooge. This was nonsense. Although he had strong Left Wing views, sufficiently strong to have made impossible his preferment in the Church of England had he been an Englishman, he was first and foremost a Churchman. He immediately began a programme of renewal. He insisted that the clergy, many of whom were uneducated and idle, should be retrained. He transformed the theological colleges. He set up a department for foreign relationships, with the result that leaders of Churches and of all faiths, including Jews, Muslims and Buddhists, poured into Bucharest.

Justinian and President Ceausescu respected one another. The

President, who has a reputation for independence in foreign affairs, is a hard-liner on domestic issues. Being a realist he decided to reach an accommodation with the Church because, atheist though he is—even to the extent of foolishly refusing to be present at the saying of grace when he visited London—he accepts the fact, it is said, that "Christianity will be hanging around for a long time." He did what most Governments have done since the inception of Christianity, he rendered harmless the critics and promoted the obsequious. The bishops live in a style which has been unknown in England for decades. The clergy are well paid with many privileges, and church buildings are excellently maintained. The critics are in prison, or in small country parishes. Justinian, like Agag, walked delicately, but I think it likely that by accepting defeat on some issues he was the victor. In any case, I am reluctant to criticise, it is difficult for us who have comparative freedom to appreciate the circumstances of those who live under a dictatorship.

What has always heartened me have been the vast congregations that have packed the churches. In particular I remember an Easter service in Sibiu Cathedral which lasted several hours, beginning before dawn. It was said that there were fifteen thousand people in and around the building.

While the primary purpose of my visits to Rumania was to learn more of the Orthodox Church, to become impregnated with its spirituality and to further ecumenical relationships, I occasionally had difficult missions to fulfil. Attempts were sometimes made to use the Rumanian Church in London for political purposes. This led to serious difficulties. I was cast in the role of troubleshooter and had to travel between London and Bucharest to seek solutions. Although there was plain speaking between myself and the Rumanian authorities, both religious and secular, relationships remained unimpaired. On one occasion when the situation had become tense, those taking part in the dispute adjourned for a luncheon in my honour. The Government representative, the Minister of Myths, as I called him, said how surprised he had been by the warm reception I had received from the workers on a building site. In fact it was not surprising because the Rumanian bishops remain aloof and do not mix freely as do English bishops. In reply to his toast I said, "Of course you are surprised, just as they were surprised. Why? Because for the first time in their lives they had set eyes on a genuine socialist." Fortunately it brought the house down and further toasts were drunk.

Although I had easy relationships with the people who were

allowed to meet me, it was impossible to visit private homes. Even the most innocent associations could be suspect. I was present in Sibiu Cathedral at the ordination of a young priest; to safeguard him I call him Peter. He was overwhelmed that an Anglican bishop had taken part in the service as he had had no dealings with Westerners. He gave me a small icon on the back of which he wrote: "This icon is an expression of my deep respect and gratitude." A year later he heard I was staying with the Archbishop, so he waited outside the house to give me a parcel. It contained a photograph of the baptism of his child together with a coloured Easter egg. At once he was ordered to go away. I insisted that I should talk with him, explaining I was the guest of the Patriarch and that I already knew the young priest. We did have a brief conversation, but he never wrote to me again, and when on my next visit I asked after him, I was told that he had left his job and that his whereabouts were unknown.

On most visits I was accompanied by two guides, Jivi and Dorian, who worked for the Patriarchate. They were excellent. To repay their many kindnesses I asked that they should be my guests in London. They were intelligent, spoke English and had read theology. I was assured that everything would be in order, but it required from me a catalogue of letters, visits to the Rumanian Embassy in London, and the intervention of the Archbishop of Canterbury before they arrived. The interesting point is that Jivi had frequently been to the West for ecumenical conferences and for post-graduate studies. On these occasions he was a member of a delegation and presumably under supervision, whereas in England he was staying in private houses. I can understand the reluctance of the Rumanian Government, which is trying to drag the country into the twentieth century, to allow its brightest citizens to seek more prosperous jobs in the West, just as I think we are foolish to allow our citizens, upon whose education the taxpayer has lavished thousands of pounds, to pursue wealth in America without returning the taxpayers' money. But there can be arrangements between Governments to prevent these abuses while allowing friendly visits to continue. Moreover if the communist society is as attractive as it is claimed by its dictators, Rumania should have sufficient confidence in the loyalty of its citizens.

A country that has always fascinated me is Ethiopia. This interest became a matter of concern after our betrayal of Haile Selassie by the toasting in Rome of the King of Italy as Emperor of Ethiopia by Lord Halifax. Chamberlain and Halifax paid their thirty pieces of silver by allowing Haile Selassie to come to England. He arrived at Victoria but, for fear of annoying Mussolini, Halifax arranged for him to be taken through the back streets in order not to be applauded by the sympathetic crowds. He was despatched to Bath. As a young priest I wrote to the chaplain and asked if I could meet him to learn more of the Abyssinian Church, its history, customs and liturgy.

Christianity was brought to Ethiopia in the fourth century but it developed on independent lines, cut off from the rest of Christendom. For instance, the Abyssinians observe many Jewish customs, especially the observance of the Sabbath, the distinction between clean and unclean meats and circumcision. Pontius Pilate is recognised as a saint on the supposition that had he not sentenced Jesus to death Christ would never have become the Saviour of the world. The clergy, whose numbers are incalculable, are illiterate, apart from a few. They are a mixture of priest and witch-doctor.

It was to be more than thirty years before my wish was fulfilled. I was asked to lead pilgrimages to Ethiopia on two occasions during my Christmas holidays. It is difficult to describe the sheer beauty and romance of the country. While I deplore the viciousness of the Marxist régime that has enslaved the country, a revolution was inevitable. Haile Selassie, with whom I had long talks on two occasions, was a benevolent autocrat who, in his old age, had lost his grip and surrendered his powers to the nobility. They lived in luxury at the expense of the poverty-stricken peasants and they were corrupt. During one of my visits I was followed by the secret police and, being stopped for questioning, disposed of them with a present.

The great festival in early January is the Epiphany, but their customs are unknown elsewhere. In each Ethiopian church the chief object of veneration is the ark which contains the Book of the Law, the Ten Commandments. On the eve of the festival the people of the parishes combine to carry their arks in procession to the nearest lake or river. The bearers of the ark are covered in gorgeous silks and crouch down in order that their faces shall not be seen. When they reach their destination by the water, the ark is put in a tabernacle or tent, and only priests are allowed to enter. I am told it was due to the Patriarch, or Abuna as he is called, that I had the exceptional privilege of being admitted to the tent. I did not remain for the vigil, but on the following morning I stood for hours in the great heat, wearing cope and mitre, while the priests blessed the waters in memory of Christ's baptism, and those who wished jumped into the water. A group of mischievous boys seized the opportunity to dive into the lake and smilingly splashed my cope. When the procession eventually set out on its return, numbering thousands, I whispered to my chaplain that I had had enough, and since we were about to pass the hotel it was about time to quit for luncheon. He discreetly informed the police who, as indiscreetly, brandished their canes and beat the faithful to make a gangway to hasten my retreat.

The following year I went to a similar ceremony in Gondar, the ancient capital of Abyssinia. I called at the Bishop's house to pay my respects. I was told that he was still at Jerusalem, in a convalescent home, as he had been on my previous visit, and was unlikely to return. I was not surprised, because it was alleged that his predecessor had been poisoned by the evil-eyed Abbot who had put a potion of 'no-return' on the bread of the Sacrament. I called on the Abbot, whose hut was stacked with empty whisky bottles. He asked me to talk to his theological students, who sat on their haunches in a mud cabin and began to kiss my feet until I insisted they turned their attentions to more savoury tasks. When I asked for questions a boy asked me whether it was true that a man had reached the moon. Before I had time to answer the evil-eyed Abbot interrupted with the remark that it was only the Marxist anti-god propaganda press that had made such a claim.

I returned to my hotel, glad to be beyond the reach of the evil eye and thankful that, as an Anglican, I was not permitted to receive the Sacrament at his hands. However at midday the Abbot phoned to say that he wished to kill a sheep in my honour and asked me to dine with him. I thanked him but explained I had to return to Addis to have luncheon with the British Ambassador.

I had several talks with the Patriarch. He was a wily man, in the pocket of the Government, as most Archbishops of all denominations in every Government have been and are. He admitted the illiteracy of his clergy, but was fearful that education might lead to unrest, as it certainly would. He was content that the Church should prop up the Emperor's régime. Poor man, he paid the price. Haile Selassie was imprisoned and is said to have been smothered. The Patriarch disappeared and one can only guess his ghastly fate at the hands of his Marxist torturers.

In 1978 I went on a parliamentary delegation to the USSR. I was glad to be included as I had been on the black list of the Russian Embassy in London for some years. I had made a point of inviting ambassadors to dinner at Bishop's House since my early days. These parties occurred twice a year and were not limited to the Western powers, although I had the pleasure of entertaining several of their representatives. The others came too—the Soviet Union, Czechoslovakia, Poland, East Germany, Rumania, Cuba and the

Chinese. I was particularly attracted to the Czech Ambassador, Dr Ruzek. The ambassadors reciprocated my hospitality, but Dr Ruzek would ask me to lunch alone with him at his private house on Saturdays, and we would discuss philosophical and religious questions, perhaps for four or five hours. Ironically our last discussion was on the amount of freedom that it would be right to allow citizens to have in a country that was committed to a socialist revolution. Ruzek was worried. He was too discreet to show his hand but I think he leaned towards Dubček's socialism with a human face. At the same time he was concerned with the group selfishness which always betrays socialist dreams. He thought that while liberty was the goal, it had to go hand in hand with responsibility. If it did not, then a Government would have to acquire absolute authority until such time as the people had become sufficiently adult to behave responsibly and to work for the common good. We were agreed on the principle, but we differed as to where the line should be drawn. The question was answered for Czechoslovakia when the Russians invaded it a few weeks later and reduced it to a vassal state. I made a scathing attack on the Soviet Union in a speech in the House of Lords which was widely reported. Invitations to the Russian Embassy were immediately terminated and it was a long time before I was to enjoy its caviar and vodka. However the opportunity came when, in 1977, I was chosen to be a member of the delegation. The Ambassador was a little embarrassed but not nearly as much as his colleagues in the Kremlin, who found it difficult to understand how a man wearing clerical clothes and a pectoral cross could be in a parliamentary delegation. Communists in the East, like capitalists in the West, are always embarrassed by a crucifix.

On the first evening we went to the Kremlin to discuss our tour and to suggest places to which we should like to go. Each gave his list. Cledwyn Hughes and Richard Luce joined me in the wish to visit a church. Our host thought it might be difficult. I added that as I had a letter from Donald Coggan, the Archbishop of Canterbury, for the Patriarch, I expected to call on him. I was immediately told he was out of Moscow. "How curious," I said. "It was the same when I made a similar request twenty-four years ago to deliver a letter from the Archbishop of Canterbury, Geoffrey Fisher, to the previous Patriarch, Alexis. Perhaps you will bear in mind the unfavourable impression that will be created if I do not see him." An hour later while we were touring the magnificent chamber for the Soviet delegates, our host told me that the Patriarch had just returned unexpectedly to Moscow: "How curious," I said. "Just as his predecessor did twenty-four years ago." But that was not the end of the affair. The meeting was fixed for our last day in Russia at 3 p.m. on April 25th. On the evening of April 24th we were told that the President of the Soviet Union had invited us to an official luncheon on the following day. I knew that as this would be an occasion for a lengthy menu with toasts galore and speeches, the chances of finishing in time to keep my appointment with the Patriarch were remote. So I asked our host if he would ask the President to excuse me at 2.30 p.m. He was far from pleased. But as I was determined to go, I said, "I am sorry if I appear to be discourteous, but I am in your country in a double capacity, first as a bishop and second as a parliamentarian. My duties as a bishop take precedence." And that was that. "I shall expect a car to be awaiting me."

It was indeed a splendid luncheon. There were eight courses. I am afraid it makes our State dinners in Britain seem a little dreary and 'Third Worldish'. Here it is:

> Caviar
> Salmon
> Assorted game and vegetables
> Bortchok
> Sturgeon baked with shrimps
> Filet mignon
> Ice Cream
> Fruits
> Tea, Coffee

I left about halfway through, so I was unable to toast the workers' paradise, the socialist way of living, and the equals who are more equal than the other equals. When I reached the taxi the driver said he did not know the way to the Patriarchate. I said, "Then you had better ask." I think his ignorance was genuine. Eventually, after several stops, we reached a house which I believe had been the German Embassy at the time Stalin had made his pact with Hitler. Outside was a sentry box and my papers were examined. Patriarch Pimen struck me as a simple and godly man who was appointed with the consent of the Government on account of his political reliability. But perhaps he was sufficiently acquainted with English history to have become aware of the fate of Primates such as Becket, Cranmer and Laud who had stepped out of line, and perhaps he thought it wise to emulate those divines who had never embarrassed the State, but had been content to provide spiritual sanction for the status quo. Caiaphas has his equals.

Our introduction was amusing. We had to pretend we had never met before. We had. I had come to Ethiopia for a religious festival, and so had Pimen. The airport officials made a mistake, thinking I was the Russian Patriarch. Pimen was the next to arrive, supposedly the Bishop of Southwark. We were not allowed to meet. Next day I read in the press an address given by Pimen that was clearly written by the Soviet Foreign Office with a few religious platitudes to top and tail it. It is not always realised that while the Patriarch of Moscow is ignored in his own country, and so far as the media is concerned does not exist, he is used by the Government to travel abroad in considerable style to plug the party line.

The conversation I had with Pimen and his colleagues was virtually a repeat performance of the one I had had with Patriarch Alexis twenty-four years before. The same soundtrack. The State was based on atheistic principles, and the Church was sorry about that. However the Orthodox Church was free to go its own way. Only Christians who indulged in anti-Soviet politics were punished. It was not the Orthodox practice to keep statistics, so they could not give me details of the numbers of baptisms, priests, churches.

There was, however, a notable difference between Alexis and Pimen with regard to the openness of their opposition to Marxism as a philosophy. Here is the record of my conversation with Alexis.

"Your Holiness, what are your views on Marxism?"

The wily old man fixed me with his eye and said, "Marxism—I really don't know anything about it." And then, giving an infectious chuckle, with a devastating wave of the hand, he exclaimed, "It's all about politics, history and capital."

"But do you feel it is compatible with Christianity?" I asked.

And here the Patriarch revealed himself in his true colours. He remained a statesman without compromising himself as a Christian. "The Church is not concerned with politics, and in so far as Marxism is a political matter, we pass no judgment. But when it comes to a materialistic analysis of man, there is, of course, a conflict between the two systems."

"And what is the Church doing to combat materialism?" I enquired. "Your children are brought up in atheistic schools and Christianity is ridiculed. They know nothing about God."

"It is difficult, but the Orthodox Church has never been an evangelistic Church or a militant propagandist. We emphasise the importance of the liturgy, and we leave it to God to do the rest. But you must not think we are losing. We are always having enquiries. Professional men, engineers and scientists are abandoning their careers to enter our theological academies. A distinguished doctor, a Stalin prize-winner, joined the other day. I admit the dangers of materialism. People are so occupied with improving their living standards that they have little time for God. But that is not a weakness peculiar to the Soviet Union. Materialism seems to be as firmly entrenched in Britain and the United States."

"That is true. The main difference between us is that we like to ignore the fact and pretend we are a Christian country."

Pimen was not so forthcoming, but he is not such a strong character as Alexis. Moreover, since the intensification of religious persecution and the imprisonment of dissidents the Patriarch's primary concern seems to have been to keep the Church in existence to sing the liturgy and to provide the sacraments. And if the Church is primarily a cultus system and an end in itself, there can be no argument. That, of course, is what Caiaphas sincerely felt about the Jewish Church and that is why Jesus, who took the opposite view, was crucified. But who are we in the West to criticise? For most Christians our profession costs us next to nothing. The Russians pay with their lives.

A fascinating incident in a hair-dressing salon in the hotel where the delegation was staying inclines me to think that both Alexis and Pimen are right in thinking that nothing will eradicate a basic Orthodox faith, even if it is little more than the remnants of a folk religion. I had taken an electric razor with me on the parliamentary delegation. It ceased to function and as it was of American origin it was not surprising that I could not find the necessary spare part to repair it. I had no alternative but to go to the large salon in this rather grand hotel to be shaved. There were two dressers, one of either sex. The man already had a client. Here was a dilemma. I am enthusiastic for sex equality, even when it comes to the ordination of women; but to be helpless in a chair with a woman wielding a cut-throat razor is another matter. However I had no alternative and I know now what real commitment means. As the soap-coupled beard mounted on the blade, the woman looked intently at me, especially at my pectoral cross and episcopal ring. She consulted her partner at the neighbouring chair, and hurrying back, asked me, through an interpreter, whether I was a bishop. It was the Easter season and the Orthodox Church, perhaps more than the others, celebrates the Resurrection with intensity. Taking my cross in her hand she kissed it, next my ring, and then raising the razor blade aloft, with the soap

137

and my beard still on it, called out, "Christ is Risen," whereupon the other customers joyfully responded, "He is risen indeed." I thought, "Poor old Brezhnev, sixty years of atheism and still the Galilean conquers!"

Although we do not associate persecution with the Churches in the Western democracies, problems do occasionally arise which bring Churchmen into conflict with the State.

I was in New York to lecture to the clergy at the height of the Civil Rights Campaign. We started with a dinner at the Astoria Hotel, where I found myself sitting next to Paul Moore, then an assistant bishop of New York, but now the diocesan. As I had not met him before, I broke the ice by asking him how he had spent Easter Day. "In prison," he replied. "So did I," I said, because I usually celebrated Holy Communion at Christmas and Easter at Brixham or Wandsworth gaols. "I don't mean that," said Paul Moore. "I was inside with the others for campaigning for civil rights." He told me that people of all denominations were with him and they celebrated Easter Communion with prison bread and cocoa in an enamel mug. He was interested to learn from me that, although I had not suffered, I had recently visited Bertrand Russell and one of my former servers of St Matthew's, Bristol, who were in prison for sitting down in Trafalgar Square at a demonstration organised by the Campaign for Nuclear Disarmament.

My visits across the Atlantic were not frequent, there being a regular queue of bishops and clergy on the dollar track. Our hosts treated us generously, meeting our travelling expenses and paying us business rates for our addresses. I thought it wiser to develop my interests in the Orthodox Churches in the Communist bloc, to which few had admission. But I enjoyed my times in Canada and the States, especially in Dallas. On one occasion I was there during the election of a suffragan bishop. There were three candidates. It resembled a presidential campaign. Each had his electioneering organisation and the meetings were rowdy affairs with streamers, music, banners and the usual paraphernalia. There seemed little evidence of the operation of the Holy Spirit. At least that was the view of the diocesan bishop who was appalled by the result. However, I am not sure that our present procedure in the Church of England, though less outwardly vulgar, is better—unless one believes that the Holy Spirit works through lobbying, wire-pulling and political manipulation.

My final trip abroad was in May 1979 as the guest of the Lutheran Church in both Germanies. I started in East Berlin. I was impressed by the quality of Christian witness among the laity and by the youthfulness of their synods. It was a refreshing change. The clergy had encountered many difficulties and rebuffs until the Government established a *modus vivendi* with the Church a few years ago. But it must be difficult for the people to keep up their courage under a grim and oppressive régime, made worse by the fact that they see another way of living beyond the prison wall that encircles them. And yet I felt there was more spiritual drive in the East. The Church in the West is too wealthy and comfortable.

A difference between the two régimes is illustrated by the remarks made by the wives of the two Bishops of Berlin. In the West we were asked what we would like to eat; in the East we were told that it was not known what might be on sale in the shops next day. The one provides choice, the other only necessities.

By good fortune the Archbishop of Canterbury, Dr Donald Coggan, joined me in East Berlin for two days as he was on a European tour. It was the festival of the Ascension. He celebrated Communion and I preached. As we were walking up the aisle Donald said, "Let's take off our robes here and we'll go straight into breakfast." I told him it was impossible as the zip fastener of my trousers had disintegrated during the service. To which Donald said, "Come to our room. Jean is very good with zips."

8

Honest to God

The largest file I possess concerns John Robinson. It is filled with letters of protest, denunciations for heresy, and pleas for a trial and for his immediate dismissal from the bishopric of Woolwich. Not having looked at the file for several years I find it astonishing that his book could have caused such a reaction, bordering on hysteria. Although Dr Robinson has not changed his basic beliefs he is now regarded as a conservative New Testament scholar and his book *Honest To God* as a contribution to the interesting and necessary theological debate that was engaging the Church in the early 60s.

Robinson joined my staff in Bristol in 1945. He had had a distinguished academic career and I at first wondered how he would cope with my down-to-earth parishioners. I quickly realised I had no need to worry. He was excellent. Like all curates he was asked to submit his sermons to me, and occasionally I suggested that he should use the language of the *Daily Mirror* or indeed of the *News of the World* rather than that of *The Times* or the *Observer*. He kept us on our theological toes. He provoked intelligent argument. He was a dedicated pastor. In short, he was the curate for whom a vicar prays although rarely gets.

He and his wife, Ruth, were much loved in the parish. The three years of their shared ministry passed all too quickly. We went our different ways until we renewed our relationship at Cambridge in 1955. I as Vicar of the University Church and John as Dean of Clare College. When I was appointed to Southwark, the Bishop of Woolwich informed me that he had already told my precedessor of his intention to resign. It was my responsibility to replace him. The custom is for the diocesan bishop to submit two names to the Prime Minister to pass to Buckingham Palace for approval, on the tacit understanding that the first name will be selected. It was not until Margaret Thatcher, a Nonconformist, with little or no knowledge of the Anglican Church, went to Downing Street that a Prime Minister exercised her prerogative to reverse the order when it came to the appointment to the diocesan bishopric of London. It will be interesting to know whether a socialist successor, perhaps an atheist, rather than a Nonconformist, will do the same.

As a matter of courtesy I informed Archbishop Fisher of my intention to appoint John Robinson. In my letter to him I said,

> I want as Bishop of Woolwich a man (i) who understands what I am trying to do (ii) who has the intellectual competence and theological knowledge to advise me (iii) who is accustomed to the teaching of ordinands (iv) who, in addition to his special concerns and experimental work, will diligently carry out the normal pastoral and routine duties of a suffragan bishop. At Southwark there is a strong team at the centre. I have already established happy relationships with most of them and I know they will be a great help to me. But they are essentially conventional Churchmen. I use the word 'conventional' in no unkindly sense, but to describe an attitude. But in addition to the six men I want a seventh who, while realising the importance of the conventional approach in large areas of the diocese, will appreciate the need for a new approach in places like Rotherhithe and Bermondsey. I must have somebody to whom I can talk, with whom I can discuss and argue, and on whom I can rely. It would be unfortunate if I felt I had to keep this part of my episcopate to myself. Moreover being made as I am, I can always work best when I can put my mind against another man's mind.

Geoffrey Fisher was not convinced. He saw John Robinson and subsequently wrote to me on March 19th, 1959:

> (i) I think for a time longer he ought to put his undoubted abilities to the theological life of Cambridge. (ii) I am not satisfied that there is any final reason why you and the diocese should have his services at this moment. (iii) There is John Robinson himself. He is only thirty-nine. Is it right to bring him at this stage of his experience and activity into the machine of ecclesiastical and episcopal authority? I told him all that, and I added that having said it I should be perfectly content, and that he and you should judge as best you can. Having given him my own advice I have done all that is proper for me to do.

Although the Archbishop insisted throughout our correspondence, which covered several weeks, that the decision to nominate was mine and not his, I felt that both John Robinson and I should

141

carefully consider his hesitations. So on March 20th 1959 I wrote to John.

> As I see it, you must decide whether you want to continue teaching theology at Cambridge to people who may or may not be able to implement it in their parishes; or whether you feel called to devote your abilities and energies to that section of English life in which theology means next to nothing. If you think you are called by God to devote yourself to this other pattern, I shall be pleased to submit your name for nomination. While you are trying to make up your mind I am sure you will carefully consider the points that have been put to you by the Archbishop. I am particularly anxious that he shall not think that I have been bringing unfair pressure upon you. If you think you should stay in Cambridge I shall accept your decision without question—and with respect.

John Robinson's answer came a few days later.

> After a good deal of thought I have decided to accept your very kind and indeed overwhelming proposal that you should submit my name for the bishopric of Woolwich. It has been one of the most difficult decisions of my life. I suppose the thing that finally weighed down the scales on this side was the recognition that however important it might be to keep the theological bridge-head open at the Cambridge end, at the other end it virtually did not exist at all. There must be something into which ideas and people from this end can engage if any traffic is to take place.

The Archbishop was about to leave for Japan on March 25th and he asked me to phone him at noon. I told him of the outcome. I added. "I hope you won't be disappointed, Your Grace." Typically Fisher said, "The decision is yours not mine. You have made it. I shall support you." What I liked about Fisher, in spite of the occasional rows, was his scrupulous fair-mindedness. I always knew where I was with him. He was incapable of deviousness, still less of politicking.

Just as the storm clouds had gathered over me on Chanctonbury Ring, so clouds of another sort gathered over John Robinson on the eve of his consecration in Canterbury Cathedral. His wife was taken seriously ill and there was cause for grave anxiety. Fortunately the crisis was surmounted, but on the actual day there was uncertainty. I suspect that those of us who were there will never forget the sight of the Archbishop's wife, Rosamund, leading John's young family up the great aisle of the Cathedral to her pew.

With Ruth in hospital, the Fishers had John and his children to stay at the Old Palace. Again, how typical.

The explosion came in 1963. Dr Robinson had attracted little attention in the national press during his early years. Then he was busily engaged in getting to know his parishes, holding study groups for his clergy and helping to launch the Southwark Ordination Course. Occasionally he wrote articles which, like his books, were applauded for their lucidity and theological insight. One day he talked to me about *Honest To God* and asked if I would like to read the script and comment on it. I told him that while there was no obligation on his part to submit his work to me I should be interested. I was; I think I made a few suggestions. It never occurred to me that there would be trouble. The views expressed in his book were more or less my own. I felt sure it would help the sort of enquirer who had come to Great St Mary's and the students I was meeting in London. Although Dr Robinson had an open mind on some traditional interpretations of Christian doctrine, it was not unusual. Distinguished theologians like Charles Gore, Hensley Henson, William Temple and Charles Raven had maintained a discreet agnosticism. Moreover much of what Robinson said was little different from what I had heard from the pulpit of the University Church Sunday after Sunday. It did not occur to me that there would be accusations of heresy. But accusations there were and pressures were brought on me to arraign him for heresy in the consistory court. The Bishop of London, Robert Stopford, told me that he had been asked to instigate an inquisition if I failed to do so. The Bishop of Willesden, appeared in a face-to-face confrontation on television, and the intellectual disparity was so marked that it was difficult to decide whether to laugh or cry.

The Archbishop of Canterbury, Michael Ramsey, was inundated with letters from all over the world and it is not surprising that he over-reacted, as he admitted later. The trouble was, many of the critics who wrote to him and to me had never read *Honest To God*. They had been content with headlines in the secular press, or worse still, in the Church press. I remember, for instance, Robert Mortimer, the Bishop of Exeter, who had a well deserved reputation as an intellectual, making a forthright attack on television within a matter of hours of the publication. Mortimer was a close friend of mine. I saw more of him than most of his colleagues. Years later when he was staying at my house he noticed a copy of John's book on the table. "You know, Mervyn," he said, "I must be one of the few bishops who have never got round to reading it. I must one day." That was the trouble. Churchmen, including bishops, jumped to conclusions through ignorance, supposition or prejudice.

In Convocation the Archbishop allowed himself to be drawn into the controversy. Here is part of his address:

> With great reluctance I refer to the matter of the Bishop of Woolwich. I would far rather not do so, but there is an obligation not to allow the position of our Church to be obscured and to prevent the spread of serious misconceptions about the Faith to which we are pledged.
>
> I was specially grieved as to the method chosen by the Bishop for presenting his ideas to the public. We are asked to think that the enterprise was a matter of being 'tentative', 'thinking aloud', 'raising questions' and the like. But the initial method chosen was a newspaper article, crystal clear in its argument, and provocative in its shape and statement, to tell the public that the concept of a personal God as held both in popular Christianity and in orthodox doctrine is outmoded and that atheists and agnostics are right to reject it. Of course the association of this thesis with a Bishop of the Church caused public sensation and did much damage. As to the book, I repeat that the questions discussed in it are real questions and the effort to open up new modes of contact between our Faith and a secular age is one with which I feel much sympathy. We state and commend our faith only in so far as we go out and put ourselves with living sympathy inside the doubts of the doubting; the questions of the questioner and the loneliness of those who have lost their way. But, again, the first thesis of the book is that the concept of a personal God as expressed in the Bible and the Creed ought to be rejected. In place of the doctrine of God which is to be rejected there emerges instead some doctrine about God and the deity of Christ. But I doubt whether the most ingenious argument could show that the doctrine which so far emerges is properly the same as the doctrine of the Church. The Bishop, however, assures me that he upholds the Biblical and Catholic faith and that the thought of the book is tentative and exploratory. It is fair and right that I should say this as clearly as I have made my criticisms.

Archbishop Ramsey informed me of his intention to make a statement in his Presidential address. However, as no copy was sent to me, I decided not to be present, refusing to be put in the position of making ill-considered comments. Instead I wrote a letter in which I said:

> As the Bishop of Woolwich works in my diocese two points occur to me: If you state publicly that the doctrines of God and the deity of Christ in Robinson's book are incompatible with the doctrine of the Church, it is possible that pressure will be brought to bear upon me to take action against the Bishop. If this were to happen I should have to make up my mind about what action, if any, to take. I have and am consulting theologians but there is a division of opinion. I shall, of course, treat your verdict with the utmost respect but, until it has been carefully considered by our best theological minds, I cannot at this stage commit myself. It is my hope that a situation will not develop which might lead to estrangement between my Diocese and the Province, with the possibility of the Archbishop and the Diocesan Bishop on different sides, and perhaps in open conflict.
>
> So far as my Diocese is concerned I am striving to bring the different parties together to talk over their viewpoints. I am refraining from saying anything that might be interpreted as an official pronouncement because it would hinder constructive discussion and encourage men to harden their attitudes.
>
> Although bishops have been receiving many letters of protest from the critics, we must not be allowed to forget the people on the other side who have not written. My guess is there will be a reaction, perhaps a strong one, in favour of the Bishop of Woolwich. This could be disastrous as it might lead to the sort of situation that existed a hundred years ago at the time of *Essays and Reviews* when the book was condemned synodically in Convocation, when eleven thousand clergymen declared their hostility to the doctrines it expressed and when only three bishops were willing to take part in Frederick Temple's consecration. No doubt we shall be more circumspect today, but the cleavage might be as serious.

My chief adviser was Max Warren, the greatly respected General Secretary of the Church Missionary Society, who had recently been appointed to a canonry at Westminster Abbey. He wrote to the Archbishops of Canterbury and York, Ramsey and Coggan. He discussed the drafts with me. Whether or not the drafts were altered I don't know, but they are of interest as they reveal Warren's mind. In the draft to Canterbury he wrote:

What has so distressed so many in the past weeks of the controversy about the Bishop of Woolwich's book is that so few have sensed his deep missionary concern. I have known him well during his time in Cambridge and Southwark and I know that this missionary concern to confront men with the Christ and so lead them to God is the very heart of his ministry.

So much of the comment on his book, so it seems to me, has picked on sentences which, taken out of context and of the missionary purpose of the book, cannot but be disturbing to many devout souls. For such I have nothing but sympathy. Set against that, however, is the fact of which I have myself had ample evidence, from a surprisingly wide selection of people no less devout, that the book has been not only a stimulus to their minds but also a reinforcement of their faith. The point where I find myself most at one with the Bishop of Woolwich is in regard to that realm where so many live today, that spiritual twilight where there is no sense of sin because there is no awareness of the holy, of God.

In the draft to Archbishop Coggan of York he wrote:

One of the really shocking features of the case is the number of otherwise reputable, honest, intelligent and presumably honest ecclesiastics who went into action without ever having read the book at all. That in itself did probably more to discredit Christianity in the eyes of honest men than anything that the Bishop said in his book. It was one more illustration of the utterly deplorable way in which far too many Christians yield to panic. I hold no brief at all for some of John Robinson's expressions but in the main they have been taken right out of context.

John is deeply and passionately concerned with that very great company of thoughtful men and women today who can make absolutely no sense whatsoever of the traditional language of orthodoxy and who, when the terms are used, just give up listening. What John Robinson has attempted is a breakthrough into their consciousness so that within their thought world the possibility that Jesus Christ has something final to say about the ultimate nature of reality can be a proposition treated with

146

respect. What I am concerned with is to defend John's attempt to get right out on this dangerous frontier with a view to winning men for Christ. It is that passionate concern which has been totally over-looked in the preposterous correspondence which has disgraced the *Church Times* and the good name of the Church.

I write this strongly because I was genuinely appalled at the thought of the mischief that could be done if anything remotely approaching an accusation of heresy were to be made at this moment. It would shake the confidence of countless people in the leadership of the Church.

On the evening of May 6th, after Michael Ramsey's Presidential address to Convocation, Max, John, and I met for dinner in Putney to decide what to do.

As I was being hounded by the press and inundated with letters asking me to disassociate myself and the diocese from the Bishop of Woolwich, and with petitions to inhibit him from his episcopal duties, I knew that something would have to be said or done to express my support for him. At the same time the three of us were anxious not to embarrass Michael Ramsey. We regretted his Presidential speech but we sympathised with his predicament. And we were determined to match the spirit of charity with which he had spoken. Of course the Bishop of Woolwich was responsible for the statement he issued on the following day, but it was a consequence of our informal conference. Here it is:

The Archbishop of Canterbury has spoken of my book with reluctance and charity. It is in the same spirit that I feel obliged to clarify my own position.

I am bound to say that some of His Grace's statements appear to me to misrepresent what I believe. In particular I would draw attention to two points:
1. The intention of the book is a missionary one. Its whole argument depends on the fact that I am trying to help those who are on the fringe of the Faith or outside it. This concern determines almost every line of what I wrote. In the light of this event I regret the Archbishop's statement that "the book appears to reject the conception of a personal God as expressed in the Bible and Creed." I would insist that my arguments do not lead to this conclusion. On the contrary I affirm in my book as strongly as I can the utterly personal character of God as the source and

147

ground and goal of the entire universe. I wholly accept the doctrine of God revealed in the New Testament and enshrined in the Creeds. My sole concern is to question whether the doctrine must necessarily be expressed in certain images and categories which might have the effect for many in our generation of making it unreal.

2. The Archbishop disputes "whether any argument could show that the doctrine which so far emerges is properly the same as the doctrine of the Church." His Grace refers to my doctrine of God and to the deity of Christ. I maintain that what I have said is both Biblical and in conformity with the Creeds. I have for instance, categorically affirmed that I stand with Athanasius against certain liberal humanist views. This, I say, can never add up to saying that Christ was of one substance with the Father, and on that line Athanasius was correct in seeing that the battle must be fought however much one may legitimately deplore the categories in which the ideas of orthodoxy had to be framed. To explore new ways in which the truths for which he stood may be communicated is not to quarrel with the truths themselves.

I regret that the tentative character and obscurities have led to these misunderstandings, and I hope in due course to write more fully to say how the ideas that have been partially expressed in *Honest To God* are compatible with the doctrines of the Church of England. Meanwhile I reject emphatically any suggestion that what I have written is contrary to the Catholic Faith. As a Bishop it is my duty to defend it. This I do. And it is my earnest wish to commend it to those who are as yet unable to accept the Living Christ as their Lord and Saviour.

Oil was temporarily poured on troubled waters and a few days later Michael Ramsey and John Robinson were among the guests at my fiftieth birthday party. During the festivities the two men, with glasses of champagne in their hands, were observed with their free hands to draw imaginary concentric circles on the doors of an antique cupboard, the Archbishop remarking, "Up there and in here—yes." The Bishop remarking, "The ground of our being." Clem Attlee, sitting on a chair by the cupboard said with his usual economy of words, "Never read the book."

But Harold Macmillan, who was Prime Minister at the time had, and he sent me this letter:

My dear Bishop,

It was very kind of you to send me Bishop Robinson's book which I have read with great interest. I have also given it to one or two friends to read, including a very devout and intelligent Roman Catholic. I like the first half of the book and dislike the second.

I think the great fault of the treatment is its somewhat materialist, almost naïve approach. If we use symbols at all I do not see much more difficulty in imagining God up there than God down here. As I said to the Archbishop of Canterbury at the Mansion House (who seemed rather tickled at the notion), it is only the difference between the bomb which is obsolescent and Polaris! If you don't use the symbols at all and try to think more metaphysically, I do not see that there is anything which the Bishop is trying to say which was not already better said by St. John. What it is, however, that impresses me, with the exception of a few rather cheap witticisms, is the reverent approach which underlies the somewhat H. G. Wellsian style (incidentally it is incredible to me that anyone could take H. G. Wells seriously nowadays.)

It is of course very difficult for people of different generations to understand each others' problems and it may well be that for the youth of today we need different symbols; instead, for instance, of the traditional religious art, whether the grand and terrifying Byzantine mosaic or the mild beauty of Renaissance painting. For instance a modern abstract painting of God might be more attractive to young people than the traditional form. Nevertheless whichever it is, it is only a symbol and whether God is represented as God the Father in conventional painting or as a series of triangles and circles, it is still only an attempt to use the material to represent the infinite.

Another thought strikes me. How tremendously important it is nowadays to strengthen the discipline of the Church. It is on the authority of the Church and tradition that so much depends, and this has been weakened in our Church. Therefore confusion and uncertainty come into many people's minds.

Nevertheless, I am glad to have read the book and I think it is a very sincere effort. I have not read Bonhoeffer, but the Bishop of

149

Woolwich seems to lean very heavily on him. I do not know how seriously he is taken by theologians.

Yours very sincerely,

Harold Macmillan

When I came to write this autobiography and read through the letters I was surprised that Michael Ramsey had taken such a harsh line. It was untypical. Ramsey, although a High Churchman like myself, was basically a liberal. Indeed his success with the student world was and is due to a proclamation of the Gospel which was tempered with tolerance and flexibility. So I wrote to him in September 1981 to ask him to give me his considered opinion. It is with his gracious permission that I print his reply:

16 South Bailey,
Durham,
DH1 3EG
September 10th 1981

Dear Mervyn,

You ask about *Honest To God*. My initial reaction was very harsh and very unsympathetic and 'over-reacting'. Very soon, within a few months, I came to see the matter differently and with, I think, more understanding, and I blamed myself for my initial attitude.

I think the difference was between the two kinds of 'wavelength' in approach to the book. Approaching it as a kind of 'doctrinal statement' one found it very inadequate and said "A bishop ought to know better than this!" Approaching it as a way of moving towards Christianity for people 'outside the camp' the book was seen very differently and its value became apparent.

I think my own trouble was that I started on a wavelength right in a traditional way but wrong for the understanding of what was involved. John Robinson knew this fairly soon but I thought I had over reacted and somewhat mistaken the issues.

Some of my subsequent writings dealt with the question more constructively, and you would find an account of how I came to see these issues in a book of mine, *Canterbury Pilgrim* (SPCK 1961), the final chapter: "Lessons of a Pilgrimage". I am not surprised that you find my letters at the time unduly harsh.

150

Michael Mayne is doing very, very well at Great St. Mary's—
how good that you were there and too good that you moved to
Southwark.

With our love,

Michael

Within a matter of days I was involved in another doctrinal
controversy. Once again it was the Thirty-Nine Articles and the
necessity of a priest to 'read himself in', just as I had to do at
the University Church. Cyril Garbett, who had been Bishop of
Southwark years before I came on the scene, had said, "I have never
concealed my own wish that some other standard of doctrinal
orthodoxy might be accepted for the Thirty-Nine Articles are in
many cases ambiguous and in some cases inconsistent with modern
knowledge. I doubt if anyone can accept from his heart every
sentence in these Articles."

Canon John Pearce-Higgins, whom I had appointed as Vice-
Provost of the Cathedral, certainly could not. He told me of his
dilemma and I suggested that when I called upon him to make his
general assent to the Articles he should add the words, "In so far as
the mind of Christ permits." This is the advice I was already giving
to the clergy with troubled consciences. Furthermore I told them I
would not enquire whether they 'read themselves in' on their first
Sunday. I hoped they would not. Within minutes of the conclusion
of the installation there were protests from the hard-line evangelicals
and fundamentalists, whereupon Pearce-Higgins made a statement
to the press. It is worth quoting:

The Thirty-Nine Articles are a Reformation document, origin-
ally set out in all sincerity within the limitations of thought and
under the stress of the theological and social pressures of the time,
and reflecting the views of the Church of England four hundred
years ago. I believe them to be in need of revision and restatement
as they are no longer consonant with the new insights both into
the nature of the world in which we live and into the origin of our
faith which we have acquired.

While Justification by Faith has always been a keystone of
Protestant belief, the expression of that belief in the Articles is
unsatisfactory, especially Article 13 which appears to condemn
all non-Christians to eternal punishment. Article 19 on Pre-
destination gives, I believe, a totally false picture of God's love

151

for His children. If I were to be convinced that the belief that God had predestined a large number of His children to eternal punishment was an essential part of the Christian faith, I would resign my Orders at once. I cannot therefore give the appearance of condoning under the form of general assent these Articles which are included among others to which I take little exception.

I hope and pray therefore that the strong feeling already expressed in many quarters, of which my own public protest, which is entirely my own personal responsibility, is symptomatic and may lead to the abolition of assent as a condition of office, and thus to gain in spiritual and intellectual integrity which will be of immense blessing to the Church we love and seek to serve.

This temperate statement did nothing to pacify the Protestant minority who, as always, took the line that its interpretation of Scripture and dogma was the only correct one in the Church of England. Indeed it claimed an infallibility that led it to suppose that it had the right to catechise and denounce anybody who disagreed. An infallibility never claimed by the Pope!

The letters poured in from all parts of the country, and I treasure with amusement one from a clergyman in the neighbouring diocese of Rochester informing me that he was providing a Scriptural haven for refugees from the diocese of Southwark.

I answered the letters and the protests as reasonably as I could and I invariably quoted the words of my predecessor, Cyril Garbett. But it was to little effect. They were impervious to reason. Every jot and tittle of the Thirty-Nine Articles were sacrosanct and anybody who dared to question them was in error.

Today the hopes and prayers of John Pearce-Higgins have been fulfilled. The clergy are no longer required to assent to the Thirty-Nine Articles. I like to think that his protest in the Cathedral played a small part in winning the battle for intellectual freedom and integrity. And I am glad that I supported him publicly.

While the battle of the Articles was raging, another started. Again it began in the Cathedral. One of the canons, Douglas Rhymes, in a series of talks on Christian morality, mentioned—among other things—the need to rethink the Church's attitude towards sex. His basic contention was the need to reverence human personality and not to isolate the sex act. Divorce, pre-marital sex, homosexuality should be studied within the wider context of loving, caring relationships. Unfortunately the word 'sex' is to many Churchmen what a red rag is to a bull, or whatever may be the equivalent for its female counterpart. Indeed I sometimes had the impression that in their opinion the main purpose of the Gospel was to condemn what they considered to be sexual irregularities. Social injustice, apartheid, nuclear warfare, economic exploitation, slums, illiteracy were trivial ills as compared with the horrors of 'bed'.

Inevitably those who took this view were appalled. The words 'South Bank Morality' were coined, as though Douglas Rhymes was seeking to fill the Cathedral with harlots, strumpets, lechers and, if not gaiety girls, at least gaiety boys.

The High Churchmen, through their chairman, Canon Charles Smith, asked to see me. We had a helpful conversation. He thought that what Douglas Rhymes had said could be misunderstood; his friends had decided to publish a booklet for general distribution. It was intended as a guide to the younger generation who might be careless in their sexual standards and unaware of basic Christian standards. I assured him of my approval and support.

The Evangelicals were different. They wanted a meeting to which all could come to discuss a range of subjects including *Honest To God*, the Thirty-Nine Articles and Douglas Rhymes. I refused to have a meeting in a public place because I knew the press would be there and would come out with sensational headlines. Instead I invited them to Bishop's House on the understanding that it would be a private discussion within the family circle. Providing they respected confidentiality, I assured them they could open their hearts to me and that I would do my best to listen to them with charity and understanding. About seventy came. Within five minutes of the conclusion of the meeting someone telephoned a report of the proceedings to the press, or gave it to the reporters and photographers who had surrounded the house for three hours. Next day one headline was "The Exit of the Stifled Seventy."

I had made some general points with regard to the comprehensiveness of the Church of England and of the need to live and let live, and to try to understand one another instead of making public denunciations in pulpit and press without even talking things over with the persons concerned. I asked them how many had read *Honest To God*, or knew what Pearce-Higgins and Rhymes had said in the cathedral. Very few. It was mostly hearsay and ill-informed gossip.

I took their three complaints in turn and summed up by quoting the words of my predecessor, Bishop Garbett, who on another occasion had said,

We have in our Church a number of biblical scholars, philosophers and moral teachers who are relating the ancient faith to modern thought. To do this they need both freedom and courage; sometimes they will make mistakes, at other times the novelty of their opinions may startle and alarm. The Church must have great patience, there must be neither witch hunting nor heresy hunting. Through free and unfettered research and open discussion, the Spirit of God will lead the Church in each generation into a deeper understanding of the Truth. Those of us who are not students must sit at the foot of men more learned than ourselves and gratefully use their work in commending the faith to men and women who do not understand the terms of the old theology, and only are able to do so through the use of categories of thought with which they are familiar. This freedom of research and expression is one of the distinctive characteristics of our Church.

Looking back on these upheavals, I did not enjoy them; although it was assumed that I was more than ready to go into battle, I was easily distressed, perhaps over-sensitive. Nevertheless, I am sure they were inevitable. The 1960s was a decade of protest, of questioning, of the rejection of convention and tradition. The universities, the arts, moral standards, political and philosophical attitudes came under fire. The Church could not escape. The fearful sought refuge in fundamentalism, either of the Church or the Bible. Just as when I was a boy Father Stothert had tried to anaesthetise my critical faculties and to get me to accept without question what he considered to be the truth, so now conservative Churchmen tried to silence the pioneers because they were frightened that 'South Bank Religion' would undermine the faith. One bishop put it to me like this: "Why upset the faithful? Most of them are simple people." In fact they were neither as faithful nor as simple as he supposed. The Evangelicals were the most alarmed because their literalist attitude towards Scripture was the most vulnerable. Fortunately out of the conflict emerged a new school of Evangelicals which, while continuing to make a distinctive contribution, was open-minded and flexible. By the time I left the diocese I had appointed men from this new school to some of the most responsible positions. What is more, the quality of its ordinands was as impressive as those who came from other traditions, perhaps more so.

The impact that these battles made upon me can be summed up in a paragraph from Professor Herbert Butterfield's *Christianity and History*, "There are times when we can never meet the future with sufficient elasticity of mind, especially if we are locked in the contemporary systems of thought. We can do worse than remember a principle which gives us a firm rock and leaves us the maximum elasticity for our minds: the principle: Hold to Christ, and for the rest be totally uncommitted."

It was the end of July and as I wanted to escape from the controversies and barrage of letters, I went by cargo boat across the Atlantic and up the St Lawrence to stay with my brother in Canada, and then with the Bishop of Dallas. There were about a dozen passengers on board and as some were Churchmen I asked the captain if I could hold a Communion service in the mess room. He immediately agreed and asked if the officers would be welcome. "Of course," I said, "and the crew as well."

"I don't think that would be appropriate," he said, "especially with a bishop on parade."

9

The House of Lords

The previous chapter may give the impression that much of my time was taken up with ecclesiastical controversy. That was not so. The greater part of each day was devoted to pastoral work, visits to the parishes and diocesan administration. In 1963 I had a new interest, the House of Lords; and from the day of my introduction until my resignation seventeen years later I attended as often as I could.

Although I did not favour the second Chamber as at present constituted, not believing in a hereditary peerage, I took the view that so long as it existed it should try to fulfil a useful purpose. And it often did, especially when it dealt with matters of major social and humanitarian concern.

Again while it may be a historical anachronism for some bishops of the Established Church to have the right to a seat in the Lords, it gives them an opportunity to express views that are independent of party. There may have been a time when the bench of bishops attempted to provide the spiritual sanction for the status quo of the Tory party, but that is no longer so. Like my colleagues I accepted no whip and there were many times when I voted against the Labour party to which I belonged. I think all of us examined each case on its own merits and voted as we thought fit, no matter what the Government or Opposition may have wanted.

Unlike the Commons, any member of the Lords who wants to speak in a debate does so. He sends his name in beforehand and a 'batting order' is arranged through the 'usual channels'. The advantage of this procedure is that no time is wasted on the preparation of speeches which, as in the case of members of the Commons who fail to catch the Speaker's eye, may never be delivered. Even so, there is a formidable difficulty. If a member of the Lords decides to speak it is expected that he will remain throughout the debate to await the Government's reply to the points in all the speeches. If the matter under discussion is of general importance there may be thirty speakers or more. Such occasions play havoc with one's diary. For instance, when the House debated

Rhodesia at the time of Ian Smith's rebellion against the Queen, the Archbishop of Canterbury and I had to stand by from early afternoon until well after midnight. We received short notice of debates. Often it was impossible to put down my name to speak because I had arranged, perhaps a year previously, to take a confirmation service or fulfil a diocesan engagement. I might drop in during the afternoon to show interest, but I could not join in the debate. However if the subject was of exceptional importance I would try to find a retired bishop to take the confirmation. For these reasons I was sorry that when I resigned I automatically ceased to be a member of the House. I wish that those of us who wanted to remain could be treated as life peers because in retirement we could devote more time to our parliamentary duties and play a greater part in public life. In addition we could deputise for those bishops who find it inconvenient 'to take prayers'. Proceedings begin with prayers. Unlike the Commons, the Lords have no chaplain. The bishops take it in turn on a weekly rota. This means that a bishop may have to spend two or three weeks in London during the year to fulfil his duties. Many of them resent this enforced absence from their dioceses. In my case it was no problem as I could reach the House within thirty minutes and if I was not interested in the business of the day I would leave immediately. I had two disasters. In my early days I had not understood that sittings of the House were sometimes advanced. On this occasion when the Lord Chancellor took his place on the Woolsack, thirty minutes earlier than usual, I was not in my place—a nearly unforgivable sin. After what was subsequently described to me as an embarrassing silence the Lord Chancellor took the book and said the prayers. The ensuing debate was on penal reform and I was taking part. I began my speech by saying, "May I crave the indulgence of your Lordships by apologising to you for not having been in my place. I stand in a white sheet; I crave the forgiveness of the House, and I only hope the noble and learned Lord on the Woolsack will not despatch me to the Tower."

On the second occasion I was not to blame. It is the custom for a large book containing the psalms and prayers to be placed by a steward on the Woolsack for the bishop to use. No deviations are permitted. Alas there was no book. I looked helplessly for the steward, but he was rushing around the House searching for the key of the cupboard in which was the precious book. In came the Lord Chancellor's procession. My mind went blank. I made an effort to say the psalm, "The Lord is my Shepherd", but got stuck halfway.

Then I tried the Lord's Prayer, but got muddled with the different versions. After that the Hail Mary came vividly to mind, but an immediate sense of diplomacy restrained me.

The debate on penal reform in which I took part was in November 1964. It makes dismal reading in Hansard. There were excellent speeches with valuable suggestions put forward by men with considerable experience. The Government appeared to be enthusiastic in its reply. But nearly twenty years later the position is little different from what it was.

Penal reform has been a special interest of mine because of my association with Wandsworth and Brixton prisons. Not only have I taken part in debates but I have had talks with successive Home Secretaries. The conditions in some of our prisons are worse than appalling. They breed criminals because they deprive men of purpose and dignity. The last thing they do is to prepare prisoners to play their part in the life of the community and to become useful citizens. We have not lacked enlightened Home Secretaries and prison staff, but we have lacked the determination to foot the bill. It would seem that all Governments have financial difficulties and are compelled to make cuts. Too often the prisons are the first to suffer. The state of our prisons is a moral scandal.

I note with interest, in view of the events of 1981, what I said in my speech in 1964 about the police in Brixton. "The police have an unenviable task, which in the majority of cases they discharge with courtesy, patience and wisdom. Even so, great importance must be attached to establishing better relations between the police and the public." I did my best to convince the police in the years that followed and I warned them that unless they changed their tactics there would be an explosion. I knew many of them and admired them; but I wondered whether their training was adequate. Like that of the clergy it was better suited for a situation before it had changed beyond recognition. Home Secretaries agreed with me—but did nothing.

Allied to my concern for penal reform was my determination to be rid of capital punishment. Before speaking in the Lords I thought it wise to address the House of Bishops, as I knew a few of the older ones were in favour of retaining the rope while others thought that 'the time was not yet ripe' (as it never is in the Church of England) to make a change. As one of my colleagues said: "Nobody respects the Bishop of Southwark more than I do. But he has yet to balance his enthusiasms with the adage 'more haste less speed'. He must realise that public opinion is not ready for the abolition of the death penalty. I am sure all of us agree with his ultimate goal, but hanging must continue for the time being." A few more corpses and then I should be home and dry! I dreaded a divided episcopal bench in the Lords on this issue as I knew how our differences of opinion could be exploited by the retentionists. So I pressed for a compromise. It was that capital punishment should be suspended for five years and then reviewed, as I felt sure that once the practice had been discontinued it would not return. And I added a further clause: "that there should be compensation (financial) for the dependants of the victims of homicide."

In my speech I surprised some of my colleagues by reminding them that the debate had continued for a hundred and fifty years and I was doing no more than ask the Government to write the final paragraph.

Their ears were alerted when I told them that at the beginning of the last century there were two hundred and twenty capital offences. In 1808 a boy aged seven and a girl of eleven were hanged for stealing; in 1814 a man was hanged for cutting down a tree; in 1832 a boy of nine was sentenced to death, though subsequently reprieved, for stealing two pennyworth of paint.

They looked embarrassed when I went on to say that whereas the temporal peers in 1810 introduced a bill to abolish the death penalty for stealing five shillings and over from a shop, the Archbishop of Canterbury and six bishops voted against abolition. And as for tree-felling by the poor to keep themselves warm, the Primate was sure that without hanging England would suffer the perils of disafforestation.

Next I quoted from a series of reports and commissions, before listing the countries that had abolished the death penalty. After that a silence—and then, as I sat down, the throwaway remark—"Of course, Soviet Russia has retained the death penalty, as you would expect."

To what extent I played a part in the successful outcome I don't know. What I do remember is the moving speech in the Lords by Robert Mortimer, the Bishop of Exeter. On a previous occasion he had voted against abolition but in the final debate he explained his change of mind. It was a *tour de force*, as most of Mortimer's speeches were.

I regarded attendance in the Lords as a priority when matters affecting London were being debated, particularly homelessness, unemployment, ethnic minorities and the inner city. Housing, the conditions and the lack, had been the concern of the Church for decades. In the 1920s, Cyril Garbett had headed demonstrations and marches from Lambeth Palace to Westminster. In my earlier years the Bishop of London, Robert Stopford, and I, together with the Lord Mayor of London, led a torchlight procession from St Paul's Cathedral to Southwark Cathedral. In my last years the next Bishop of London, Gerald Ellison, and I led a procession from Marble Arch to Lambeth. What were we trying to do? Perhaps the short answer is to be found in a speech I made in the Lords in March 1977:

> With regard to housing. Look across the river. There are too few houses. It is difficult to estimate exactly, but we need to think not in terms of tens of thousands, but in hundreds of thousands. That is the first thing about housing. The second thing is that there are too many sub-standard houses. In Wandsworth, thirty-five per cent of the applicants on the lists have no living rooms; in Lambeth, forty-six per cent share a bathroom; also in Lambeth, fifty per cent share an inside lavatory; whereas in the Borough of Southwark, forty per cent have no inside lavatory at all. The third thing about housing is that much of the new housing encourages anti-social behaviour at enormous cost. Come and visit some of our new housing estates, with their bleak corridors, their vandalised lifts and their appalling sense of isolation. Much of it badly planned, much of it badly maintained and much of it, alas! so badly managed. These three items on the agenda showing the desperate housing situation are, in all conscience, enough; but I have to add a fourth: the lack of rented accommodation for young people, one-parent families or immigrants. Yet the latest figures show there are 50,000 properties empty—30,297 being in Southwark borough alone. Some have been empty since 1973. What an appalling state of affairs.

A few months later Trevor Huddleston, the Bishop of Stepney, and I tried to shock Londoners into a realisation of the human tragedy of homelessness by having a human crib in Trafalgar Square on Christmas Eve—a young married couple and a baby in a plastic tent with a donkey tethered. Whether the presence of the donkey was misunderstood by the authorities I don't know, but Trevor and I were told there was no need for a crib in Trafalgar Square as there was already a very beautiful one there with a lighted Christmas tree nearby and carol singers on the steps of St Martin-in-the-Fields. Instead we could have our human crib in a remote part of the park. It was remote and it was a cold Christmas Eve. As on the first occasion at Bethlehem, few people saw it.

I returned to the matter again in July 1977. Especially I stressed the needs of the thousands of young unemployed who had nowhere to live:

I wonder how many of Your Lordships have gone out on the streets at night and met some of the young people who roam around the city in their hundreds during the early hours of the morning? I encourage my own young clergy to do what I call 'take the plunge'. They are shoved out on the streets of London for two days with only £1 in their pocket. It is a shattering experience for them. Certainly they are very careful afterwards about the criticism which they make regarding people who are supposed to be intentionally homeless and enjoying what is supposed to be the fun of wandering around.

I tried to be in my place when the House was discussing unemployment, which it often did. The debates were more constructive than in the Commons because, there being less need to make party capital, speakers were concerned with long-term cures. They knew that, no matter the colour of the Government, the assumption that a person has the right to work has been impaired by the scientific revolution. It is not easy to see the solution. Obviously there must be a massive movement from traditional jobs to jobs dependent upon the new technology. In the transitional years it will be difficult. For some it will involve earlier retirement, while for others it will necessitate re-training. Even those who are fortunate enough to find employment must expect a drastic reduction in working hours and an extension of holidays. Hence the country is faced with an urgent social problem that cannot be solved unless there is a revolutionary attitude towards leisure. As our major preoccupation becomes our free time rather than our work, we shall become a different sort of society. Instead of spending the greater part of our day in the office or the factory or at the bench, we shall be faced with the problems of using time usefully or killing time uselessly.

I was keenly interested in overseas affairs especially when the British Government had an opportunity to help the oppressed, either by resisting a dictatorial régime or by supplying aid. The late Lord Astor initiated annual debates on refugees and he asked me to make myself responsible for the Middle East. Although I had worked with Victor Gollancz to support the Jews that had escaped from the Nazis, I was now as keen to help the Palestinians who had been deprived of their homes and livelihood by the Israelis. It saddened me that those who had suffered so much at the hands of Hitler could be inhuman in their dealings with Arabs. Perhaps we should be nearer to a solution, both in the Middle East and in Ireland, if the power and finance of the American lobby were to be diminished.

Racial discrimination has always appalled me. It is foolish because it cannot succeed. It is inherently self-destructive; it is wrong because it makes nonsense of the concept of the brotherhood of man. For a Christian it is evil because it is incompatible with the teaching of the New Testament. When we are baptised we join a supra-national society, the Catholic Church. It claims our first loyalty.

The Communion table brings together people of all colours, classes and nations. We cannot share bread at it sacramentally unless we are prepared to share it, and all that bread represents, in daily life. Holy Communion necessitates the goal of a holy community.

I took every opportunity, both inside the House and outside, to protest against the practice of apartheid in South Africa. I spoke in Trafalgar Square with Michael Foot and Fenner Brockway, friends over many years. I joined in protest marches and spoke in university debates. Shortly before I left Southwark I was invited to the South African Embassy to be told by the Ambassador how anxious he was to learn my views. In fact he spent two hours explaining his. Of course there are difficulties when black and white find themselves in the same country, but in South Africa it is the exploitation of the black by the white. Just as we prospered when we had an empire which produced goods for us with cheap labour, so the whites in South Africa maintain a standard of living which would be impossible were it not for the evil doctrine and practices of apartheid, both of which affront the dignity of human beings. I doubt whether the enthusiastic labours of so many of us achieve much, if anything. I always felt that in the last resort the British Government, like the American, would do little more than utter platitudes. They were, and are, too afraid of Soviet influence to take active steps to change the régime. How short-sighted. Our failures to bring pressure on South Africa inevitably hastens the day when the blacks in their desperation will summon the Marxist forces to their rescue.

Rhodesia was a different matter. When Ian Smith rebelled against the Crown to establish white supremacy, we had an opportunity in Parliament to oppose him. Perhaps the most exciting debate in which I was involved was in December 1965, three days before Christmas. The issue was oil sanctions. Tory peers, led by the Marquess of Salisbury, were against the imposition of sanctions.

They may not have approved of everything Smith had done but they sympathised with him. Their line was that as the Africans were not capable of governing themselves the whites should be the interim authority, even though Smith had said that there would be no change in his lifetime; indeed one of his colleagues had said not for two hundred years.

Lord Salisbury was held in regard and respect in all parts of the House. It was not easy to joust with him. However as I felt as strongly as he did on the other side I was compelled to engage him. I had been placed low down on the list of speakers. In fact it was to my advantage. When I rose from my seat late at night the House had been filling up during the previous hour for the vote. It was now packed with members sitting on the steps of the throne. I decided to take my stand on Christian principles. I spoke quietly and I hope with courtesy. I challenged Lord Salisbury on his doctrine of God and his doctrine of Man. I asked him how he could relate the actions of Smith to what we as Christians were supposed to believe. The Marquess retaliated by asking how I could justify what was happening in Ghana. To which I replied, "There are many things that happen in Ghana, in Russia, in Franco's Spain and in South America of which, as a Christian, I strongly disapprove. But one wrong does not make another right. Also we were being told by the noble Marquess that these Africans were more or less savages. If that is true, perhaps they may be excused for their uncultured behaviour. But the white people, we assume, have many generations of civilisation behind them, and so I say to the noble Marquess straight out that their conduct is not as excusable as that of the coloured people—the noble Marquess is hoist with his own petard."

There were further interruptions especially from Lord Colyton who talked about flesh and blood and the British stock with the inference that we were a superior creation. I countered by reminding the House that in forty-eight hours it would be Christmas Eve: "We shall be making our way to our Churches and Cathedrals for the Midnight Mass, when we shall be reminded of the occasion when, according to legend, three Kings, white, black and yellow, gathered together before the Child who was the Prince of Peace. Our purpose is the reconciliation which will bring white and coloured together in one living community." Later I asked whether in the interval between the debate and the Midnight Mass the noble Marquess and their Lordships who supported Smith would take their tins of whitewash to change the colour of the black and yellow kings at the crib. It was a tense moment. There was no interruption, just silence. I sat down.

C. P. Snow told me years later that in his judgment it was the most dramatic moment he had experienced in Parliament.

I enjoyed the debate partly because of the importance I attached to it, and because of the occasion and setting. Usually peers wander in and out of the Chamber. I remember one occasion when my speech was cut short by a lengthy Government announcement. I found the House was almost deserted when I resumed. In a sense the Lords is like a railway station, with its noble passengers on the move, especially when the time has come for tea and crumpets in the dining room. The Chamber is no place for the orator. It is too large and because the benches face one another a speaker never sees the faces of more than half his audience. It takes a long time to master the art of addressing their lordships. Archbishop Ramsey once said to me that he thought Donald Soper was the outstanding success. I agree. He was brief, concise, factual with an attractive voice. Although he spoke on many subjects he was so well informed and had such a retentive memory that he never had a note in his hand. He was as effective when he spoke in the open on Tower Hill. He captured the attention of the passers-by and he outwitted the hecklers.

The Lords were at their best on such controversial humanitarian matters as divorce and homosexuality. They could say what they liked as they did not have to look over their shoulders at their electors, and many had had to cope with these problems as lawyers, doctors or priests.

The Divorce Reform Act which came into force in 1971 owed much to the Bishop of Exeter, Robert Mortimer, whose report, *Putting Asunder*, was published five years earlier. The basic recommendation of his committee was that the one ground for divorce should be the irretrievable breakdown of a marriage rather than matrimonial offence. While the courts would take into account what used to be called matrimonial offences, it would do so not as ends in themselves but as possible evidence of the allegation of irretrievable breakdown.

I was keen that the Church should play an active part in changing the law because Christians should be foremost in fostering right relationships with the home. On the assumption that for most people to become integrated personalities, they require a partner, marriage is the corollary. But, and this is crucial in the debate, marriage, when approached from this angle, must be seen to exist for men, and not men for marriage. Our primary interest should be a stable relationship that enables two people to live together in a constructive partnership that impinges positively not only upon their children but upon all who come within its ambit. This is the idea, but ideals do not necessarily make good laws. And if we try to enforce them the result may be not the fulfilment of love but a condition of guilt and hypocrisy.

The State, like the Church, must begin with human beings as they are. Most couples when they become engaged envisage a permanent relationship, but not all of them are sufficiently mature to prepare for it. What is more, few or them realise the length of years involved. Inevitably there are failures, and breakdowns that are irretrievable, which if words mean anything, means the end of the partnership. To hedge the couple around with laws that try to make them live beneath the same roof can turn home into hell. That, and more, engaged the House in its debate. Nobody thought that the Divorce Reform Act would solve all problems but it was a genuine exercise in compassion for the casualties.

Unfortunately the Church of England has a matrimonial discipline which is far from compassionate and needs to be modified. For years it has tried to prevent divorced persons from being remarried in church, and time and again I referred to the matter in Parliament, in the General Synod, in the diocese and in the press. It has been a long and uphill struggle, but I expect the change to come during my life.

What few people know is that this rigid attitude is comparatively new. The remarriage of divorced persons in church was allowed in previous centuries, and it is allowed in other provinces of the Anglican communion. Moreover in the Eastern Orthodox Church a man or woman may be married a second and even a third time, although the previous partners are alive.

The bishops of the Church of England have been divided in their views but in the days when each petition for divorce had to go to the House of Lords, there is no record of a single episcopal dissentient vote, even when three of the petitions came from Anglican priests. And in old registers there are records of the marriages of divorced people. In St George, Hanover Square, in the nine months previous to May 1800 there are three second marriages and no distinction was made between 'innocent' and 'guilty' parties.

Later in the century the saintly Bishop King of Lincoln, the embodiment of High Anglicanism, said to his clergy that he was "unable to accept the conclusions of those who would make marriage absolutely indissoluble and so forbid the remarriage of those who have been separated under any circumstances." And King was not the only one. Mandell Creighton, the formidable Bishop of London, with a still more formidable wife, wrote, "I could not advise any of my clergy to refuse to solemnise a marriage of an innocent person who genuinely desired God's blessing. I prefer to err on the side of charity."

With the setting up of divorce courts and with an increase in the number of broken homes the attitude of the Church hardened. When in 1937 the Matrimonial Causes Bill, intended to clarify the position on divorce, for which A. P. Herbert was largely responsible, came to the House, Hensley Henson, the Bishop of Durham, welcomed the Bill and in a vigorous speech gave two reasons for doing so: "1. It is time we cleared our minds of the figment by which marriage is considered as something independent of the possibility of the partners exercising any of the purposes for which marriage exists. 2. The marriage union is made for man and not man for the marriage union." The Archbishop of Canterbury, Cosmo Lang, refrained from voting, but he welcomed a conscience clause which allowed clergy *not* to marry a divorced person. That is still law, though few people seem to realise it. A clergyman need not marry a divorced person, as previously demanded by the law, but he may if he wishes. Alas, most bishops, supported by Convocation, reacted the other way, and the Herbert conscience clause was twisted— with the result that it was thought that no priest was allowed to marry a divorced person except one whose conscience demanded that he should. It was the exact opposite to what Herbert intended. Worse still, the clergy who had the courage to stand by their legal rights often found themselves in trouble with their bishops, with the result that they feared for their careers. It was little short of episcopal blackmail. As Herbert said towards the end of his life, had he known how his conscience clause would have been interpreted by the Church of England, he would never have agreed to it. He felt he had been conned by Cosmo Lang and he despised the duplicity of the bishops.

I took action as soon as I arrived in Southwark. I informed the clergy of their legal rights and, at the same time, explained the official attitude of the Church. It was a matter for their conscience and I had no wish to be involved. I added that on rare occasions I had married divorced people, but only when I had been convinced that they genuinely desired to establish a Christian home. I expressed my opposition to marriage in a church, either for the second or the first time, of couples that had no real faith but wanted a 'white wedding' for custom's sake.

I am glad to say that my regulation was appreciated in the diocese and when some years later I asked in an anonymous questionnaire how many had married divorced people, I found that more than a hundred had done so. Others had contented themselves with a service of blessing after the ceremony in a register office. This strikes me as humbug. If God can bless a divorced person as he sets out on his second venture the marriage cannot be wrong. So why not have the marriage service instead of a hole-in-the-corner affair? I am sure that the answer lies in the obsession that so many people in the Church have about the sex act. Just as there was a radical change of attitude amounting to an about-turn with regard to contraception, so there will be with regard to remarriage. I like to think that the Southwark diocese was among the pioneers.

Homosexuality was another bone of contention. The Wolfenden Report had suggested the law should be changed. The existing situation was ludicrous. If a man committed a sexual act with another man, even in private, he could find himself in prison, whereas a woman who had a lesbian relationship was free, within limits to pursue her inclinations.

I had no doubt in my mind where I stood. The over-riding consideration in all relationships must be reverence for personality. How two people express their love for one another must be for them to determine. It may be physical or it may not. In the Scriptures we read that Christ had a special affection for John, "the disciple whom Jesus loved, who had his head on Jesus' shoulder at supper."

So much had come to light in recent years as a consequence of sexual and biological research. The man who is wholly heterosexual is probably in the minority; more likely he, like a woman, is to some extent bisexual. He can be attracted sexually to members of either sex. Whether or not he expresses himself physically, perhaps only in a kiss or a hug as on the football field, is his business. Not even apostolic succession confers upon a bishop the right to spy through bedroom keyholes.

However I did not approach the problem at that level. My concern was for the man who, knowing that he was homosexual, should have the liberty to live with a man he loved, and be accepted by society in the same way as women already were. As one who had always lived by himself I knew that many would find such loneliness difficult or intolerable. If a man is made to love and to be loved he must be free to find a partner, unless he has a special vocation to do otherwise. To suggest that he can solve his problem by 'finding a nice girl' is pathetic. Made as he is, no girl, however beautiful, will attract him. More likely he will try to conform outwardly, but will satisfy his nature in the least desirable ways. Hence the hundreds of squalid convictions in the police courts, the intense unhappiness, the blackmail and the suicides.

The Wolfenden Report recognised the facts, and attempts were made in Parliament to deal with them. The debates continued, and continued, and continued. Before a law can be changed there must be agreement in both Houses of Parliament in the same session. There were delays galore. Intentionally or unintentionally the Bill having passed through one House did not reach the other House in time. It fell to the ground. It had to start from the beginning in the next session. I took part in a number of them. A friendly antagonist was Field Marshal Montgomery. He was utterly opposed to what he told me was the 'Buggers' Charter'. But we had a good relationship. Soon after Nye's death I took his young nephew, Vincent Stafford, to luncheon in the House of Lords—as he was anxious to compare it with the meal he had had with his aunt, Jennie Lee, in the Commons. Montgomery passed our table and he spoke to Vincent. In fact he sat down and picking up a menu card, the cover of which was a photograph of the Queen opening Parliament with himself as sword-bearer, pointed to himself with a fork and said to Vincent, "That's me."

Sometimes when he and I would leave the House together I would offer him a lift in my car as he lived on the route to Bishop's House. At the time I had a German driver who had been taken prisoner after the African campaign. On his release he married an English girl and settled down here. Montgomery used to talk war strategy to him as though Karl, an ex-private, had been Rommel's closest adviser. "Of course," he would say "what you fellows ought to have done was so-and-so." Karl, then a middle-aged man, told me that he little thought when he was a young private in the German Army that he would one day be treated as an equal by the fabulous British General. Such was Monty's charm.

Even so, Monty didn't like Wolfenden or his works. Still less could he understand bishops who wanted to change the law. He was appalled that the Primate, Michael Ramsey, had supported the charter. When the Bill was read a second time and returned to the House for the committee stage he tried to render it harmless by suggesting that the age of consent should be raised from the age of twenty-one to the age of eighty, adding with a disarming smile that he himself would achieve four-score years at his next birthday.

The supporters of Wolfenden thought that at last we had achieved our goal. Nothing remained but the third reading, which is usually a formality. However on the morning I had an urgent message from Lambeth Palace to be in my place as it had become known that backwoodsmen were heading for London in the hope of taking the House by surprise and throwing out the Bill. I cancelled my engagements and went to Westminster. Yes, the enemies of Sodom were scattered around the building hoping to capture its battlements. Unfortunately for them the troops of Gomorrah had been alerted. There was an onslaught, with the bows and arrows from the public-school armoury of long ago, but Monty and his friends, like Lot's wife, were reduced to pillars of salt. We won by a small majority.

For years more the Church of England continued to debate the subject but the battle had been won in Parliament. I doubt whether anybody cares what the Church says or does not say. Instead of leading the way to a new understanding the Church limped helplessly behind as it had on contraception and divorce. But what else can one expect of a General Synod with a membership which is above middle-age, some in their late seventies, and drawn from such a closely knit social group, which has never been acclaimed for its prophetic gifts or its enlightenment.

In 1973 I became involved in the campaign for entry into Europe and the Common Market. I was a keen supporter. While I was not competent to express an opinion on the economic factors, I thought that had the European Community come into existence a century earlier we might have avoided the two World Wars and my father, and millions more, would not have been killed. That is still my view.

Soon after I went to Southwark I met Sir Oswald and Lady Mosley. A curious friendship developed. Nobody could have been more opposed to the British Fascist Movement than I was in the 1930s. I detested it. On one occasion two Mosleyites in uniform came to my church in Bristol because I had advertised an address in which I intended to denounce their racist views. At the point in my sermon when I said that nobody who claimed to belong to the Catholic Church could tolerate discrimination between Jew and Gentile, on the grounds that for the Christian such discrimination is heretical and blasphemous, two men rose from their chairs and, facing the altar on which was the figure of Christ on a crucifix, gave a fascist salute as they clicked their heels together. I said from the pulpit, "Good evening, gentlemen, I am glad to note you are saluting a Jew." Members of the congregation were less tolerant. They pursued them, tackled them and brought them down to the ground, and banged their heads on the kerb stone. A week or two later they returned and, standing on a chair in the street outside the church,

169

harangued the crowd. A famous character of the locality, 'Our Liz', who wore a cap, a sack around her middle and heavy boots with no laces, took a lighted candle and set fire to the speaker's trousers. He ran for his life with 'Our Liz' tapping him on his head and his backside with a boot. I warmly applauded.

Years later when I was at the University Church I was asked to debate with Mosely in the Cambridge Union and I refused. I would not be in the same room, still less debate with him. Then I went to Southwark. For private and personal reasons, and because I had met Mosley's son, I accepted an invitation to dinner. Although my views on fascism had not and have not changed, I became fond of Oswald Mosley and his wife, Diana. To dine with them, as I did about twice a year over a long period, was an intellectual excitement. Mosley was one of the most brilliant men I have ever met and I can understand why his contemporaries of different political parties have said that if only he had played his cards differently he could have been Prime Minister. Perhaps his brilliance was his undoing. As a young Cabinet Minister he despaired of the incompetence and banalities of Ramsey MacDonald and went into the wilderness. He saw the country lurching towards disaster under a Premier that he, like others, considered to be mentally inactive.

Again like others before and since, he had a messianic compulsion to save Britain from disaster. Alas, democratic methods go ill with such aspirations. To what extent he approved of fascist methods and anti-semitic propaganda I do not know. When I raised the matter with him he insisted that the tough methods of his bully boys had no purpose other than to protect his followers from the attacks of the Marxists who tried to disrupt his meetings. I just do not know. When he launched his biography, Bob Boothby and I tackled him for hours at a dinner in the House of Lords, but even Bob was reduced to silence, no mean feat. My guess is that he was so impressed by the achievements of Mussolini that he thought similar autocratic methods rather than the bumblings of a MacDonald or a Baldwin were necessary to overcome the ghastly unemployment of the 30s and to save Britain from war. Had he lived earlier, he might have been accepted. But it was too late. Our democracy prefers to put its faith in a Government which can be rejected at a general election rather than to commit itself to an individual. That Mosley should have despaired of MacDonald is understandable. Had he been ten years older he might have been content to wait until he could have achieved a democratic leadership by democratic methods. It was a tragedy.

Oswald Mosley was kindness itself to me. Except when I raised controversial matters of the past, we concentrated on the present, especially on Europe. He was an ardent European and a powerful propagandist. He had facts and figures at his finger tips and he transmitted his enthusiasm. I sought his advice when I spoke in the Lords on our entry into the Common Market and some of my speeches were drafted by him. On one occasion I was warmly congratulated by members of all parties but I thought it wise to conceal the source of my inspiration.

In 1973 I became impatient with the attitude of Harold Wilson towards the European Community. He seemed to shilly-shally, the epitome of indecision and vacillation. I understood Douglas Jay, who had always been an out-and-out opponent and with whom I had discussions, but Wilson seemed to be incapable of making up his mind. I regretted the growing difference between us because we had had happy relationships for several years and I knew him as a man who was capable of much personal kindness. He also did me the honour to invite me to address his Cabinet colleagues on two occasions in the Crypt Chapel of Westminster before the opening of a new Parliament. But I felt that the political coinage was being debased. To me the Labour party meant men of the integrity of Cripps and Attlee.

The crux came with Dick Taverne's election in Lincoln. With Bernard Levin I spoke on his platform. I expressed my support of his adherence to the ideal of a United Europe and I accused the Labour party of duplicity, though not those members who had been consistent opponents. Until Jim Callaghan became Prime Minister my relationships with Downing Street were strained. I was no longer honours' list material. Perhaps I was too honest!

10

Later Years in Southwark

Since my early years in the ministry I have always been interested in para-psychology because I believe it provides a key to a fuller understanding of consciousness, widens horizons and makes life less of an enigma. Unfortunately intelligent discussion can be difficult because too often it is assumed that psychical research involves 'spooks' and the exploitation of superstition, to say nothing of the increasing number of practitioners in black magic and obscene occultism. This encouraged me to persuade people to take the subject seriously. In Bristol and Cambridge I gave a course of lectures, which attracted large audiences, besides writing in the press. When *The Times* published two articles of mine on psychic phenomena I had so many letters, running into hundreds, that I had to seek extra secretarial help. Among the correspondents were Sir Alister Hardy, the Professor of Zoology at Oxford, President of the Society for Psychical Research, and the director of the religious experience research unit at Manchester College, Oxford. He invited me to a private weekend conference in Gloucestershire which did much to help me sort out my ideas.

There are three basic questions.

1. Is it possible when making observations to by-pass the normal mental processes, which are rooted in a verifiable physical world?
2. Is the concept of a psi-component, existing independently of flesh and blood a valid one?
3. Does the psi-component, if it exists, survive the disintegration of the body at death?

I admit that what is usually regarded as reliable proof under test conditions is not easy to obtain. The imponderables are too many. As matters stand we must be content with signposts and not conclusions.

I am often asked whether I am 'psychic', but I find it a difficult question to answer as I believe most of us have occasional experiences or extra-sensory perception. We 'know' things without going through the usual processes of thought, and we make decisions because we have been 'prompted' to a conclusion.

Let me begin with intuition, or telepathy, though both are question-begging words which cannot be satisfactorily defined. Sometimes I know the contents of a letter before I open the envelope, or I know what a person will say to me before he speaks. Of course it may be intelligent guesswork at the subconscious level, but that does not explain everything. I give two examples. The first concerns a priest in Southwark who came to see me at his own request. As he entered my study I said, "I know what you want to tell me. You are about to become engaged." He was astonished. So was I. I knew nothing of his matrimonial affairs, nor that he was interested in a particular girl. The only light I can throw on the incident is that these hunches occur more frequently when I have kept my rule of silent meditation in the early morning. Perhaps silence increases sensitivity.

Meditation does not account for the second example. It was a Saturday night in 1956 when I was vicar of the University Church. I had been asleep for two or three hours when I awoke with a sense of horror. I was so frightened that I turned on the light. One thing was clear to me—I must call on the dean of King's College as soon as possible. I got up early and arrived at the college gates soon after eight o'clock. I was met by the porter who said that the dean had committed suicide during the night by throwing himself from the turret of the chapel.

Some years later I was told by two people living in Cambridge at the time that they too had woken up terrified. All three of us could claim to be no more than casual acquaintances of the dean.

Intuition leads to another aspect of the psi-factor, precognition, from the perception of what is happening to the perception of what will happen.

The crudest form for precognition is the booth at the fun-fair—usually nonsense. Most of the palmist's prophecies deal with marriage and money. On a Brighton pier, for instance, I was told to withdraw proceedings against my wife and to return to her and my three children immediately. Poor comfort for a bachelor! But it is not always rubbish. Before I was ordained, still an undergraduate at Cambridge, I was told by a gipsy in the Isle of Man that I would finish in the House of Lords, sitting near the throne. Even if as a young man I had had dreams of episcopal purple, I had never set foot in the House of Lords, nor did I know that the bishops' bench was close to the throne.

Precognition is not confined to fun-fairs. It needs to be treated seriously. Why is it that some people can look into the future? More important, to what extent are our futures predetermined?

Turning from what is happening and what may happen to what has happened, I think that people with a developed psi-faculty are capable of tuning into the sub-conscious or into a 'pool of memory'.

When I have engaged in tests I usually give to the medium, or whatever name is the most appropriate to describe a person who is a developed psychic, a sealed envelope containing the name of the person who may be dead or alive. Time and again I have had detailed descriptions of things we have done together, places visited and people met, perhaps thirty years ago, perhaps only a month previously. The quick explanation is that the medium gets the information from my sub-conscious. Perhaps so. But nobody has yet defined adequately the sub-conscious, or explained how knowledge is extracted from it.

The alternative solution may be 'the pool of memory', a pool with which all can be linked as donors and recipients. In this pool is a continuing existence of all that has happened. I think of it as a vast library of television recordings which, under certain conditions, appear on the screen.

Perhaps that explains the ghost or apparition at Bishop's House. I saw the apparition twice—an elderly, sad-looking woman. I doubt whether 'it' was a contemporary happening, i.e. the spirit of the person today; more likely 'it', as in other hauntings, is the tangible expression of a memory which is contained within the pool and becomes identified with a particular place.

I asked my friend, Tom Corbett, who has a developed psi-faculty, to visit the house. He described the woman as I had seen her, told me she had come from overseas, and pointed correctly to the room in which she had appeared to me.

When I mentioned this in a newspaper article, an elderly woman in Dublin wrote to tell me that during the First World War she had lived opposite my house and had got to know a Polish refugee who was given hospitality by the people who used to live there. She added that the refugee was a woman who longed to return to her country and was unhappy in London.

I was interested in the apparition and was planning to make a careful study of her and, if possible, to take photographs. Unfortunately I had to exorcise her. Munir, an Arab from Jerusalem, had just joined my household. Although I never mentioned the apparition to him he became convinced there was a ghost in the house. I treated the matter lightly, but as the weeks went by I realised that he would not remain unless I 'did something'. As it is easier to obtain the services of a new ghost than those of a new cook, 'do something' I did—and Munir remained for many years.

I turn to the more controversial aspect of the psi-component; does it enable us to communicate with the dead, or—as I prefer to say—with those who because they have broken free from the limitations of their physical bodies, like a butterfly from a chrysalis, are more alive than we are? I believe the answer is yes. But first let us deal with three points about which there is misunderstanding and prejudice.

First, the phrase 'communicate with the dead' raises a host of irrational fears. It suggests darkness, witches, Macbeth! It need not mean any of these things. When I 'talk' with those who have passed to a fuller life I usually do so in broad daylight, through a friend who has developed a psi-faculty and to whom the next dimension is an inescapable reality as it was, for instance, to St Paul or Joan of Arc. We sit facing one another and the psychic describes the people he can see around me and reports their conversations. It is as un-emotional as filling in an income-tax return, though less complicated! Only occasionally does the medium go into a trance.

Secondly, it is said that to become involved in communications with the dead means necromancy and evil spirits. Not necessarily; it depends upon motives. If a person dabbles in these matters for the wrong reasons there may be trouble. In fact I cannot stress too strongly the folly of those who for kicks consult dubious mediums and the so-called 'witches' who traffic in black magic. There are depraved personalities in every sphere of existence who are always ready to destroy us. If we look for them, we shall find them on both sides of the grave. There are enough evil-intentioned persons in this world without seeking out their counterparts, perhaps potentially more dangerous, in the next. I have seen the results among groups of young people who thought that table-turning, Black Masses and the invoking of Satan constituted a lark. On one occasion I was asked by the police to help in a town in the diocese where devil worship had become the latest craze. The results were not pleasant. For whatever reason two of the youths died within a matter of months and a third became mentally disturbed. Psi-investigation is a serious matter and demands as much discipline as any other branch of scientific inquiry.

Thirdly, sceptics emphasise the banality of the alleged communications. If people survive death, it is argued, they ought to have something better to discuss than the trivia of their former lives. Perhaps so; but what else could they talk about that we should understand? Reunions are usually retrospective and boring, as any old boys' association knows. Since leaving school, university or regiment the members have little in common. To keep the conversation going they have to look back. Inevitably the recurring question "Do you remember . . .?" is the point of meeting.

And there is another difficulty. Just as it would be impossible for a child who had left the womb to describe earth conditions to a child still in the womb—supposing such a ridiculous situation to be possible—so is it illogical to suppose that a man who has discarded his physical body and entered a new dimension can speak coherently to a man who is ignorant of his experiences.

When I try to write of my experiences of 'communication' I am in a predicament. Some of the communicators have been well known in public life, while others have been unknown except to a small entourage; but both have relatives who might be distressed. Reticence is inevitable and I must confine myself to examples which will, I hope, cause pain to nobody. In some instances I have changed names.

1. When I sit with a sensitive I am usually told my father wants to speak to me. He joined the army in the First World War. He was killed in 1916 when I was three. Apart from two or three memories, he is almost unknown to me. It may sound hard, but I feel about him what most of us feel about an unknown grandfather. How could it be otherwise? Yet I have received from him detailed information about persons and things which occurred in his lifetime before I was born, which meant nothing to me but which, upon enquiry, proved to be correct. The few communications I have had with my mother, who died at a great age, were more vivid and detailed. But I was less impressed because the medium may have got the facts from my sub-conscious, whereas in my father's case this was not possible.

2. A medium, who was unknown to me and who was under the impression that I was someone else, told me in trance that a relative of mine, a priest, who did not live in England, had died of a lung disease. The only priest in the family apart from myself was Charles Stockwood, the Archdeacon of the Isle of Man. I had no idea he had been ill and was planning to spend my summer holidays with him and my aunt. When I reached my vicarage in Cambridge on the following day there was a telegram from my aunt. I instantly phoned her. The medium was right. He had died of a lung disease just before

I had the sitting, but news of his death had not reached England, or been published on the island.

3. Mr and Mrs Jones, as I shall call them, had been happily married for many years. He was a wealthy and distinguished businessman, she was a charming hostess who knew how to spend his money. He died, and she did not know how to cope. When I was sitting with the medium he 'came through', giving me precise details about the disposal of his property and private papers and mentioned by name people of whom I have never heard. He asked me to pass on this information to his wife. Mrs Jones, to her subsequent advantage, followed his advice.

4. A vicar in Southwark died of a heart attack in his early forties. I buried him. Some months later his successor complained of odd happenings—noises, footsteps, crying. I went to the vicarage with a friend who had a developed psi-faculty. He told me that the dead man—of whom he knew nothing—was deeply troubled because, although he had given the impression of being a faithful parish priest, he had in fact been involved in all sorts of tragic practices. I found the story difficult to believe as it was out of keeping with everything I knew about him, but when I made enquiries I discovered it was all too true.

5. A canon of the Cathedral died in a motor crash; the circumstances were unusual. He was a brilliant and gifted man, but he had a prickly and a cruel tongue which caused many problems. In my sermon at the Requiem Mass I restricted myself to his good points. When a few months later he 'came through' he gave me details of the fatal accident and then added with characteristic humour and cynicism, "I attended my funeral service in the Cathedral. I enjoyed your sermon, but I didn't recognise myself in your description of me."

6. The final example is different from the others. No medium is involved and no message. Just a strange occurrence. Among my friends none was more amusing and outrageous than Richard Blake Brown. As a theological student he went to a garden party given by the Chancellor of Oxford University for Ambassadors, Cabinet Ministers and top brass. For a while he had been with the Old Vic and had acquired an ability for impersonation. On this occasion he dressed up as the wife of a diplomat from a little known country and apologised to the Chancellor for the absence of 'her' husband on account of illness. This was typical. I knew Richard for forty years and every encounter was hilarious. As an undergraduate he had been at Magdalene College, Cambridge with Norman Hartnell who was to become famous as a dress designer. It was because of my friendship

with Richard that as a young man in my twenties I got to know Norman. When he died in 1979 I buried him and preached at the memorial service in Southwark Cathedral. The following March, Norman's successor, George Mitchison, invited me to make use of Norman's house at Ascot for the weekend. Everything was as it had been on the day that Norman died. On the Friday night Andrew Henderson, an old friend from University Church days, stayed with me. When we were sitting around the fire after dinner a jade ornament at the end of the mantelpiece suddenly fell on the floor. Andrew, even more of a sceptic than myself, thought it was due to the heat of the fire. On the Sunday the Bishop of Woolwich, Michael Marshall and the Bishop of Kingston, Keith Sutton, joined me for what was alleged to be a staff meeting. Again we were sitting around the fire and, in passing, I told them about the jade ornament and Friday's happening. Almost immediately it descended on to the floor a second time. Perhaps it was the heat of the fire, perhaps it was coincidence, but I would not put it beyond Richard Blake Brown, who had died a few years previously. It was precisely the sort of thing he would do—and, with Norman's approval—just for the fun of it!

It would be misleading to suggest that all sittings have been as impressive. Quite the contrary. I have attended seances which have been an insult to the intelligence, a fraudulent and shameful exploitation of grief and ignorance. At least these bogus mediums should be required to enter their doubtful gains on their income-tax returns, as they must get away with a tidy packet.

As an example, when I was vicar of the University Church a well known medium, who produced voices and physical effects, had a seance in the town. Trumpets whizzed, lights fluttered, bells sounded, a child-spirit moaned sentimental ditties. The medium belched 'ectoplasm'. Some months later I was in Brighton and seeing an announcement of the medium's performance paid up and went. It was a repeat performance word for word.

Soon after my arrival in Southwark I was asked to meet a man who was supposed to be exceptional—he was indeed in matters of fraud and bluff. The lights went out, and a luminous trumpet came through the air, allegedly on its own initiative and rested on my lap. I broke the rules. Instead of keeping my hands linked with those on either side, I grasped the end of the trumpet. The medium, who had left his chair, was holding the trumpet and my hand collided with his. He quickly dropped the trumpet and collapsed into his chair. The seance came to an end. Later at supper he looked a little embarrassed as I fixed my eyes on him over the prawn cocktail.

The third example concerns Cosmo Lang, the Archbishop of Canterbury who had been involved in the abdication of Edward VIII. I was told that the late Primate had a message for the Church of England and had spoken through a physical medium. It was thought that as a bishop I should make it known. A tape had been made. I was assured that his voice was astonishingly life-like. I agreed to listen to the tape, but as I was doubtful about anybody's ability to express an opinion on the tone of voice of a man long dead, I took the precaution of obtaining from the BBC a recording of Lang's Abdication sermon. The two voices had nothing in common. Nor had the grammar. I do not believe that the intentions of those who wished to win my support for the authenticity of the tape were anything but honourable—but it just shows how necessary it is to approach the subject with a questioning mind, and to be inclined to believe nothing unless otherwise convinced.

In the light of these contrasting experiences, do I believe in life after death? I do, while recognising that it is difficult to distinguish between an existing entity and a materialisation from a possible pool of memory. In giving this answer, I write as a private individual who has tried to make an honest appraisal of psychical research, leaving my religious convictions on one side. If I were asked to express my views as a committed Christian I should express myself differently. For reasons which have little or nothing to do with psychical phenomena but are rooted in my faith, I believe, *ex animo*, in "the resurrection of the dead, and the life of the world to come." In any case 'survival' has little in common with what Scripture means by 'eternal life'. The latter is something which is experienced now and brought to fruition later.

What do I mean by life after death? A former Dean of St Paul's, Dr W. R. Matthews, who was a helpful friend to me on my pilgrimage, puts it thus: "We cannot say much about the spiritual body because we cannot imagine what it would be like to have a body different from that which we now inhabit, but it seems to me reasonable to believe that we are now weaving our spiritual bodies as we go along. They are being formed by our thoughts and acts of will and imagination during this life."

This is not incompatible with a view I expressed some years ago and to which I still adhere: "I am inclined to believe that personality expresses itself through two bodies—a carnal body of flesh and blood and a spiritual, or, as some would call it, an etheric body,

179

which, penetrating the carnal body and transcending our earthly limitations, acts as an intermediary between two dimensions. And I further believe that in the process of death the etheric body disengages itself from the carnal body and is set free for the next stage of its development."

At a London technical college I was asked: "Does a belief in a future life give you comfort and does it strengthen your religious convictions?" Whether or not it brings comfort depends upon values, priorities and motives. If we think in terms of progress and evolution I want to break free from the imprisonment of the body and to experience the splendour of another dimension—with more dimensions, up or down, to follow. But I have no desire to survive if the disappointments, the sadnesses and the heartbreaks of this world, which inevitably increase with the passing of the years, are to be projected into the next.

As for religion, I doubt whether psychical phenomena much affect it. If a man, contrary to his expectations, finds himself continuing after death in another sphere of activity it does not follow he will be led to a belief in God. He will recognise his new status as a fact, without necessarily placing a theistic interpretation upon it. The acceptance of the reality of God depends upon other factors. What psychical investigation can do is to drive a coach and four through a crudely materialistic view which assumes that life on this planet is the sum total of human experience; instead of seeing it as part of something greater in the context of an evolutionary process and of an extension of personal and collective consciousness. As the philosopher Dr C.E.M. Joad said, when reflecting on this subject: "If these things are true then the universe must in some respects be totally other than what one is accustomed to suppose."

Perhaps the most valuable outcome of my interest in psychical affairs and of my experience is the sensitivity to help the bereaved. Time and again people at every level of society have come to me in their grief for a word of comfort and healing. If they are believing Christians, I turn to Scripture and remind them of the wonderful Biblical promises. But most are not believing Christians and in their moments of agonising despair they want reassurance of another sort. The fact that I have been able to tell them that I believe I have had communications with people in another dimension has given them hope, and the strength to pick themselves up to start again. And it is not only the unbelieving. Even those who put their signature to the creeds can be shattered by grief. A brother bishop, now dead, of conservative views, after a meeting at Lambeth, sought

180

me out and said, "Mervyn, tell me, do you think I shall ever see Mary (a fictional name) again? Do you really believe there's another life? Mervyn, help me." He cried in despair; so did I in sympathy. If the reader thinks this is an extravagant story I could mention similar instances from among my people in East Bristol, the dons in Cambridge, the members of all parties in the House of Lords. Death and grief are levellers. And so is the loving sympathy which tries to heal the wounds.

I find it difficult to understand why many students of Scripture keep psychic studies at arm's length because the Bible is packed with illustrations in both the Old and New Testaments. To mention but two, the Transfiguration and the Resurrection. In the first instance we have clairvoyance and clairaudience. The disciples saw Jesus with Moses and Elijah, both of whom were dead, and heard him communicating with them. If that is not some sort of seance I do not know what is. In the second, Jesus appeared to his disciples after his crucifixion, talked and apparently ate with them, and yet passed through doors and disappeared. I do not find these incidents difficult to accept. There are so many worlds inter-penetrating one another. Perhaps Jesus could move freely among them, able to transmute the instrument of expression, his body, in such a way that he was recognisable at each dimensional level.

My interest in the psi-faculty was a help to me when the charismatic movement hit this country. For those who have not had the experience of pentecostalism, let me give a brief explanation. Many things happened in the Church in New Testament times which people brought up in traditional ways do not expect to happen now—speaking with tongues, the interpretation of tongues, prophesying, casting out devils, miracles of healing. If they think about them at all they believe them to be untrue, or as evidence of unwholesome hysteria. The opposite view is that on the first Pentecost the Holy Spirit became so active among the first Christians that all these unusual happenings were manifestations of His abiding power. Holders of this view point to periods in the history of the Church when there were similar manifestations. They expect them to occur now. And, in their opinion, occur they do.

In the early 1960s I found a few clergy and laity speaking in tongues, interpreting tongues, prophesying and holding healing services and practising exorcisms. As one of them put it to me, "When we pray 'Come Holy Spirit, Our souls inspire and lighten with Celestial Fire,' we really expect something to happen. It is as though we are electrified by the power of the Holy Spirit."

181

The numbers grew. I knew it was my duty as diocesan bishop to work with them. The bishop is the focal point of unity and no matter how the spokes of Anglicanism may seem to differ—High, Low, Middle, Catholic, Protestant, Modernist—he must be the hub into which all fit. Now there was the new Pentecostal spoke.

The group came regularly to Bishop's House for prayer, Bible study, discussion and meals. I attended their services. Although I am too much of a traditionalist to feel completely at home in their methods of worship with the guitars, choruses, physical jerks and the uninhibited acclamations and other manifestations of religious fervour, I was impressed by their sincerity and above all by their commitment to Christ. Enthusiasm may not be a characteristic of the Anglican tradition, but these people had such an enthusiastic belief in the Holy Spirit and His pentecostal gifts that lives were changed and parishes revitalised.

Twice a year they had a pentecostal Eucharist for anybody in the diocese who might be interested. Hundreds attended and I usually celebrated. As they had an insatiable appetite for lengthy services, I left it to them to conduct the first and third hours. I appeared for the middle hour, during which I performed the essential parts of the Mass. After distributing the Sacrament, I anointed with oil, or laid hands on anybody who came forward. This was an interesting mixture of traditions. The pentecostalists usually laid hands on those who sought a gift of the Holy Spirit, just as a bishop does in confirmation. I was glad to follow their custom, but I sometimes feared that the less well instructed might regard it as a second, or superior 'confirmation'. I preferred anointing as I had learnt it in the Eastern Orthodox Church. Whereas in the West anointing is usually reserved for the sick and dying, in the East it is available at all times. The sole condition is that the recipient should desire to be strengthened by the Holy Spirit. A man might drop into a church to be anointed because it is his birthday, the anniversary of his wedding, because he is ill, sad or glad, because he wants to pull himself together and make a fresh start.

Believing as I do in the inter-penetration of dimensions, I regard the sacrament of anointing, or to give it its proper name 'unction', as a symbolic gateway into the area in which the Holy Spirit operates for particular purposes. The word 'charisma' is carelessly used. A charismatic person is usually regarded as exceptional. That should not be so in the case of Christians. All of us who have been baptised in the Holy Spirit should bear His charisma, and it is His charisma that should mark us out as different.

When I took leave of the diocese in 1980 I spent two days in each of the twenty-one deaneries. At the main service I provided an opportunity for unction. I must have anointed hundreds of people. It was my hope to bequeath to my successor a spirit-filled diocese. I shall always be grateful to our pentecostalists for the contribution they made. A bishop has two strips hanging down on the back of his mitre. They are supposed to represent the tongues of flame which came upon the disciples of the first Pentecost. In short, as a successor of the Apostles he should incarnate and mediate the pentecostal experience. He should bring fire to frozen hearts and energy to drooping spirits. And what is rightly expected of him should be expected of all Christians. No wonder Pope John prayed that the Church should be hit by a new Pentecost and that it should begin with the person who offered the prayer.

I had hoped that my closing years in Southwark might have been free from the controversies which had characterised the earlier period. But it was not to be.

On reflection I do not regret the explosion over the issuing of the Archbishops' pastoral letter and my reaction to it, unpleasant as it was, because it gave me the opportunity to explain and try to defend my attitude towards the political involvement.

Donald Coggan and I had been good friends for many years and I welcomed his appointment to Canterbury in 1975. I think he would agree with me in saying that he, Jean his wife, and I had a close and affectionate relationship. I saw more of him than of his predecessors. When he returned from his long and exacting journeys overseas, I invariably arranged for a bottle of iced champagne to await him on the steps of Lambeth Palace—just as I had for Michael Ramsey.

Donald and I had different ecclesiastical backgrounds. He was basically an Evangelical who had broadened with the passage of years, whereas I had started as a High Churchman who had moved to a more central position. Although both of us were non-party men, our origins did not desert us. Donald retained his evangelical enthusiasm for what seemed to me to be a near-Billy-Graham attitude towards organised missions for personal conversion. I had my doubts about such missions. I thought they were too simplistic in their approach. As Archbishop of York he was responsible for an evangelical crusade, *The Call to the North*; when he moved to Canterbury he and his successor at York initiated a similar campaign for the whole country. Unfortunately the Archbishops drew up their message to the nation without consulting their colleagues. When they informed us of their decision, some of us expressed our concern and urged a reconsideration. We accepted the view that the Archbishops had the right to address the nation, but we thought that, as the whole Church of England was involved, the bishops, some of whom had had long experience, should be given an opportunity to discuss the document before it was issued. After all, it is said that even the Pope, who claims at times to be infallible, consults his Curia before issuing important statements!

When the call to the nation was made public, the inevitable happened. I did my best to defend the Archbishop on television against the Left Wing critics, one of whom described him as a 'trade-union basher'. I admitted that he had by-passed the grave social ills in society and had not emphasised sufficiently the factor of economic circumstances in determining man's conduct. The attack on Donald Coggan continued in the socialist press. On October 17th Gordon McLennan, the General Secretary of the Communist party, wrote to me enclosing an editorial from the *Morning Star* of the previous day which had launched a savage attack: "It would have been much more in the interests of the working people, and indeed of the Church if Dr Coggan had taken the opportunity of the present grim situation in relation to unemployment, cuts in the social services and lowering of living standards. The tone and content of his appeal can only be interpreted as indicating he is taking the side of the Establishment, of the rich and big business."

In my reply to Gordon McLennan I said, "I have sympathy with what you say but I do not think you are altogether fair to the Archbishop of Canterbury. I readily agree with your main thesis but I am sure we cannot ignore the personal issues that Dr Coggan has in mind. Knowing Dr Coggan as well as I do I am sure that he had no intentions to bash the trade unions or to set his imprimatur upon a capitalist society. Nevertheless I agree that his words were capable of such an interpretation. Perhaps he does not share the view which you and I hold that the patterns of society and of morality are largely determined by economic situations. If you think an article along the lines of this letter would help I should be glad to write something for the *Morning Star*."

I passed copies of the correspondence to the Archbishop and in my letter to Donald Coggan I said, "As you may know I had a difficult time on Thames Television with the trade unionists. Their denunciations were vigorous and unfair. I subsequently had a more kindly letter from Gordon McLennan, the Secretary of the Communist party. He is a man for whom I have considerable regard and have complete trust in his integrity."

On October 31st my article appeared in the *Morning Star*. Here it is:

The Archbishop of Canterbury's pastoral letter spotlights a basic problem for all who are concerned for the future of Britain. I regard the letter as unsatisfactory and I wish it had not been issued in its present form.

Having said that, there is no point in being rude to Dr Coggan: instead, let's keep a cool temper and make a dispassionate criticism.

The Archbishop has taken a look at our country and there is a lot going on in it that he doesn't like, violence, baby-bashing, mugging, widespread burglaries, stealing, drug taking, alcoholism.

Dr Coggan is not alone. Any serious-minded person must be worried about the decadent features in our society.

Moreover those of us who have visited socialist countries in Europe know that if a communist Government were to be established in Britain the West End would be cleared up overnight and the ugly features of our permissive society would be changed within a matter of days. And heaven help the porn merchant and all engaged in the making of fortunes through the commercial exploitation of sex.

Having conceded this much to Dr Coggan we must go on to ask why people behave like this. Of course there are bad apples in every basket. There always have been and probably always will be. And they are to be found in the U.S. and Europe just as they are in the Soviet Union and China.

But, and this is the vital point which Dr Coggan seems to overlook, a man's character, be it good or bad, is partly if not largely determined by his environment, by the social and economic circumstances in which he is placed.

My favourite flower is a camellia. I have half a dozen lovely shrubs in my garden bearing red or white flowers similar to roses in January and the early spring. My friends admire them but often add plaintively, "we tried to grow them but they died." I'm not surprised. Camellias are difficult to grow as they need the appropriate soil and they must be safeguarded against the rigours of the climate. Human beings are like camellias in that they need the proper soil and the proper conditions if they are to ripen and mature.

Now let the Archbishop and the rest of us have a look at Britain and ask whether our society provides the right soil for the growth of the citizens. In my judgment the answer is emphatically no.

An economic system which is based on selfishness and greed and which leads to class divisions, injustice and unemployment is bound to produce social chaos.

It is this system, more than any other single factor, that is producing the evils that Dr Coggan so greatly deplores. If he is right in thinking that our country is heading for disaster let him draw the attention of the nation to the system that is largely responsible for it.

I live in South London and I am well aware of the mugging and the violence. Not for one moment do I try to condone what happens: it is wicked and innocent people suffer.

But those responsible for these atrocities are often youths who have grown up in overcrowded homes, are unemployed and feel that they have no stake in the country.

Not long ago a former Cabinet Minister was denouncing the miners for what he considered to be extravagant wage demands. A few days later we learned he himself had received a golden handshake of more than £150,000 via the Cayman Islands. That is a parable of our sociey.

And so long as it remains true there is little hope for the future of our country. It is only when the people of Britain know that the country really belongs to us and that all of us have a stake in its future that we shall achieve our true destiny.

Meanwhile I have no intention in shoring up a society which because of its basic injustices is at last crumbling in ruins.

On the following day, the article was given priority treatment in news bulletins and an outraged article appeared in *The Times* under the heading "Sad, Silly and Wrong". As far as I could make out, little attention, if any, had been given to what I had said. What caused the fury was the fact that I had criticised the Archbishop and had published the criticism in the *Morning Star* rather than in a respectable paper like *The Times*, the *Daily Telegraph*, or possibly the *Guardian*.

Private letters of abuse poured in to Bishop's House, the subject engaged the attention of editors, and the correspondence columns of *The Times* continued the battle for nearly a fortnight, and graffiti appeared on the walls of churches where I was booked to speak. There was a motion of disapproval in the House of Commons, sponsored by many Conservative members, and I was denounced in the House of Lords by a Tory peer. And a brother diocesan bishop refused to eat with me, although he had accepted an invitation to do so. Of course I had my supporters, but for the most part they were unaccustomed to write letters to the quality press.

On November 3rd I replied to the Editor of *The Times*. Here is the letter:

Sir,

Your leading article, "Sad, Silly and Wrong" is before me. I can only assume that you never read my piece in the *Morning Star* or if you did that you jumped to conclusions before you had studied it.

Let me put the record straight by giving you the facts which you would have obtained from me had you wished to do your homework.

You wonder why I chose to write to the *Morning Star*. Here is the answer: on the night of Dr Coggan's first broadcast I was asked by Thames Television to discuss it. One of the participants made a fierce denunciation of Dr Coggan and described him as a "trade union basher". As the Secretary of the Communist party lives in my diocese I sent him a letter in which I wrote: "I do not think you are altogether fair to the Archbishop of Canterbury. Knowing Dr Coggan as well as I do I am sure he had no intention to bash the trade unions or to set his imprimatur on a capitalist society." And then I added, "Perhaps he does not share the views which you and I hold that patterns of society and of morality are largely determined by economic situations." I concluded by offering to write an article to clear these points and I sent a copy of my letter to Mr McLennan to the Archbishop of Canterbury with a covering note. The fact that I wrote for the *Morning Star* no more implies that I identify myself with its editorial policy than it does when I write for *The Times*, the *Daily Telegraph*, or the *Evening Standard*.

Now I turn to your main criticism and to your implications that I am a supporter of the communist régimes.

1. Dr Coggan called for a return to moral standards. I agree with him, but I believe that his appeal will have little response at certain levels unless we attend to two matters in our society.

a) We must stop the exploitation of human weakness for financial profit. Most of us find it difficult to be good even in the best circumstances; how much more difficult it is when we are encouraged in the opposite direction. For instance,

187

The Exorcist may be a money-spinning film for the promoters, but it has done immeasurable harm. Only last week a murderer attributed an act of violence to it. We already have censorship in this country, but those who are supposed to act for our well-being seem to have some curious standards.

b) We must alter the social and economic conditions which make for irresponsibility and ugly behaviour. If Dr Coggan and I, and even you, Mr Editor, had grown up in an overcrowded room in a house teeming with several families, and if, after an inadequate education, we had found ourselves unemployed and among London's thousands of homeless, I doubt whether a pious tract or a moral pep talk would have made much impression on us, and even the freedom to express our views in Hyde Park and to demonstrate against the Government would not necessarily make us worthwhile supporters of our democracy.

2. With regard to the communist régimes. I made a statement of fact. I said that if a communist régime were to be established in Britain, the West End and the porn merchants would be out of a job. In saying this I neither approved nor disapproved the communist régime. It so happens that I have on many occasions spoken against Soviet tyranny and the Police State and the suppression of personal freedom. In fact, because of my denunciation of the Russian invasion of Czechoslovakia in my speech in the House of Lords, as reported in Hansard, I have been on the Soviet blacklist for several years, and, unlike some of my critics, who do not hesitate to go to the Russian Embassy for their receptions, I am no longer invited.

3. The fact that I deplore so many things in our society, be it homelessness, unemployment, social injustice or—as we witnessed last week—the spraying of poison on thousands of tons of fruit to prevent people from eating it, does not mean that I want the Kremlin to occupy Downing Street. What it does mean is that I want our country to learn from other systems—communist, non-communist and Mr Dubček's socialism with a human face— and to press ahead with the re-formation of our own society, so that its values approximate more closely to those of the Kingdom of which Jesus spoke, and for which he died.

Yours truly

+ MERVYN SOUTHWARK

Some of my colleagues, including the present Archbishop of Canterbury, Robert Runcie, sent me kindly letters. Others who were as opposed as I was to the issuing of the Call of the two Archbishops regretted that I had criticised the Primate in public, more precisely in the *Morning Star*, a newspaper which in most instances I suspect they had never seen, still less read.

The idea that a bishop must not criticise the opinions of his Archbishop is entirely new and contrary to tradition. I doubt if it goes back further than the reign of Archbishop Fisher, who by nature and profession was a headmaster who strongly resented criticism, especially by the bishops, whom he regarded as his housemasters. But I was old enough to remember the arguments, sometimes fierce, that took place between Hensley Henson of Durham, Headlam of Gloucester and Barnes of Birmingham with successive Archbishops of Canterbury and York.

And it is worth quoting a passage from the biography of Charles Gore, Bishop of Oxford and perhaps one of the greatest and most saintly bishops that the Church of England has ever had: "The Archbishop (Randall Davidson), whom I love and also disagree with, exercises a paralysing influence over the bishops," he wrote. And then the biographer G. L. Prestige adds: "Gore was seen on one occasion standing on the summit of Lambeth Bridge against a sombre sunset, shaking his fist at Lambeth Palace, to the open-mouthed amazement of passing Londoners, and crying, 'As for the bishops, they are hopeless; I have done with them.'"

As for the impropriety of writing in the *Morning Star*, the critics were somewhat embarrassed when a second episcopal article appeared in its columns a few months later: not by me, but by Donald Coggan. Some weeks later Lord Selwyn Lloyd, who had been the Speaker of the House of Commons, told me that when he had met the previous Archbishop, Michael Ramsey, in a country lane in Oxfordshire Ramsey said without warning, "I think Mervyn has come rather well out of it, yes rather well." But, after all, it was Michael Ramsey who, when I had consulted him as Archbishop of York about going to Southwark, had said that if I did decide to accept he would be glad because he would know that, "There would be somebody on the bench who would say 'no, no' when the rest of us, like sheep are saying 'yes, yes, yes'."

I did not enjoy the controversy. It was particularly vicious and personally hurtful. What worried me more was the realisation that the Church of England was still inextricably bound up with the Establishment, the Conservative party and the middle classes. Most of the letters of support came from what is loosely called 'working class' which has little to do with the Church and is rarely represented on its councils and committees.

The happy memory is that the incident caused no rupture in my relationship with the Archbishop. Within weeks he and his wife came to Bishop's House for luncheon. What is more, when he spoke at the Lord Mayor's Dinner in the Mansion House he stressed the need to take seriously the social implications of the Gospel. In fact it cemented our friendship. When I next attended the General Synod, the press speculated on a confrontation between the two of us. It was to be disappointed, for, as one reporter put it, "There is obviously a close bond between Canterbury and Southwark. I saw an affectionate glance pass between them as the bishop took his seat." That may well be true, but I am not so sure of the reason. My attendances at the General Synod were so rare that Donald always gave me a modest smile of welcome mingled with surprise when we spotted one another.

Another outcome of this controversy was my book *The Cross and the Sickle*. David Owen, the Foreign Secretary, wrote the preface and I dedicated it to "Donald Coggan, friend and colleague for many years".

The controversy had displayed an almost total ignorance of Marxism, and in many cases of the Christian Gospel. When I asked a group of critics to meet at Bishop's House I began the discussion by asking them to define the two words 'Marxist' and 'Christianity'. There was an embarrassing silence. There were vague mutterings about the Soviet Union and the iniquities of Stalin. I countered by saying that their remarks were about as relevant as if I were to talk about the Vatican and the Borgias. I insisted that we had met to consider intelligently two philosophies, and unless they were prepared to do so it would be more profitable to go to the next room for refreshments and to have a general chit-chat on the prospectus of the dollar versus sterling versus the rouble. After a rambling and ill-informed, if not ludicrous conversation we sank our differences "with beaded bubbles winking at the brim and purple stained mouth and they left the world unseen to fade away into the forest dim" of Fleet Street. (I hope John Keats will forgive me for confusing nightingales with cuckoos!)

Keats ends his ode with the words "Do I wake or sleep?" That is how I felt. I found it difficult to believe that men who held important and lucrative positions could be so abysmally obtuse. Perhaps they could be excused for failing to brush up their knowledge of Marxist

190

philosophy before they met me for serious debate, but at least I expected them to understand the Christian doctrine they said I was betraying. Not only did not one of them know what was meant by 'dialectical materialism', 'the inter-penetration of opposites', 'the negation of the negation', 'quantitive and qualitative change', but they were as ignorant of the Christian vocabulary—'incarnation', 'atonement', 'pentecost', 'justification by faith'. For these reasons I decided to write a book explaining as objectively and as simply as I could the two philosophies and the differences between them—a plain man's guide. Hence *The Cross and the Sickle*.

My final controversy as Bishop of Southwark, though that is too strong a word, was prior to the General Election in 1979. It was of little importance and did not receive much attention. But it was significant. The *Guardian* published an article headed "Bishop's political faith wavers". In fact my political faith had not wavered, but my faith in the politicians who were supposed to implement that faith had. The reporter hit the nail on the head when he wrote, "His trust in the political wisdom of today's leaders is less certain. This election has been reduced to cash and to payments . . . Dr Stockwood believes that the electorate has to realise sooner or later that which-ever party wins on Thursday, things aren't going to change unless they themselves change." That was true. The idealism of the Labour party had been tarnished. Selfishness and greed had taken its place. So long as the bullies could maintain their standard of living, the poor and the pensioners could go to the wall. Worse still, more and more could be thrown on the slag heap of unemployment. There was a tragic lack of moral leadership. Gone were the days when the Labour party, based on the Christian ethic, stood four-square on social righteousness, integrity and goodness.

As a member of the House of Lords I had no vote. Now that I am retired I have. At the next election I shall vote for the man who approximates to a Christian socialist in his endeavours, a man like Stafford Cripps or Clem Attlee, whose approach is based on the teachings of Jesus of Nazareth, and who knows how to combine principle and conviction with tolerance and charity towards those who differ. Equally it may be a woman.

I joined the Labour party because I believed the Tories thought profits to be of more importance than people. Hence the appalling social injustices of the 1930s and the affront to man's dignity. It was different with the socialists. I felt, and I don't think it was youthful naïveté, that I had joined a crusade which was motivated by a deep concern and compassion for everybody and for the well being of our

191

country. Personal commitment to a vision of a Britain as it might be would be a useful consideration for all parties who are claiming electoral support to form a Government for a country riddled with a cancer of selfishness. As the Book of the Proverbs says, and as history has proved time and again, "Where there is no vision the people perish."

11

Resignation

A few years ago a law was made requiring a bishop to resign on reaching the age of seventy. But as it was not retrospective I could have remained indefinitely, like a certain Archbishop of Canterbury who was well into his nineties when he crowned a monarch. In fact so exhausted was he that he had to sit on the steps in Westminster Abbey to regain his breath. It is true that there are exceptions to the rule of geriatric diminution of faculties. How sad it would have been had John XXIII been denied the papacy on grounds of age. Nevertheless I am sure the alteration has been beneficial; in fact, the Church of England might be quite different from what it is if the members of the General Synod, including the bishops, accepted the retirement disciplines of the armed services and the diplomatic corps.

I did not seriously consider retirement until I went on sabbatical leave at the beginning of 1975, when I was sixty-one. Until then I assumed that I should remain at Southwark for another nine years—I had no intention of taking advantage of any privileged position. As the Church has said that seventy should be the age to quit I have no respect for the man who holds on to his job for no reason other than that he had been appointed before the new law. This meant I should leave Southwark in the summer of 1983.

In my previous year my suffragan bishops, David Sheppard of Woolwich and Hugh Montefiore of Kingston, begged me to go on sabbatical leave. They took the line that after fifteen grinding years in Southwark I ought to have six months absence. Perhaps they knew better than I how tired I was. After all, Archbishop Fisher had said that no bishop should remain in Southwark for more than twelve or thirteen years. So I agreed. I remember waking up on New Year's Day with a sense of relief. "How marvellous! no diocesan problems until July. Even if the curate runs off with the organist's wife, David and Hugh will have to cope. Better still, no ghastly synods and committees to attend with their boring wranglings."

After saying Mass in my chapel, I went off to Sussex to join David and his wife Grace to make my pilgrimage to Chanctonbury Ring.

We discussed possible moves in which he might be involved during my absence. I had been warned that he was a likely candidate for Coventry or Liverpool. Then we discussed my plans. I was off to Spain in a fortnight to Moraira, where I was to have a house party at the lovely home of my friends Philip and Susan Richardson. They had often lent me their house and I had been there with John Robinson, Hugh and Eliza Montefiore and John Betjeman. After that I was to head for China for two months to write articles for a Sunday newspaper.

Unfortunately my plans were wrecked. While I was in Spain I slipped a disc. In Moraira the neighbours allowed us to use their heated swimming pool. We went there most days. Forgetting my age I foolishly accepted a challenge to join in a race, most of the contestants being years younger than myself. The inevitable happened—I slipped a disc. The local doctor lived several miles away but he said there was a sort of nurse in Moraira who would inject me. In fact he was a burly builder and the owner of the local bulldozer. Nevertheless General Franco allowed him to jab me with a needle. I went to his small house on the quayside and waited in the passage with six other jab-seekers, among whom was the wife of one of Hitler's Admirals. When my turn came, he prepared the needle and then, just as he was about to stick it into me, put it down, took out a packet of tobacco, rolled some shreds, made a cigarette, and had a smoke. Thus encouraged he set about his work. As might be expected, there was no significant improvement. I returned to London and went to doctors and osteopaths. Occasionally there was temporary relief, but no cure. I knew that China was off and that I had to remain in England. I travelled the country visiting old friends but I had to return to London each week for treatment.

Although I kept away from diocesan affairs, I knew it would be unwise to remain at Bishop's House for Holy Week and Easter. Inevitably people, not knowing the facts, would be puzzled by my absence from the Cathedral. So I went to Walsingham, a lovely village in Norfolk where there is the famous shrine in honour of the Virgin Mary. It attracts thousands of pilgrims each year and, as at Lourdes, there is a holy well. As I was an episcopal guardian of the shrine, the Master, Colin Gill, invited me to make use of his house for a fortnight.

The purpose of my visit was to keep the most solemn period of the Christian year as a private individual. For years I had played the leading role at the great holy week ceremonies; now I had the opportunity to take a back seat as a member of the congregation.

194

Above all I wanted a fortnight's protracted silence in which to say my prayers. I had not gone to Walsingham for healing. I had already made arrangements to continue treatment on my return to London. However I went to the holy well most days, but only as an act of devotion. Be that as it may, when Easter came I was cured and put away my stick. Of course the sceptic will say that it would have happened in any case. The result would have been no different had I gone to Brighton or Benidorm. I cannot logically refute him. Nevertheless I believe it was another of those instances, to which I have already referred, of dimensions inter-penetrating one another. It could have happened at Brighton or Benidorm—possibly at Blackpool, if free from political conferences—but perhaps Almighty God in His wisdom wants us to make the effort to go on pilgrimages to sites hallowed by prayer if we are to achieve, through a receptive serenity, His healing gifts.

As my disc trouble had wrecked my plans for travelling abroad, and as I had to spend many hours lying flat on my back, I had had time to think. I had been busy for such a long time, moving from one engagement to another, to say nothing of the round of countless letters and interviews, the preparation of sermons, addresses and lectures, that I had rarely considered the deeper issues with regard to my ministry. Now was the opportunity.

It was a disturbing experience. Although I loved my pastoral work and did until the end, I felt I was being caught up into an ecclesiastical bureaucratic machine in which I believed less and less and which, alas, I almost came to hate. This is no criticism of my colleagues or those who staff the machine, many of whom are close personal friends. They are doing what they are paid to do. The fault is the machine, and the guilty are those who insist upon the retention of the machine. As Cardinal Suenens put it, "I have now come to a clearer realisation that Christianity is not an 'ism' but a someone. And that Someone is the living Jesus." To that definition I would add that, "Christianity is a way of living each minute of the day in the presence of the living God." I know every movement has to have an organisation of some sort, but as I lay on my back and turned things over in my mind it seemed that the organisation had usurped the place of God.

Part of the difficulty is that I am not an ecclesiastically minded person. I remember Bishop Wand of London saying how he looked forward to Friday mornings with eagerness as it meant the arrival of the latest copy of the *Church Times*. To me such an argument is incomprehensible. I have bought the paper from time to time to make sure that it had remembered to include my advertisment for domestic help, and occasionally to refer to an article about which I have been told, or to answer a letter, but my mind runs along another level. I doubt whether I have read more than forty copies of the paper in as many years. I am more concerned with what is happening in the secular world. If the Church is newsworthy and has done something to deserve attention the facts will reach the serious daily press.

Then I thought of the amount of time I had spent just 'keeping the show going'. I often wonder how the laity endures it. Busy men, who have little enough time with their families, are expected to hurry from work to committees and synods or parochial organisations. To what purpose? Of course I am not dismissing the necessity for some committees, but when in the war they were reduced to a minimum, it is possible the Church garnered more spiritual fruit than it does today. It certainly wasted less money and time.

Increasingly I felt a loner. I knew that basically I was bored; not with the things that Scripture associates with the ministry but with the bureaucratic machine. It was as though an ecclesiastical vampire was draining me of spiritual energy and obscuring my vision of God. To me the business of being a Christian is simple, no matter how difficult it is to apply and impossible to accomplish. It is to walk through life with the Risen Christ tabernacled in our hearts and seeking to radiate His truth, His hope, His joy, and above all His love in every situation and to everybody.

In the summer I was often alone with my thoughts on Chanctonbury Ring and I came to the conclusion that I would have to go. The question was, when? I was determined not to cause hurt. Although there was much in me that wanted to start a new life then and there, I knew that such precipitate action would be misunderstood. Moreover, while I felt suffocated by the bureaucratic octopus, my deep devotion to the Church of England was in no way impaired. Apart from anything else, the Church of England is the only Church in which I was at home, and which was generous enough to contain me. C. of E. can be interpreted in many ways. My favourite definition is Comedy of Errors. I felt myself to be contributing to the Comedy, my critics more likely thought it was to the Errors. Especially also did I consider my diocese. I loved my clergy, even if I did not like the more tiresome, and I was always glad to be with them and their people on pastoral occasions. Hence my duty to Southwark was the top priority. I decided I must remain three years, until early 1978. I would then be sixty-five and nobody would think my retirement at that age would be unreasonable. Having made the decision, I was subsequently informed there were to be great diocesan jubilee celebrations in 1980 and I was expected to lead them. My heart sank, but I knew the date of departure had to be postponed for another two years.

It is not easy for an autobiographer to know how much he should reveal of his private life, his joys and sorrows. There is a part of me that counsels reticence; there is part of me that counsels honesty. It is because some people think that bishops constitute a special breed with a privileged existence, knowing nothing of the deep inner conflicts which confront the ordinary mortal that, after much thought, I have decided to write a little of the next five years in the hope that those who go through similar experience will be encouraged. But only a little.

Having been free from the machine for six months during my sabbatical I returned to the diocese without enthusiasm. I had enjoyed my status as a backbencher in a pew, and I had revelled in my freedom to pursue interests usually denied me for lack of time. I have always loved the theatre, and Lew Grade allowed me to go to any of his theatres as his guest. Another delight was supper on Sunday nights at Lord Goodman's house. Arnold kept open house when he was in London on Sunday evenings, but I rarely went, I being busy in the diocese. During my sabbatical I made the most of the opportunity, usually accompanied by Jennie Lee, whose friendship I had enjoyed since those far off days of political campaigning during the war. Next I visited galleries and went to concerts. I have always loved painting and music, but I was abysmally ignorant. I asked a friend who was an authority on both to instruct me. He told me he considered me a willing pupil, but was aghast at my lack of knowledge, and enquired of my education. I am not surprised. Like me, he considered the public schools of my generation to be battery farms for Spartans, not Athenians.

Of the rest I single out the visits to foreign Embassies. I had often attended ambassadorial receptions but without the opportunity for serious discussion. Now I was free to spend quiet evenings with Ambassadors and members of their staffs, to ask questions and to listen. It was an enlightening experience. I also got the chance to sample the wines and delicacies of their countries. Perhaps most memorable was the Chinese Embassy. What I assumed was the entire meal proved to be no more than the first course.

During my absence David Sheppard had gone to Liverpool and I had submitted the name of Michael Marshall, vicar of All Saints',

Margaret Street, to follow him. He was young for preferment, aged thirty-nine, and he was thought to be an inflexible Anglo-Catholic. Pressure was brought upon me to reconsider my choice. I did not. I knew that Michael would provide verve and dash—as did his immediate predecessors in their different ways—John Robinson and David Sheppard. And I was aware that if I were to survive another five years I would need in the suffragan bishop of Woolwich the qualities we associate with champagne rather than plonk. Nobody could accuse Michael of plonkishness. Moreover he was not an intransigent High Churchman. Although he and I differed on some doctrinal matters, he was essentially a truly charismatic figure whose one interest was the spiritual renewal of the Church. Much the same could be said of my last episcopal nomination, Keith Sutton, to the Bishopric of Kingston. After an outstanding ministry in Uganda he became principal of Ridley Hall, the evangelical theological college in Cambridge. He was everything that was wanted in a successor to Hugh Montefiore.

Soon after my return to duty in July 1975, I was hit by a very deep depression which did not lift until after my resignation five years later. It is not easy to write about it. I seemed to be immersed in depths of despairing gloom. At night I often had a temperature and had to change my clothes because they were wet with perspiration. In the morning the temperature was back to normal and I was in my seat in chapel for Matins and Communion at 7.30 a.m. Eventually I went to my doctor who sent me to the Westminster Hospital. There was a strike among the staff over pay, and matters were made worse because the Minister involved in the dispute was due to arrive at the hospital on the same day for an operation. In fact the building was besieged with reporters. Fortunately I was in collar and tie and when a press-man, aching for a story, asked me to disclose my identity, I said I was a reporter for the *Church Times*. A nurse then whisked me out of the hospital and told me to return later when the mob had departed.

My time in hospital made no difference. The symptoms remained. Worse was to follow; I became covered with eczema. I felt like Job with his boils.

I am sure there were many causes for the depression. For the sake of those who find themselves in similar predicaments, I list the following:

1. My sabbatical had caused me to ask basic questions about my work which I was unable to answer, still less to act upon.
2. I wondered whether I should or could devote the remainder of my

life to a Church about which I had so many reservations and which seemed to obscure rather than to reveal God, His glory and His purposes. I had less and less interest in organised religion. I began to doubt whether the message of Jesus could be institutionalised.

3. Chemistry. My knowledge of medicine is negligible, but I understand that as the years pass physical chemistry can affect one's personality.

4. Loneliness. A bishop, especially an unmarried bishop, no matter how many friends he has, is necessarily a lonely person. And it is not easy for a lonely man to carry such heavy burdens for twenty years. I had had a succession of devoted domestic chaplains, most of whom had lived at Bishop's House, but I had insisted that out of working hours they should be free to enjoy their privacy in their own quarters and to live their lives independent of me. I was determined not to be a burden to them. The same was true of the other members of my household who gave me such loyal service. We were a happy household. We began each day around the dining-room table for a bible-reading and prayers, followed by a few minutes gossip and chit-chat. We always celebrated one another's birthday. The Christmas parties were remarkable and so were the summer picnics. Yes, there was a happy background, but it did not lessen the sense of ultimate isolation. Perhaps nothing does.

No matter what the reasons, I accepted the fact that just as the saints had written about the dark night of the soul so lesser struggling Christians like myself had to expect to be tested. Now that the clouds have lifted and I have found happiness and peace I am glad I was put to the test. I suspect it is the necessary price for inner serenity.

As I have said, it is difficult to write about these experiences. While passing through these bouts of deep depression I was determined to keep them to myself. I knew that if I once admitted to them it would soon be known in the diocese and become an occasion for gossip. My duty, as is the duty of all who are in positions of leadership, is to bolster morale and never to generate gloom or despondency. It means striving to have dreams in our bones instead of marrow, and hearts of bronze instead of flesh. It requires an iron personal discipline. I was not very successful in the struggle but fortunately I am a reasonably good actor and I think I got through these years without anybody knowing. I worked as hard as ever and tried to bring fun and laughter to the dozens of parties to which I went or which I continued to have at Bishop's

House. Outwardly everything was normal. Of course the depressions occasionally lifted and I regarded these times as oases from which to find refreshment for the next stretch in the desert. It was difficult and I often felt bereft. Nevertheless I was concious of some sort of divine radar that piloted me through fog and darkness.

I told the Archbishop of Canterbury in the autumn of 1978 of my intention to resign. He urged me not to do so. He thought I should remain a few years longer as he doubted whether I should be happy in my retirement. I remember Donald saying, "And you, Mervyn, of all people, to think of *you* in Bath of *all* places!"

Out of respect for him I dithered, but I knew I had to go. I found myself like a schoolboy already counting the days before the end of term and the start of the holidays. I have a clear recollection of standing in front of the mirror while shaving and shouting to the cat, "Thank God, only another five hundred days!" I felt like a caged animal in an ecclesiastical zoo.

I knew I should miss my household and the people of the diocese because I cherished my relationships with both, but one of several confirmations of my decision came in November 1978 when the General Synod 'debated' (that is scarcely the right word) the ordination of women. The synod had already determined that there was no theological objection to their ordination. It was now a question of timing. In some parts of the Anglican Communion—the United States and Canada—the practice had already started. When should the Church of England follow suit? The opponents were determined it should not. Fair enough. What appalled me was the methods used by some to achieve their ends. They joined with other members of the General Synod in praying for the guidance of the Holy Spirit but apparently had no intention of waiting upon the Holy Spirit, or of listening to the arguments, for already papers had been circulated advising fellow opponents when to applaud, when not to applaud— and much else. The fact that I was on the opposite side is of no consequence. I should have felt as appalled had we stooped so low as to give an onlooker the impression that we were not a synod seeking prayerfully as brethren to learn the will of God, but a sanhedrin of political manipulators. Of course it would be unfair to make a general condemnation. Among the opponents were people such as Graham Leonard, the present Bishop of London, who stated his case with dignity and deep spiritual conviction. He would have deplored the Tammany Hall tactics as much as I did, and there were those who came with open minds and, having listened to the

arguments, decided against. All honour to them. However it confirmed my intention. Like Gallio, "I cared for none of these things".

I waited a year before announcing my retirement; I have never
believed in lengthy engagements or disengagements. I met the press
at the end of November 1979. It was the right moment because,
although the date of my resignation was almost a year ahead, the
diocese was on the point of entering upon the jubilee year, when the
parishes, like myself, would be much too busy with the celebrations
to think about my departure. It was an exacting programme and
each week I had dozens of engagements taking me to all parts of the
diocese. The climax was the outdoor High Mass on the centre court
of Wimbledon. It was the only sheltered ground in the diocese large
enough to take such a vast congregation. As the centre court was a
sacred preserve for star tournaments, we approached the authorities,
though with little hope of success. We knew that the court had never
been used for other purposes. To our delight they said 'yes' and,
what is more, refused to charge us for it.

As I had nothing to do with the preparations for the service,
which were spread over several months, and can take no credit for
the results, I feel free to say it was as magnificent and colourful, and
yet as homely and intimate as a Communion service could be. It
happened the week after Borg had scored his triumph and one wag
put up a notice: "Borg out, Mervyn in." The efficiency was a
remarkable tribute to the organisers. Although there were more
than ten thousand communicants the administration of the Sacrament
took not more then ten minutes. There was a vast altar in the middle
of the centre court at which I, together with the suffragans and
assistant bishops, celebrated, while hundreds of priests standing at
the end of each row of the stands concelebrated with me. The
consecrated bread and wine were immediately passed along the
rows, each person communicating his neighbour.

The weatherman was to be congratulated. For days it had poured
with rain and it was still raining when I looked out from my
bedroom window on the Sunday morning, but by the time I had
dressed the rain had stopped, and through the black clouds was a
chink of light which had given way to blue skies and brilliant
sunshine by the time I reached Wimbledon. It reminded me of that
New Year's Day so long ago when on Chanctonbury Ring I had seen
the glorious sunset and the threatening storm clouds. It was a fitting
finale. Finale it was, because there was little left for me to do. I spent
much of August and September calling at the homes of the clergy
who had been with me throughout my episcopate and had become

beloved friends. In October I went to Spain for a Southwark house party at the Richardsons' home at Moraira. I returned for a farewell dinner at a livery hall, at which toasts were proposed by the Archbishop of Canterbury, Barbara Cartland and Frankie Howerd. It was followed a few days later by another memorable party given by the Provost and the Chapter. And so to the last service on the Eve of All Saints' Day in the cathedral where twenty-one years previously my ministry had started. Halfway through the Eucharist, at the Offertory, the Bishop of Woolwich presented me with a token farewell present—a double magnum of champagne. There had been many failures and disappointments, but at least I had tried to bring a little fizz into the diocese. The service ended with the processional hymn "At the Name of Jesus", sung to Elgar's music for "Land of Hope and Glory".

Next morning I slipped quietly away to Gloucestershire and to walk on the Cotswolds. The following Sunday was All Souls' Day, when I celebrated Holy Communion in a little Saxon church and preached, as circumstances dictated, on life after death. In a sense it was a present experience. The curtain had come down on forty-four years in the ministry and my official corpse had been sent to the undertakers. And that was that. But it was also a beginning. I was starting a new life and I wanted it to be as creative and exciting as it could possibly be.

Retirement is a curious business. I had a number of letters, especially from my former colleagues, commiserating with me. Two bishops told me they had never settled and pined for their dioceses. A possible explanation is that many people who have been in positions of responsibility retire to places where, in the days of great pressure, they have sought peaceful holidays—the Lake District, Dartmoor, Snowdonia. These places they recall with happiness. But to live there permanently is another matter. Too often there is nothing to do, and few people with whom to talk.

I decided to return to the West Country because my roots were there, and because I love it. I thought of living in Bristol, but it had become too big. The planners had wrecked it. And I wondered how I would cope as I grew older. Bath was the answer. Not only was it near Bristol and to friends of former years, but in my judgment it is, after Venice, the most beautiful city in Europe, even more beautiful than Florence, which I know well.

The first month or two were difficult, but not traumatic. I missed Bishop's House, especially Peter, my chaplain; Mary, my secretary for nineteen years; the faithful Munir, my chauffeur and cook;

and Maggie, the "woman that does" and who had "done" on and off since my Cambridge days at Great St Mary's. And I missed Pushkin and Midge, the cats who often slept on my bed and to whom I told the most private secrets about the clergy in my diocese, my fellow bishops and the Primate of All England. They were not particularly interested unless my stories were accompanied by saucers of milk and other goodies.

Perhaps the most difficult fact to accept was that I now had to look after myself, cope with a large correspondence, and deal with all the problems of greasy domesticity.

However I quickly adjusted. By Christmas I had become so involved in Bath that I had little time to think about London. I was appointed to the Council of Bath University and became a patron of the Theatre Royal, where an exciting reconstruction associated with the National Theatre is taking place.

As far as the Church is concerned, I help when I can, but only at the pastoral level. The Bishop of Bath and Wells, John Bickersteth, began his ministry as my curate in Bristol. Now the roles are reversed. I take confirmations on his behalf, and I enjoy taking services in village churches on the Mendip hills. I have invitations to preach in many parts of the country, especially in universities and schools.

But the greatest joy in my early days of retirement was to return to the church of my boyhood, All Saints', Clifton. The vicar had recently resigned and there was a long interregnum. For six months, beginning at Christmas, I presided at all the great festivals until the following Whitsun. My exit on the institution of the new vicar was not without amusement. The Bishop of Bristol in his announcement paid a small tribute to me: "I know you were all delighted to have Bishop Mervyn with you in recent months." I smiled, raised my mitre and thought no more of it. But at the bun-crush afterwards a man said to me, "It was a great honour to have you here tonight, my Lord. Such a step forward in the ecumenical movement! I have an even greater honour ahead of me, my Lord. Next week you are to confirm me at St Bonaventure's." Somewhat abashed, I said, "I don't think St Bonaventure is on the C. of E. calendar. I think you must be confusing me with Mervyn Alexander, the Roman Catholic Bishop of Clifton." "I apologise, my Lord." "Not at all," I said, "We are both Catholics of a sort, but he's Low and I'm High. To be precise I think I'm six inches taller."

I maintain my links with the Church overseas, and it was because of my association with the Anglican Church in the United States that I became involved in a controversy that hit the headlines of the New York press in December 1981. As the incident may be of some historical interest, here are the facts:

In 1978 I ordained Elizabeth Canham to the deaconate for work in the diocese of Southwark. She wished to proceed to the priesthood, but in England it was impossible. I told her that I was tied and bound by the rules of the General Synod.

After my resignation Elizabeth told me that she had been accepted by the Bishop of Newark, New Jersey, John Spong, as a candidate for the priesthood. In the summer of 1981 Dr Spong invited me to preach at the service and to take part in the act of ordination by joining with him in the laying-on-of-hands. I gladly accepted and in so doing broke no rule. The Anglican Church in America is independent. It is, therefore, free to ask any bishop in the apostolic succession to take part in an ordination. The Church of England has neither the right nor the wish to interfere. Nevertheless as a matter of courtesy I informed the Archbishop of Canterbury when we were guests in a country house in July. In the previous month, John Andrew, the rector of St Thomas, New York, who had been a chaplain at Lambeth Palace, wrote to me. He, who is an opponent of the ordination of women, said that he had read in the *Church Times* of my forthcoming visit to America and added: "Well, it's a free country, but would you like to come and stay with me and preach. I should love to have you." So keen was he that he phoned me from New York and on August 6th wrote a further letter asking me to preach on "Heaven, or Hell?" I was surprised by the invitation as St Thomas's is a pillar of traditional orthodoxy and John Andrew, who must be among the best paid clergymen in the Anglican Communion, is doing excellent pastoral work on conservative lines. I had, and still have, a high regard for what he has achieved. However, I wondered if John appreciated the likely consequences of his invitation to me. It was not only the *Church Times* that was aware of my intention to take part in the ordination; there had been several references to the matter in the British press. I suspected that his congregation might not be best pleased; but that was his business, not mine.

When I arrived in New York in December I was interviewed by the press and by television, as I had been in England six months previously. Although the media were primarily interested in Elizabeth Canham, they took note that I was the first Church of England bishop to take part in the ordination of a woman to the priesthood. After all the Church had set up its headquarters at Canterbury in

597, and it had taken 1,384 years for a bishop to disregard sexual discrimination at the altar! It was not surprising that the report of the event appeared on the front page of the *New York Times*.

After the ordination I went to Toronto to stay with my brother, before returning to New York to preach at St Thomas on the following Sunday. One morning, John Andrew phoned me, very agitated, informing me that I should return to England from Toronto without breaking my journey at New York. I immediately had a word with the Bishop of New York, who apologised on behalf of his diocese for the rudeness with which I had been treated. He put me into the picture. It was as I had suspected.

John, in his first letter, had said that the United States was a 'free' country. But it all depends upon the definition of the word. I was reminded in 1938 when I was banned from pulpits for my views on Chamberlain's appeasement policy. And I was reminded of the churches in Southwark who at the time of the *Honest to God* controversy warned me that if I sent the author, John Robinson, Bishop of Woolwich, to take their confirmation services, they would stop their financial dues to the diocese and withdraw their candidates! Some did.

I felt sorry for John Andrew; he was in a dilemma. I hope he found a suitable substitute to preach on "Heaven, or Hell?"

The fracas meant I had three extra days in Toronto before returning to England. I was asked by a black priest to celebrate Holy Communion and to preach at the Church of the Good Samaritan—a settlement that concerns itself with the homeless, the deprived and the misfits. I doubt whether they were concerned with ecclesiastical arguments about the sex of a priest. What they needed was love. As for myself, well, it was within a few days of Christmas, and although I was sad not to be with John Andrew at St Thomas, I felt that the humility of the shepherds, the perseverance of the wise men, the joy of the angels and the peace of the Christ Child became real at the holy table of the Good Samaritan, in the downtown parish of Toronto, perhaps more so than in New York.

What more can I say? Here I am in Bath, this glorious city. I have a house on the canal and at the bottom of the garden are the steps that lead down to my small boat, 'The Jim Storey'—named after a worker priest who was greatly beloved in the diocese, but who died of a heart attack at an early age. As I sit at my desk and look out of my window I see across the canal and the playing fields Bath Abbey, floodlit at night and nearby is Saint Mary's Church where I happily take my place.

For many years I have had the practice on waking up to think of three things for which to return thanks to God, partly to counter-balance the list of horrors and disasters that are vomited from the BBC's seven o'clock news and which spread the microbes of misery and despair. I find increasingly that I begin by saying, "Dear God, what have I done to deserve such a fate in bringing me to such a lovely place?"

But this is not quite the end; the curtain comes down with Chanctonbury Ring as a background and with Midge on my bed.

On New Year's Day 1981 I walked the Sussex Downs to Chanctonbury Ring. It was a glorious morning, blue skies, brilliant sunshine and a wind that reminded me of Pentecost. Twenty-two years had passed since the New Year's visit prior to my consecration. Something happened; I don't know what. The depression of several years was lifted and I found inward happiness and peace.

Yes, but we must come back to earth. Pushkin and Midge, who used to sleep on my bed. I did not bring them to Bath because I thought they would miss the garden at Bishop's House, and I would not know what to do with them when I went away. The new Bishop of Southwark and his wife said they would adopt them. I was grateful, but I feared the outcome—at least for Midge. She was a godless cat. Occasionally she would venture into the chapel during Communion and jump on the holy table. One day, bored with the service, she made her exit through the window and scrambled to the top of the roof to defy the fire brigade to bring her down. In the circumstances I was not surprised when my successor pronounced the sentence of excommunication. Steeped in Scripture, I believed that a prodigal daughter, like a woman priest, has the same rights as a prodigal son to forgiveness, and that it was my duty to slay the fatted mouse and to welcome her home, even though she be not penitent— which she certainly was not! Fortunately her misdeeds became known to the media and the citizens of Bath were alerted to her excommunication. I received immediate offers of help, advising me that she could be assured of free bed and breakfast in nearby houses, while the butcher, Mr Aplin, would send her meaty Easter offerings. So Midge arrived in a basket. She joins me most days on the gangway to my boat, while I throw bread to the swans, ducks and moorhens. At night she sits on my bed while I tell her stories of the Bishop of Bath and Wells and the local clergy. But she quickly gets bored and falls asleep because there are no spicy scandals as in the old Southwark days.

Occasionally she wakes me up to ask impertinent questions.

"Do you think it was worthwhile?"

To which I reply. "I hope so. But God's mathematics are different from mine. When He adds up columns of figures of successes and failures, He arrives at a number which is not to be found on a human computer."

"If you had your time over again, would you reverse your collar?"

I think a long time. "Well, Midge, the point you see is this: *yes*—if I could be convinced that the Church of England would leave me free to be a minister in the living Body of Christ; but *no*, if it meant being an undertaker for a decomposing ecclesiastical corpse. Of course it is unlikely to be a stark alternative, but there must be a convincing emphasis."

Credo—A Postscript

Those who do not share my religious beliefs may not want to read this postscript as it deals with matters of personal spirituality and with ideas which may be alien to them, or which they have rejected. But there may be others who will sympathise with a stumbling pilgrimage.

Jesus, described in the Scriptures as 'The Prince of Life', was concerned with fullness of life. When he called men to be 'holy' he called them to 'wholeness'. The words mean much the same. We cannot achieve our destiny on this earth or beyond it unless we are true to our calling. We are created in God's image and life makes sense only when we recollect the image and are true to it: "The Son of God thus Man became that men the sons of God might be." There is a verse in Scripture that puts it quite simply: "The Spirit of the Lord will come upon you in power, and you will be changed into a different person." (1 Samuel, 10.6) A new world requires new men. That is why to me prayer is not merely important but essential. Our beings must be rooted in it. Not only does it bring us into communion with God but it gives the perfect mind of God an opportunity to feed our mental and spiritual powers.

As I said when I wrote on psychical research, I believe we have a physical body and another body—'spiritual', 'etheric' call it what we will. In this life these two bodies are entwined, but maybe at death the other body disengages itself from the physical and becomes the medium through which, in another dimension, we express our personalities. Before this disengagement takes place, in fact throughout our earthly existence, both bodies have to be nurtured. The diet for our physical bodies is a matter of constant concern to ourselves, to the nation and to dozens of interested parties. But what of the diet for our spiritual bodies? As Jesus made clear, eternal life can begin now, and it is eternal life that must engulf us. The medium is prayer. Without prayer our spiritual faculties shrivel and we become insensitive to the image of the Divine. We lose the glorious liberty and freedom of the sons of God.

I am often asked to define 'prayer', but it is too difficult and personal. Instead I can try to indicate what it means to me by referring to methods I have found helpful, though I constantly vary them.

1. *Imagination*. I stand against a wall and, breathing deeply, relax. Then I try to dedicate my whole being to God. I lift my hand and place it on my forehead with an incisive motion, to cut out all worldly thoughts and to submit my mind to Him. Next I pass my hands over my eyes to submit them; then my mouth and power of speech; my arms and hands and powers of activity; my heart and powers of affection. Then I pass my hands in a circular movement around my body to signify the intention of entire commitment.

2. *Affixation*. By this I mean the effort to fix our minds on the life of Jesus. I believe psychologists call this inducing the power of an expulsive affection. When a man loves another at the deepest level, it is likely that his love will act as a furnace to heighten his unselfishness and to restore his disfigured self. Hence the purpose of the prayer of affixation on Christ is to allow ourselves to be consumed with love for Him, and for all that is contrary to His will to be expelled from us.

For the clergy the source of this practice should be the Daily Office. We are required to say Matins and Evensong each day of our lives. I have never been able to understand how such an undertaking can be set aside as, alas, it sometimes is. However there is a difference between *saying* an office and *praying* an office. I see no point in consuming what Dean Inge used to call "undigested slabs of Holy Scripture". Better to do nothing unless we are prepared to read, mark and learn and inwardly digest. One of the joys of retirement is having the time to say the Offices slowly, to ponder and to apply. But even when I was at Bishop's House my chaplain and I were accustomed to have half an hour's silence in the chapel after daily Matins and Mass for meditation. The Bible is the word of God and if approached with eagerness and with prayerful longing we can be certain that the Holy Spirit will open our eyes.

3. *The Jesus Prayer*. I learnt this prayer from an Eastern Orthodox priest when I was a boy and I have discovered much more about it as a result of many visits to Orthodox monasteries in Rumania.

Basically it is a more intense method of *affixation*. It is based on breathing. As we draw in, we say "Jes", as we let out, "us". Jes-us, Jes-us, Jes-us. If we had not experienced this form of prayer it may seem odd, but I know that if we persist it can become part of our being. As we set about our work, do the chores at home, sit in the bus, meet our friends, walk along the streets, we will find we are breathing, thinking and saying the Jesus Prayer. Best of all, the heart of Christianity will cease to be an 'ism' and become a Person.

4. *The Prayer of Association*. Here is an example. We have in front of us an object, it may be a saucer of water or a lighted candle. As we fix our minds on the water, the sayings of Jesus pour in: "If you know the gift of God, and who it is that says to you, 'Give me to drink'; you would have asked of him, and he would have given you living water;" "In that last day, that great day of the feast, Jesus stood and cried, saying, 'If any man thirst, let him come unto me and drink. He that believes on me, as the Scripture has said, out of his belly shall flow living water.'"

Or the candlestick. We sit in the dark and fix our eyes on the flame: "In Him was life, and the life was the light of men." "I am the light of the world: he that follows me shall not walk in darkness, but shall have the light of life." "Let your light so shine before men that they may see your good works and glorify your Father in heaven."

These Scriptural references cascade into our minds until we feel our beings are illuminated by the Light of God Himself.

5. *The Prayer of Union and Identification*. This is not easy to explain, but this is how it was put to me. Suppose every human being had a microphone in front of him and we had in our living room a similar number of radio sets the size of a pin's head or less, the population of the world, or most of it, would be in the room. Go a step further: if we could balance all the pin-head radios on our little finger, the population of the world would be on it too. But it already is. And if we had extra-sensory perception we could be aware of it. Everybody is in us and we are in everybody. But it's not only people—it is animals, trees, flowers, beautiful things, hideous things, saints, sinners—the lot. The lie which is the cause of our predicament says that we are isolated individuals, separate and apart, whereas the contrary should be true, we should be part of the whole. We belong to each other, we belong to nature, the trees in

my garden, the swans on the Bath canal, the homeless family at the reception centre.

Whatever may be the truth of the Genesis myth and of the Fall—and I am reverently agnostic about both—we know we are alienated from God, our fellow men, the animal world and creation. "Eat of this apple and you shall be as gods." That is man's tragedy and dilemma. Instead of being in the orbit of creative love in proper juxtaposition with everything in creation, man has usurped the position of the Deity and put himself at the centre of the universe. By so doing he has broken the golden thread which binds him to his creator and creation, and has placed himself in destructive isolation. Hence the need for the prayer of union and identification.

A way to overcome this sense of alienation is to consider our relationships with the things around us. For instance, I look at the table on which I am writing this chapter. I pass my hand over the surface and I know that we are both part of the creative process; I talk to Midge, who is sitting on the table urging me to give her yet another saucer of milk, and I know that both of us owe our lives to one creator and are therefore related. My eye passes to the sixteenth-century Florentine candlestick, by the light of which I am writing, and I know that in some sense I am *en rapport* not only with it but with those who years ago fashioned it. I look at the picture of Chanctonbury Ring above the mantelpiece and there is another door for communication.

It would be wrong to give the impression that prayer is concerned only with God and Me and my personal attitude. Far from it. Prayer is unselfish because it is rooted in Love. We must 'go into God' so that we can 'go out into the world'. Karl Barth put it into a nutshell when he said, "I take the Bible in one hand, the newspaper in the other, then read the paper in the light of the Word of God." I heard Barth say that when I was a student. And usually I have followed his advice. Throughout my episcopate, after the morning Mass, I went from my chapel, avoiding the breakfast room, to my study and took up *The Times*. It was my hope that by so doing I should, no matter how inadequately, look at the problems of the world through prayerful eyes, to be moved with compassion and incited to action.

This sort of prayer encourages an attitude of intercession. But one must be practical. I find it so easy to love everybody in general, but nobody in particular. It costs nothing. I know that the reading out of long lists of names in church can be as boring as it is useless, but it is more realistic when we take a few names each day—birthdays of family and friends, people in need, those with whom we work. A favourite custom of mine was to keep a box for Christmas cards. They poured in each Christmas—or did until the cost became prohibitive—I had not the time to look closely at them, so I put them into a box in my chapel and each day I took out ten or a dozen of them and held them up before God. But that was not the end of the exercise, because often I found myself prompted to phone some of them, or write a letter.

But what do we do at the end of the day with the people who have annoyed, injured, misrepresented or possibly hated us? These are the people who are alienated, perhaps through our own fault, perhaps not. There is only one thing we can do, difficult as it is, and that is to accept the hate, the injury and the misrepresentation and, without complaint, offer it to God.

As I read the New Testament it would seem that when people brought their needs to Jesus he released his psychic energy upon them to meet their needs. It is my belief that when we pray for others, if we are doing it properly, we are focusing beams of energy from our spiritual bodies upon them.

As important as intercession is thanksgiving, and praise. Like the lepers in search of healing, so often we ask, but so rarely return to say thank you. Each day before I get out of bed I think of three things for which I return thanks: a good sleep, bodily faculties, food, a home and security, my garden and animals—and much more. I am convinced that one of the worst features of our national life is the obsession with disaster. So rarely do we read or hear of our achievements and of the splendid but ordinary acts of goodness, heroism, kindness and caring which should rejoice millions of thankful hearts each day of the year. Yet in the New Testament there is reference after reference to the need for gratitude and joyfulness to be hallmarks of a Christian's life. Even on the night before he died Jesus, who was in mental and spiritual agony, could return thanks to the Father and promise joy to his friends.

Linked with thanksgiving is the affirmation of faith on which it depends. I love the great words of St Patrick's Breastplate: "I bind unto myself today the strong name of the Trinity." I usually say it as I lie in my bath, slowly and with my eyes shut! It's an encouragement to face the day ahead with confidence and serenity. Even in times of depression it reduces sadness and fear.

The foundation-stone of personal spirituality must be a daily renewal of commitment to Christ. Even though I see only through a glass darkly and remain agnostic, if not sceptical, about some statements in the creeds and much else, I am firmly convinced that Jesus reveals the nature of God as does nobody else. Perhaps God has other revelations for other worlds and dimensions, but for me, as far as this world is concerned, my faith would lack point and purpose unless I could "confess that Jesus Christ is Lord, to the glory of God the Father" (Philippians 2.11). For that reason the Risen Christ requires total commitment. By that I do not mean that he makes autocratic demands but that when we apprehend in him the incarnation of Love we respond voluntarily and abandon ourselves to him, submitting to his purposes. For me the prayer of commitment finds almost perfect expression in Charles Wesley's hymn:

Jesus, confirm my heart's desire to work, and speak and
                                                think for thee;
Still let me guard the holy fire and still stir up thy gift
                                                in me.
Ready to do thy perfect will, my acts of faith and love repeat,
Till death thy endless mercies seal, and make the sacrifice
                                                complete.

I have said this prayer on most days of my life as a bishop, and sometimes many times a day. It has helped me cope with what the Psalmist calls "the destruction that wasteth at noonday"—the plague that hits most of us in middle life. It also helped me to follow St Paul's advice to 'maintain the glow' when the lamp had started to flicker.

The purpose of spirituality is union with God, or as near as we can get to it in this life. Technical phrases like 'the beatific vision' mean little to me. I know the saints are alleged to see it, but as I am in a different category altogether it is unlikely to come my way. What I do understand is a relationship with God which is as close as a hand that fits into a glove: "My heart is restless until it rests in Thee." Not that I have experienced it, but in my better moments that is my supreme yearning. I wish they came more often.

But spirituality must not be restricted to personal terms. Because of my baptism I am a member of a God-given community in which the Holy Spirit operates and opportunities for communal growth are given, especially through communal worship.

Worship means 'worth-ship'. We worship what we believe to be worth the most; God, money, possessions, sex, security, self. And what we worship determines our attitudes, thought patterns, conversations and actions. It also directs our paths towards the group whose members have outlooks similar to our own. For Christians, God, His Kingdom and His way of life are deemed of paramount importance, and therefore become the object of our worship. The reason for coming to this conclusion is our response to the Gospel of Jesus and our allegiance to Him. We know in our bones that the over-riding consideration in every situation must be obedience to His prayer that God's will and Kingdom may be realised on earth just as it is in heaven. But such obedience means the readiness to share with Christ in His life of self-giving love, supremely revealed on the Cross. And that is what the Mass, the Eucharist, the Holy Communion—call it what you will—is all about.

We meet around the Lord's Table as members of a supra-national community with no distinction of colour, class or sex. We take of the fruits of the earth and of man's labour to offer them to God as the stuff and substance, the bricks and mortar of His new world, His Kingdom. But before they can be used for such a purpose they must be taken away from the grasping hands of this fallen world and placed in the hands of the Prince of Life, who allowed His body to be broken and His blood to be shed. Only when they have been identified with His sacrificial self-offering can they be given back to us as the nourishment for our lives and the tools for our costly work. So it is that, as the Holy Community gathers around the altar, we have a foretaste and a pledge of the Kingdom of God: the world as He means it to be, life in its true quality. That is the goal of our communal spirituality.

For these reasons the Mass had been at the centre of my life. At Bishop's House, just as in the parishes in which I served, the day began at the altar. Now that I am retired, I go to a church on Sundays and some weekdays, but at other times I sit by myself at the breakfast table with my Bible at my side, and with bread and wine in front of me. Sometimes I sit with my picnic basket on Chanctonbury Ring. It makes no difference. I think of the Mass as a golden cord that begins at Bethlehem, proceeds to Calvary and the Easter garden, continues through the joys and sufferings of mankind till it reaches the Kingdom of God. As it passes over the table I know that I am pegged on to it and that, as I take the broken bread and drink from the cup, the Lord is in the midst, just as years ago He walked on Easter evening with two disciples along the road to Emmaus before making himself known in the breaking of the bread.

Perhaps some verses which appeared in a paper at the beginning of the century, and which are thought to have been written by the late Father Martindale, sum up more adequately than I can the thoughts that go through my mind as I offer the Mass:

> I lift this bread
> And lift therewith the world, myself and Thee,
> Hast Thou not said:
> 'I, lifted up, will draw the universe to me'?
>
> O heavenward Cup!
> The drops that redden in thy tiny bowl
> Could swallow up
> The ocean's undulant to utmost pole.
>
> O no demur,
> Weak fingers, to exalt this enormous load.
> Thou Christopher!
> Thy God sustaineth thee who sustainest God.

Index